PSYCHOLOGY LIBRARY EDITIONS:
AGGRESSION

I0124822

Volume 2

AGGRESSION
AND ITS INTERPRETATION

AGGRESSION
AND ITS INTERPRETATION

LYDIA JACKSON

Routledge
Taylor & Francis Group
LONDON AND NEW YORK

First published in 1954 by Methuen & Co. Ltd

This edition first published in 2025
by Routledge
4 Park Square, Milton Park, Abingdon, Oxon OX14 4RN

and by Routledge
605 Third Avenue, New York, NY 10158

Routledge is an imprint of the Taylor & Francis Group, an informa business
British Library Cataloguing in Publication Data
A catalogue record for this book is available from the British Library

ISBN: 978-1-032-77840-2 (Set)
ISBN: 978-1-032-77913-3 (Volume 2) (hbk)
ISBN: 978-1-032-77922-5 (Volume 2) (pbk)
ISBN: 978-1-003-48541-4 (Volume 2) (ebk)

DOI: 10.4324/9781003485414

Publisher's Note
The publisher has gone to great lengths to ensure the quality of this reprint but points out that some imperfections in the original copies may be apparent.

Disclaimer
The publisher has made every effort to trace copyright holders and would welcome correspondence from those they have been unable to trace.

AGGRESSION
AND ITS INTERPRETATION

by

LYDIA JACKSON

D.Phil., B.Sc. (Oxon.)

with a foreword by
FELIX BROWN
D.M., M.R.C.P.

METHUEN & CO. LTD. LONDON

36 Essex Street, Strand, W.C.2

First published in 1954

CATALOGUE NO. 5463/U

PRINTED IN GREAT BRITAIN BY
UNWIN BROTHERS LIMITED, WOKING AND LONDON

FOREWORD

The successful management of aggression has now become one of the most topical and urgent subjects in human society, not only because of the part played by aggression in the origin of delinquency, crime and neurosis, but also in the wider aspect of human relationship and aggression between nations.

Human beings are aggressive, we have descended from predatory hunters, and our predominance on the earth is partly due to our successful aggression as well as to the nervous connection between hand and eye, and the power of speech. But now it seems that some of the qualities which led to our success in the stone ages, not so long distant biologically, are dangerous to our survival. Aggression in man is now a very proper study for mankind, and Dr. Jackson's contribution is, therefore, especially welcome.

In psychiatry there are many different levels at which emphasis may be laid in the search for causation, the physical construction of the brain, heredity and constitution, the influence of religion, economic background, relation to society, sexual adjustments, present situations and infantile emotional relationships within the family, to name only some of them. The emphasis which Dr. Jackson makes is consistent with the axiom of modern psychiatry, that the personal relationships of an individual to his fellow-men are formed on the pattern of his relationship with his parents in early infancy, that destructive aggression is, in fact, an infantile response to rejection.

The very interesting and difficult problem of the similarities and differences between the neurotic and delinquent mentality has been studied here with the help of her projection tests which prove useful in therapy as well as in research.

The actual technique of therapy is here particularly clearly stated, and she very rightly emphasizes the central principle of therapy with children, that a good relationship between a child and an adult is an indispensable basis for all real improvement in the child's personality. The therapist acts, as it were, as a

5

catalyst, enabling the destructive aggression to be released and eventually resolved into creative aggression, and self-realization. Lengthy and difficult as this process is, it is worth doing and must be done, for it is at present the only way of dealing with the problem of aggression. Whether aggression is innate or acquired in early childhood is perhaps an academic question, the fact is that society is much troubled by misdirected aggression in its members, and the only reasonable time to deal with this is in childhood. Dr. Jackson's work will be a valuable help to all who have this end in view.

FELIX BROWN, D.M., M.R.C.P.

PREFACE

The modern psychological view of neurosis and insanity tends to stress the integrative rather than the destructive aspect of mental processes which characterize these states of mind. It regards them as attempts at overcoming the disintegrating forces of illness: neurosis is 'an attempt at adaptation which has failed'; insanity, by implication, is another such attempt, only more desperate, and much less successful.

In therapeutic practice one is often amazed at the striving after order and organization manifested by even the most poorly integrated adults and children. Children, who show many signs of gross instability, or even psychotic tendencies, would display a sporadic urge to 'make things', to 'tidy up', to 'mend'. However crude and inadequate such attempts, they indicate the presence of mental energy of a positive kind, which opposes disruption. In adult patients, the obvious urge they feel to justify their delusions, their 'rationalization' of their symptoms, their 'pressure' of explanatory talk, all can be taken as manifestations of the same organizing force, an attempt to bring 'system' into their 'madness'.

This approach to mental illness, based on much clinical observation, is probably nearer the truth and holds a much greater promise for future research and therapy than the earlier one, which regarded such illness as a wholly disintegrative process.

The author of this book became convinced, through her experience in psychological treatment and research over a number of years, that a similar approach is needed in dealing with the concept and problems of aggression. The older, popular view that aggression is wholly anti-social should be replaced by a more recent and dynamic one, which equates aggression with the biologically indispensable urge to self-assertion, in its meaning of self-realization. Such an approach would facilitate the much-needed research into the causes and motives of aggressive behaviour. Only through the study of

7

innate endowment and of environmental forces which influence the direction of the aggressive urge and the forms assumed by it can we hope to achieve control over these forces and over aggression itself.

That such control must be gained for the survival of our civilization has been emphasized by many outstanding men and women during the last fifty years. That humanity is nowhere near achieving it, has been made clear by recent history. Yet even now psychological research, especially in the sphere of emotional relationships, remains the most neglected branch of scientific study, with little encouragement given it, with few opportunities provided, save by the courtesy of private individuals, or, occasionally, of a progressive local authority.

This book is a record of an attempt to discover, through the study of aggressive behaviour in children, how the self-assertive urge, on which the survival of the individual depends, becomes deflected from creative to destructive ends, and how it is again re-directed into constructive channels. The majority of the subjects studied were emotionally disturbed children, who were observed and treated by the writer in various Child Guidance clinics. The emphasis is thus, inevitably, on the socially disruptive forms of self-assertion, but, lest it loom too large in the reader's mind, let him remember that, when all is said and done, the great majority of both children and adults manage to assert themselves in socially acceptable ways.

The author owes a great debt of gratitude to her subjects, and to all those who, inside and outside the clinics, co-operated so generously in this research.

L. J.

London, 1952

ACKNOWLEDGEMENTS

A special recognition is due to Miss Nance Fairbairn and Dr. J. O. Wisdom for having read the manuscript and made many helpful suggestions, to Dr. Felix Brown for having supplied the foreword and to Professor William Stephenson for his most valuable advice on my research.

8

CONTENTS

Part I

Aggression and its Interpretation

Part II

Projection Studies of Aggression in Children

Part III

Clinical Studies of Aggression in Children

9

Part IV

Interpretation and Theory

PLATES

11

Part I

Aggression and its Interpretation

★

I. THE ORIGINS OF AGGRESSION

It may seem strange to inquire into the origins of an urge which most psychologists and laymen alike assume to be innate. The modern theory of instincts, as well as the basic concepts of most religions, postulate that the human infant is born with the potentialities for anger and fear, that the blend of these emotions produces the sentiment of hatred, and leads to behaviour generally described as 'aggressive'. In ordinary speech 'aggression' usually signifies an attack, and is employed to describe both verbal and physical behaviour. The adjective 'aggressive' is used to describe people who are truculent in manner or speech, or, in a milder sense, people who are self-assertive, 'pushing' and always ready for an argument. Rarely the word is used in its older meaning—to describe an enterprising person, who 'goes forward'[1] and achieves his aims despite obstacles and resistance.

All these uses carry an overtone of disapproval, for violence and hostility are condemned by West European tradition, and are tolerated only when they can be justified by some moral principle. Yet a certain amount of admiration is often blended with disapproval, for the aggressive person is frequently successful in his pursuits and impresses people with his apparent self-confidence and strength of character. Therefore, the attitude of the man-in-the-street towards aggressive behaviour and

[1] *Aggression (adg-) ōnis (aggredior)*—a going to or towards a thing (Lewis and Short, Latin Dictionary); also 'Behold, I see him now aggress and enter into place' (Cambyses—in *Hasl. Dodst.*, Vol. IV, p. 172).

aggressive people is probably always ambivalent, and might include a wide range of emotions: from horror, disgust and strong condemnation to mild disapproval on the one hand, and from reluctant admiration to powerful fascination, on the other. Many of these emotions probably remain under the threshold of consciousness.

Psychologists, both medical and lay, have used the terms 'aggression' and 'aggressive' predominantly in the same sense as laymen. Thus the authors of a recent piece of research on causes of aggressive behaviour define aggression as 'an impulse to destroy, damage, torment, retaliate, blow up, humiliate, insult, threaten and intimidate' (48, pp. 215–95). This seems to cover many of the possible verbal and physical expressions of hostility, and thus appears to presuppose that aggressive behaviour is usually associated with aggressive emotion. Its source appears to be the emotion of anger, and its aim the destruction of the object which arouses this emotion.

Recently, however, there has been a trend towards re-examining and re-defining the meaning of the terms 'aggression' and 'aggressive', and a renewed interest in the origins of these concepts, an interest probably stimulated by the ever increasing need to control its massive outbursts during the recent years. Some of these theories and definitions are slightly modified re-statements of older views, others are attempts to break a new ground. Of the older views those of the leading medical psychologists are in my opinion of foremost interest, for they were able to study under controlled conditions the motives of aggressive behaviour usually hidden from observation. Of these, Freud, Adler, Karen Horney and Ian Suttie used their observations to formulate general theories, or hypotheses, concerning the origins of aggression.

Freud, by tracing the history of his patients back to early childhood, discovered a close relationship between the aggressive and the sexual impulses, and at one time concluded that all aggression was of sexual origin and was directed towards 'the overpowering of the sexual object in so far as the carrying out of the sexual act demands it' (18, p. 69). In his early writings he equates aggression with hate and with the destructive impulse, at the same time regarding it as a normal component of the instinct of sex (19). He soon became aware, however, of the difficulty created by this assumption, and later questioned it himself: 'How is one to derive the sadistic impulse, which aims at the injury of the object, from the life-sustaining Eros?' (18, p. 69). The attempt to overcome this difficulty gave rise to his hypothesis of a 'Death' instinct, 'an urge which every living organism has towards the re-instatement of the original, in-organic state, the impulse of every animate thing to revert to the inanimate'. According to this theory, the primary aim of aggression is self-destruction, and only after it had been 'driven apart from the ego by the influence of the narcissistic libido' does it 'become manifest in reference to the object' (18, pp. 69–70).

Clearly, this theory, bold as it is, cannot be accepted without careful verification, which, so far, has not been even attempted. The evidence should be produced in support of this hypothesis at least as strong as that which can be quoted in support of the hypothesis of the self-preservative instinct—one more gener-ally held, and shared also by Freud. Thus both the human infant and the young animal cry persistently and grope for food almost as soon as they are born; they also cling to any warm protective object near-by. A young ape or monkey has a 'fur-clinging' reaction which makes it hold fast to its mother's breast (57); a new-born human infant has a 'grasping reflex', so powerful that he is able to support the weight of his own body for a few seconds. On the other hand, perhaps only one item of infant behaviour can be adduced in support of Freud's hypothesis of the Death instinct. It is the fact that young children (but not infants under a year) sometimes react to frustration by banging their heads against the sides of their cot, which may be interpreted in Freud's words as an expression of 'primary masochism', or as 'the turning of the aggressive in-stinct against the self' (18, pp. 69–70). This reaction, however, is sufficiently unusual to have attracted special interest and discussion, whereas the more common responses to frustration, such as kicking and struggling, clearly directed to warding off danger or injury to the self, and appearing as early as eighteen months, are taken more or less for granted.

It thus appears that, in the present state of our knowledge, the burden of proof regarding Freud's theory of aggression falls upon those who advance it.

Adler's theory of aggression stresses its independence from the instinct of sex. He regards it as an instinct in its own right, but in no way identical with Freud's 'Death instinct'. Whereas the primary aim of the latter is assumed by Freud to be self-annihilation, the aim of the former, in Adler's view, is self-protection and the affirmation of the Self. He regards exaggerated aggressiveness—or Will-to-Power—as an over-compensation for feelings of inferiority (1).

These two conceptions of aggression, arrived at through the study of the same kind of material—mental disturbances in neuroses—are thus quite distinct from one another: Freud identifies aggression with an urge to destroy (oneself or others), whereas Adler identifies it with an urge to dominate and subdue. Freud postulates the possibility of its being the oldest impulse of all (18, pp. 69–70), probably present in the unicellular amoeba; Adler conceives it as a derivative of the basic feeling of inferiority, a self-protecting device.

The views of two other medical psychologists are too important to omit from this survey—those of Ian Suttie and Karen Horney. Both these writers began their psycho-therapeutic practice as followers of Freud, but later modified their views in the light of their experience with patients.

Ian Suttie (54) came to the conclusion that aggression and hatred are not primary; the basic emotions of the human infant are the feelings of dependence and need for love, to ensure security. Only when the demand for love is frustrated does aggressive behaviour arise. 'The refusal of the mother to give to the child leads to anxiety, hate, aggression (which Freud mistakes for a primary instinct), and to the quest for power (which Adler mistakes for an equally fundamental and inevitable characteristic of human nature)' (54, p. 50). 'Aggressive emotion is not an instinct but a product of a particular relationship to environment, one of refusal and rejection by the mother, or, more generally, non-responsiveness' (54, p. 51). In Suttie's view, this particular relationship to environment is responsible for 'the whole competitive, self-seeking, power-extolling character of our civilization'.

Karen Horney, like Suttie, found no evidence in her experience with neurotic patients to show that the aggressive impulse was primary. Her view is that 'the extent and frequency of destructiveness are not a proof that it is instinctual' (30, p. 127). Nor can the small children's sadistic fantasies be regarded as such a proof. 'It has to be shown', she writes, 'whether sadistic behaviour and fantasies in small children ever appear in children who feel happy and safe because they are treated with warmth and respect' (30, p. 130).

These four views on aggression, distinct though they are, have one point in common: their implied condemnation of aggressiveness as an impulse which is anti-social and life-destroying in its aims, that is, negative in its human and biological value.

It is to the students of general, and especially of child psychology, that we have to turn for the modifications of this view. William McDougall, for instance, regards the aggressive impulse as 'far from being wholly injurious'. 'Its operation', he writes, 'has been one of the essential factors in the evolution of the higher forms of social organization' (39, p. 242). It is not an instinct in its own right, but part of the 'instinct of pugnacity'.

McDougall evidently accepts, as Freud does (20), Atkinson and Lang's theory of the origins of society. He describes the positive role played by the aggressive impulse in human society in the following passage where he refers to the perpetual feud between the patriarch and his sons for the possession of the women of the tribe. This feud 'secured for the family community a succession of patriarchs, each of whom was superior to his rivals not merely in power of combat, but also, and chiefly, in power of far-sighted control of his impulses' (39, p. 246).

He believes that the custom of going to war among primitive tribes also has its social usefulness. Tribes with fewer civic virtues are exterminated by those whose members are more highly organized.

The impulse of rivalry and emulation, the emotions of revenge and moral indignation, in McDougall's view, also originate in the instinct of pugnacity. Through these emotions it is responsible for 'the growth and maintenance of every system of criminal law and every code of punishment (for there can be no doubt that punishment was originally retributive)' (39, p. 251).

We may not agree with McDougall's views on the origins of aggression—for what is 'the instinct of pugnacity', we might ask, unless it is 'an impulse to destroy, damage', etc. which other writers prefer to call 'aggression'. His important contribution to the theories of aggression is just this emphasis on its positive aspect, its socially valuable function. This aspect was not stressed for some time afterwards, until it was emphasized again by some Freudian writers (46), by the author of this book (33) and by Frederick H. Allen, in a paper read to the Congress on Mental Health, in 1948 (2).

Meanwhile, writers on child psychology were providing material for the verification of these theories—the material obtained from first-hand observation of young children. It is surprising that this obvious source—the behaviour of normal children—was left more or less untapped for so long by both medical and academic psychologists. They seemed to prefer to build their theories on, and to draw their general conclusions from, their studies of neurotic adults or from some unverified hypotheses, such as Atkinson and Lang's (36).

It would seem that the innate springs of any kind of behaviour can only be postulated on the grounds of its early and spontaneous appearance. How can we recognize the expression of the aggressive urge in the human infant and what is the earliest age at which we can place it with reasonable certainty? On the definition adopted by Sears and Hovland (48), anger would be a prerequisite of aggression, and the early appearance

18

of anger in the infant would justify the inference that the aggressive urge is innate. Darwin seemed to take this for granted. In referring to anger, he mentions frowning at ten weeks of age, and says that when his child was four months old 'there could be no doubt from the manner in which blood gushed into his whole face and scalp, that he easily got into a violent passion' (11). But even at the time when the material of child psychology was limited to a few painstaking diaries recording the development of individual children, the observers gave different dates for the first appearance in young children of the emotion they believed to be anger. Sully (53) noted the first expressions of 'anger' in his child as early as the end of the third week, Dearborn (12) at eight weeks. Much more recently, and pertinently, Valentine maintained that 'genuine anger is not convincingly shown until towards the end of the first year' (55, p. 286). The difficulty in reaching agreement on this point is obvious, for it depends on the observer's interpretation of the infant's behaviour. Such interpretations are, perhaps inevitably, based on a crude argument by analogy. Valentine is, therefore, right to call our attention to the difficulty of differentiating between anger and distress in very young children (55, p. 286), and to point out that 'the first expressions which are interpreted by some as anger—violent crying, reddening, kicking, and so forth—are general to any kind of distress' (55, p. 285).

Scientific objectivity, therefore, requires caution in the use of such terms as 'rage' or 'destructive wishes' when applied to the human infant, for his emotional states cannot be assumed to be identical with ours. His behaviour, however, might be described as 'aggressive' if the term is used with a modified connotation, such as is given it by Sherman. He distinguishes between two kinds of reaction in the new-born infant to an unpleasant stimulus—'avoidance' and 'aggression' (49). When pressure (with a finger) is applied to the infant's chin, his first reaction is to try to turn his head away. When this fails he begins to wave his arms, as if trying to get rid of the offending object. Used in this way, the term clearly implies neither anger, nor hostility, but merely an outgoing response to a stimulus, as distinct from withdrawal. Much of the aggressive behaviour of infants, described by Charlotte Buehler (7), is probably of the same type. Infants under a year placed together in a play-pen were observed to snatch toys from one another and even try to scratch one another. Such behaviour is certainly 'aggressive', in the sense that it displays initiative and vigour rather than passive submissiveness to whatever happens, but it would be rash, to say the least, to read hostile or destructive meaning into it.

This 'projection' of adult meaning into infantile behaviour is a temptation against which we cannot guard enough. Are we to accept as universally true the neurotic fantasy that an infant biting his mother's breast really wishes to destroy her, when we know that he would bite any object within reach when he is cutting his teeth? As I pondered over this, and similar notions about infants, one afternoon in public gardens, I saw two babies put down by their mothers on a patch of lawn. Both were about a year old, one, a girl, could only crawl, the other, a boy, could toddle somewhat precariously. The girl had a rattle to play with, the boy—a string of coloured discs which she coveted. He dropped it on the grass, she picked it up and played with it; he reached out to get it back, but she put it out of his reach. Again and again this happened; she was determined and resourceful, he—puzzled and hesitant, and obviously impressed by her, but of anger there was no sign on either side. Only when her mother picked up the girl and restored the toy to its possessor, were there cries and sobs of frustration and protest. As soon as the two children were again put down, the same scene was repeated with the same reciprocal reactions.

That little girl was undoubtedly 'aggressive', but the quality of her aggressiveness appeared to be very different from that implied in Sears and Hovland's definition. I thought, as I looked on, that 'destructiveness' pertains to a later age; infantile aggression appears to be merely self-protective, or self-assertive.

A study of 'temper outbursts' in young children by Florence

Goodenough (23) provides much evidence for this view. She found that in a large majority of cases she studied, aggressive outbursts in children under five were occasioned by a clash of wills, the parent demanding conformity with her or his wishes from the child, and the child refusing to accept frustration or domination by the parent (23, p. 138). The typical situation, thus, was one of frustration, met by a vigorous attempt at self-assertion by the child.

Susan Isaac's observations of young children at the Malting House School (32) also confirm the view that the self-assertive urge plays a large part in causing aggressive behaviour. She writes:

'Both motives, of power and of rivalry for love, are of the greatest importance in causing aggressive behaviour between children, and on the part of the child towards an adult, but aggressive behaviour from the motive of rivalry bulks more largely in the records than either power or possession; it gave rise to more acute tension of feeling and was more difficult to deal with' (32, p. 220).

She also found confirmation of 'the general academic view that anger and the fighting impulse are stimulated by the thwarting of any wish or interference with any activity' (32, p. 220). It thus appears that there is first-hand evidence to support Adler's view that aggression can be an expression of will-to-power, as well as Suttie's—that it arises in consequence of rejected love. Adler, perhaps, is dealing with the secondary product of early deprivation, whereas Suttie—with its more fundamental effects.

All these writers, however, consider only what is best described as the 'negative' aspect of aggression, that is, destructiveness and hostility towards a rival. The adult observer rarely can rid himself from a moral approach and from a tendency to view such behaviour as 'greedy' or 'selfish'. What should be borne in mind, however, is that the destructive aspect of aggression is not its primary characteristic, and that aggression itself is grounded in the 'Life instinct', rather than in the 'Death instinct', whatever that may be. Clearly, both the 'quest for power' and the 'quest for love', which arouse aggression, are, in the case of the human infant, the biological determinants of survival.

The biological value of aggression was recognized and stressed in earlier research, such as Ordhal's (42), while Bovet (4) emphasized its self-assertive aspect. Ordhal quotes a number of examples from animal life, with the intention of demonstrating the origin of aggressive behaviour in the instinct of rivalry. The earliest and the most primitive form of rivalry is competition for food—the basic condition of survival. Other primitive forms of rivalry—for the possession of the female, and for precedence or leadership, both found in the animal world, are also more satisfactorily explained, in my view, by the hypothesis of survival urge than by any other.

Pierre Bovet, despite his initial assumption that the 'fighting instinct' derives from the sex instinct, gives a number of instances which show that aggressive behaviour commonly aims at self-assertion. In referring to teasing among children of school age, he writes:

> 'The object of teasing is to bring about a scuffle, and so allow the teaser to *show off his superiority over his opponent*' (4, p. 56).

Further, discussing the ways in which a child tries to annoy his parents by contrariness, he states:

> 'There is no need to be very powerful *to assert one's independence towards others* by deliberately doing something which thwarts them. This is the teasing of young children. They take pleasure in exasperating their elders by their acts of disobedience . . . by doing the opposite of what they have been told to' (4, p. 60).

Some pretty examples of behaviour inspired by this most imperative urge are provided by Valentine. He writes about his daughter, aged three years six months:

> 'X is very self-willed just now. Longs to assert herself. Dances and stamps with rage if her will is crossed. One day I locked her in my dressing-room till she should stop. She was silent a

moment, so I unlocked the door and said she could come out. She would not, however, held the door and said she "did not want to come out"—a final resort to save self respect when resistance was futile' (55, p. 300).

It does, indeed, seem that by stressing the destructive, anti-social aspects of aggression, writers like Freud, Adler and Bovet, and in a lesser degree even Horney and Suttie, had unduly narrowed its meaning. This has been realized lately by some Freudian writers, who appear no longer to derive aggression from the 'Death instinct'. Thus Joan Rivière writes:

> 'Aggression, which is closely allied to hate, is by no means entirely destructive or painful, either in its aims or functioning; and love . . . can be aggressive and even destructive in its operation. . . . It seems that aggressive impulses are a radical and basic element in human psychology. . . . We can say, in fact, that both the self-preservative and "love" instincts *need a certain amount of aggression* if they are to attain satisfaction, that is, an aggressive element is an essential part of both these instincts in actual functioning' (46, pp. 4–5).

And further:

> 'Aggression and sexuality, being integral parts of human nature are bound to function for good or ill while life lasts. If the attempt is made to deny their rights and exclude them from participation in life for good, they must flow into channels of hate and destructiveness' (46, p. 47).

It is clearly indicated in these passages that aggression has other functions besides destructive ones. F. H. Allen (2) writing some years later considers these functions as characteristic and regards aggression as 'a concept of action and vitality, differentiating between animate and inanimate material'. He believes that it is necessary to distinguish between 'the constructive and destructive aggressive action and feeling'.

I expressed similar views some years earlier when I made the distinction between 'positive' and 'negative' forms of aggression and put forward the hypothesis that aggression was a manifestation of self-assertion and was grounded in the survival urge (34). Since then the research in which I have been engaged has produced more material to confirm me in this opinion. My findings are described and discussed in Parts II and III of this book.

What, however, of the theories examined in this introductory chapter? Perhaps through the nature of the subject itself they were bound to remain inconclusive. But even if one allows for that, the general impression, I think, remains that the evidence adduced by their exponents does not provide sufficient support for the concept of a primarily destructive force, which many psychologists and laymen alike are in the habit of calling 'aggression'. On the other hand, there seems to be good evidence in favour of the concept of an innate forward-driving urge which is expressed in initiative, enterprise and positive self-assertion.

Yet there is little doubt that at some time in the individual's life there occurs the splitting of this stream of vital, forward-flowing energy into two contrasting currents—of destructive and constructive activity and emotion. It is the conditions of this splitting which require investigation if we are to prevent this energy from being misused.

The question of the origins of aggression is thus not one of a purely theoretical interest, for the knowledge of its sources may enable us to determine and, perhaps, control the direction of its flow.

II. THE NEED FOR FURTHER RESEARCH

It has to be admitted that the general attitude towards aggression is one of the stumbling blocks on the way to its study. In his brilliant and moving book (54), Ian Suttie coined the phrase 'the taboo on tenderness', which he regards as characteristic of Western civilization. I believe that a parallel to this is our 'taboo on aggressiveness'. This is not surprising, for sex and self-assertion are the two most powerful movers of human behaviour and the most potent sources of enjoyment and suffering. Because they contain such tremendous potentialities for good and evil, these urges are looked upon with suspicion and fear, and because they are feared, they tend to be denied free expression even in childhood.

Taboos, we know, are imposed on things and actions which are both shameful and sacred, and to which our attitude is ambivalent. We not only fear tenderness as a weakness, we also long to bestow and to receive it. We not only fear aggressiveness as a power to hurt, we also admire it as a sign of strength and initiative.

Ambivalence is an indication of conflict, and as conflict is generally painful, we tend to repress it. That conflicts are not disposed of by repression has been amply shown by the work of Freud and Jung and their many followers. The repressed conflicts continue to operate in the mind, providing human actions with motives of which the individual consciousness remains unaware. Sometimes they give rise to symptoms and behaviour which we designate as 'neurotic' or 'delinquent'. An implicit condemnation of sexual and aggressive impulses achieves no purpose except to make their study more difficult. Only when we refrain from moral evaluation does it become possible to treat aggression and sex as any other human impulse, capable of development, and, even if only partially, of transformation, the range and scope of which is as yet unknown. Freud has shown this to be true of the sexual urge, and Adler has traced the connection between the aggressive impulse and

25

some normal, as well as neurotic, character traits. Man may be the only creature who learned to misuse his instincts, yet he is also the only one in whom the original primitive impulses can undergo a high degree of transmutation and be directed to goals very remote from the primary goal of mere survival.

This transmutation, or sublimation, as Freud has called it, is an unconscious process, which cannot be directly influenced, but can be facilitated by providing a *choice of alternatives*, acceptable to society and satisfactory to the individual. Psychoanalytical writers stress that the choice cannot be forced (15, pp. 480–8); nor, as far as the sexual impulse is concerned, can all its energy be re-directed to non-sexual ends. If it could, it would indeed make race suicide possible. As for the self-assertive impulse, there is not sufficient evidence at present for making any generalizations, but it is at least probable that its energy is no less, if not more plastic than that of sex, and that even after it has been split into the divergent currents of destructive and constructive activity, the energy used in destructiveness could be re-directed towards creative goals. Even if we found that after that there still remains an irreducible amount of destructive energy, its operation could perhaps be limited to a period of life when it could do least harm, that is, to childhood.

Research into the conditions of the split and of the re-direction of divided energies is clearly an urgent necessity. Most of the research up to this date, however, proceeded on the assumption that aggression was synonymous with hostility and destructiveness. This kind of aggression, it was found, arose 'always as a consequence of frustration' (13, p. 1). The reverse, however, is not true—frustration does not always lead to aggression. As Valentine (55) has pointed out, distress may be one of the reactions to frustration, and this is especially true of the human infant. The authors of *Minor Studies in Aggression* (47) are therefore not justified in describing the crying of a five-months'-old baby, when his feeding is interrupted as an 'aggressive' response, in the sense in which they define the term 'aggressive'.

I have explained in the first chapter of this book the grounds on which I prefer to reject this limited connotation and to employ in my own research the working hypothesis that aggression is, primarily, an expression of vitality. In so far as it is a form of self-assertion and thus one of the ways to self-realization, aggressive behaviour is a *sine qua non* of individual survival. A creature of a species incapable of aggression even in defence of its own progeny would have little chance of survival. One of the paradoxes of human behaviour, however, is the fact that the aggressive impulse sometimes takes forms which endanger that very survival by producing the anti-social behaviour of delinquency or the serious maladaptations of neurosis. On the one hand this impulse is employed most successfully in overcoming obstacles to individual development and self-realization, and in creative pursuits which are both satisfying to the individual and useful to society, that is in 'positive' activities. On the other hand, it can be directed against society and towards the injury and destruction of the individual himself, that is, employed in 'negative' activities. One of the first things we should try to find out is whether these differences in the quality and the direction of the impulse are due to innate disposition or to environmental influences, and, if to the latter, how early in life do such influences begin to operate.

Clearly such problems are most profitably studied in children, for the relative simplicity of their patterns of behaviour makes it easier to see the problem as a whole, and to control conditions of observation. There are also greater opportunities for relating their behaviour patterns to the detailed histories of their early development, which are rarely obtainable in adults. By this I do not wish to imply that I regard experimental study of aggression in adults as of little value. I merely regard it as relatively limited in scope and application in the field of mental hygiene; besides, a full comprehension of aggressive behaviour in adults nearly always requires a knowledge of the events and experiences of childhood, whether obtained through direct reminiscences or by analytical technique during treatment.

It is, perhaps, safe to assume that no human being, unless

possibly the grossly defective, is born without an urge to self-realization which would lead to aggressive behaviour. There is also sufficient evidence for the assumption that wide quantitative differences in instinctual endowment exist among individuals. Innate potentialities of the mind have been compared to packets of chemicals which would, sooner or later, open up through the process of inner growth and react to stimulation by the enviroment. Each human individual has the same number of 'packets', containing the same kind of 'chemicals', but in each individual the 'packets' differ in size. In other words, there is hardly an individual who is born incapable of affection, anger or fear, to mention only a few tendencies assumed to be innate, but some individuals are more prone to be moved to fear, anger or tenderness than others.

The innateness of quantitative individual differences has been established with regard to general intelligence, or Spearman's 'g' (50), and the common-sense view holds this to be true also with regard to temperament and the emotional endowment. No such extensive research, however, has been carried out in this field as there has been in the field of 'g'. Professor Cyril Burt in *The Young Delinquent* stressed the important factor in delinquency—emotional instability—which he thought to be inheritable, as it was characteristic of the whole family group (8, p. 605). Some of the young delinquents he studied were endowed with a capacity for exceptionally strong emotions: the eight-year-old murderer Jerry could be aroused with equal ease to excessive anger, stormy grief or demonstrative affection. Burt's later work on a group of adults (9) confirmed his hypothesis of the existence of 'General Emotionality', an innate factor corresponding, in the domain of emotion, to Spearman's 'g', or 'General Intelligence', in the domain of cognitive capacity. He also found that there was a characteristic bi-polar grouping of emotions: some individuals displayed what appeared to be a greater innate capacity for experiencing 'aggressive' emotions; others—for 'inhibitive' emotions. Those who were more easily moved to joy were also more sociable, self-assertive, prone to anger and curiosity, and

28

more attracted by the opposite sex. Those in whom sorrow was more quickly aroused were also quicker than the other group in experiencing disgust, fear, tenderness and submission. Incidentally, by listing joy, sociability, sex, self-assertion, anger and curiosity under 'aggressive' emotions, Burt clearly uses the term 'aggressive' in the sense of 'outgoing', 'expansive', 'positive', that is, in the connotation advocated by myself.

Once the existence of such innate differences in emotional endowment is accepted, it might appear possible at first glance that qualitative differences in aggressive behaviour may be quantitative in origin. In other words, a person may be so well endowed with self-assertion that he is impelled to express it in any form of achievement, irrespective of its social value, or practical expediency, and sometimes at the expense of society. The delinquent, the neurotic and the insane, on this supposition, would be individuals with an unusually strong component of self-assertive urge in their constitution, who are unable to tolerate the damming-up of the impulse owing to its excessive pressure, and so break the barriers of social custom and convention. Something of this kind is implied in Freud's hypothesis of 'the innate strength of instincts'—of aggression and sex—which he advanced to account for neurotic breakdowns (21). It would then seem probable that persons who limit their self-assertion to socially approved forms may be innately less aggressive than the first group, and thus have from the beginning less difficulty in controlling their impulses and in enduring frustration and delay.

Perhaps the only way of proving or disproving this hypothesis would be to carry out an experiment with a group of infants, beginning from the hour of their birth. They would have to be brought up in a mental and physical environment as uniform as it is possible to achieve; observed and rated for the amount of self-assertion they show in identical situations; graded accordingly, and further studied throughout childhood and, perhaps, adolescence, while environmental conditions are still kept constant, all this with the aim of discovering what forms their self-assertion would tend to assume. If the children, who were rated high in infancy on their self-assertive propensities, showed a significant correlation between it and a tendency to 'negative' forms of aggression, whereas the other group showed a similarly high correlation between low rating for self-assertion and the 'positive' forms of aggression, the hypothesis could be regarded as proved.

It is obvious that there are great difficulties in the way of such an experiment. The principal difficulty would be to keep the environment uniform for all the children involved, and this would be even greater with regard to mental environment than to physical conditions. It can now be regarded as certain that the mental development of the infant is influenced subtly and profoundly by the attitude of the ministering adult; and the necessity to ensure that every child in the experimental group receives an equal amount of attention, affection and stimulation might present an almost insoluble dilemma to those who conduct the experiment.

A way to minimize the differential influence of mental environment would be to make the experiment on a sufficiently large scale. If several such groups of children, differing in social and economic status of their parents, in nationality and race, in intellectual and temperamental endowment, were studied with the aim of determining the strength of their innate endowment in self-assertion and the forms taken by this urge during development, and if the results of the study showed significant correlations between the strength of the innate impulse and the 'negative' expressions of aggression, the concealed differential effects of mental environment could, perhaps, be discounted. Plainly, however, a study of this kind is not a prospect for the immediate future, and may not even be justifiable on humanitarian grounds.

When experimental data are lacking, a closer examination of a hypothesis in the light of common experience may be of value. We may ask: does it seem probable to a careful observer of human beings that the forms taken by the self-assertive urge depend exclusively on the innate strength of this urge? In other words, does a child who destroys persistently, fights excessively, or steals and truants appear to be more endowed in self-assertion than a child who excels in games or studies, is a leader among his contemporaries and is first to volunteer for any adventurous or competitive task? Can we say with a fair amount of certainty that an adult criminal or homicidal maniac is more aggressively self-assertive than a successful barrister, politician or army commander?

It is obvious that no answer can be given with any certainty because we are aware of a number of other factors, environmental and innate, which might have contributed to the behaviour of the child or the shaping of the career of an adult. The self-assertive urge, which is a part of personality, is bound to be affected in its manifestations by the personality as a whole, and by all the complexity of the particular circumstances which influence the development of personality. Whatever its strength, it cannot act in isolation, and it seems illogical to assume that its direction and the forms it takes could be determined exclusively by its quantity.

Nevertheless, this does not dispose of the probability that the strength of the urge is *one* of the factors determining its manifestations. In the study of forms of self-assertion, as in all studies of social phenomena, we are faced with the facts of multiple causation. We cannot expect to find a simple and clear-cut issue in a matter as complex as the interaction of environment and innate endowment in the development of human personality, but we could perhaps discover the relative importance of several factors involved, by the methods of comparison and correlation.

Adler has given much prominence to the role of self-assertion in the formation of individual 'life-patterns' (1). He came to the conclusion that the thwarting of the self-assertive urge produces one of the three types of response from the developing individual. In the first instance, attempts at self-assertion are abandoned and the child assumes a submissive, masochistic attitude towards his environment. Some measure of dominance over his environment is, however, achieved through being 'good'. In the second instance, neurotic symptoms are developed and the child asserts himself in devious ways. In the third instance, compensation for feelings of inadequacy is sought in positive achievement, and satisfaction of the self-assertive impulse obtained through acquisition of knowledge and skill in games. The factors determining the form of response were, in Adler's view, largely external, that is, social and environmental: the relationship between the child and his parents, and their handling of the child's demands upon his environment, while in Freud's view they were largely internal, that is, represented by the strength of the child's instinctual endowment and his reactions to his own impulses and to parental disapproval and prohibition of his early sexual activities and demands. By implication, Adler's theory means that a wise mother can always shape the child's self-assertive urge into socially acceptable forms. Exaggerated aggressiveness, in his opinion, is always a compensation for the feelings of inferiority, and these are grounded in the child's early experiences. Suttie (54) is even more emphatic on this point, for he derives the whole character of our civilization, aggressive and competitive in the extreme, from the 'taboo on tenderness', 'the refusal of the mother to give to the child', which arouses anxiety and fosters rivalry, instead of co-operation.

Depth psychology has established the importance of early family relationships for the formation of character, but mostly in indirect ways, through the study of neurosis in adults and the exploration of adult memories, dreams and fantasies. It was clearly desirable for the sake of verification, as well as of possible new discoveries, to explore these very relationships in the crucial phase when the emotional attitudes on which character is based are in the process of formation. The study, of which this book is a result, is one such attempt at the exploration of a particular field—the field of aggressive behaviour, aggressive fantasies and emotions in children and adolescents—and at relating them to their family background.

III. AGGRESSION AND DELINQUENCY

(a) *Previous Research*

It is perhaps not surprising that the negative forms of aggressive or self-assertive behaviour have always attracted more notice from the layman, as well as from the student of psychology and sociology, than the positive forms. Social misfits personify a sharp and striking criticism of our educational, economic and political systems, perhaps of the entire character of our civilization. Their behaviour, their mental attitudes are a challenge to society which society cannot afford to ignore. For this reason delinquents and criminals have been studied more fully and by a greater number of investigators than the specially gifted: to a dozen books on delinquency no more than one on superior ability could be quoted off hand.

That delinquent behaviour is 'aggressive' in the negative meaning of the term would hardly be disputed by anyone, though the actual amount of the aggressive component may vary with individual cases and kinds of delinquency. Such variations would obviously depend on the personality of the delinquent and on his previous history. For, contrary to the popular view, the delinquent 'type' does not really exist, although certain kinds of personality are found perhaps with greater frequency among delinquents than among the general population. This will become apparent in the following pages.

Medical men, psychologists and sociologists who have studied delinquency approached it, as might well be expected, from the standpoint of their particular interest, and, perhaps inevitably, arrived at different conclusions. Except for the pioneer inquiry of 1816, the earliest approach was through the study of bodily characteristics. The well-known theory of Lombroso was based on certain anatomical and physiological data and viewed criminality as an outcome of physiological 'degeneration', characterized by a number of stigmata, or malformations of ears, roof of the mouth and skull (38). This has since been disproved by the research of Goring (24) on the English criminal. Goring has shown that these 'stigmata' of criminality were no more common among the inhabitants of the English prisons than they were among the general population of the same social and economic status. Lombroso's contribution, however, retains a certain value as the first attempt at studying the individual criminal from the scientific point of view, and at the application of scientific methods to the solution of the problem of criminal behaviour. The methods, admittedly, were imperfect, and the conclusions arrived at somewhat premature, but a start in the right direction has been made.

The idea of innate predisposition to delinquency, although dissociated from Lombroso's concept of 'atavism', has not been entirely abandoned. It seems that Marjorie Fry was influenced by it when she described a certain type of young delinquent as *The Ancestral Child* (22) and explained his behaviour as due to a 'primitive' mental constitution. Such children, she thinks, do not clearly grasp the difference between 'mine' and 'thine': psychologically and morally, they still live in an age when most things were owned by the community, and each member could take as much as he needed from the common pool. This is not borne out by the evidence of other investigators, who found that the great majority of delinquents, far from being unconscious of the distinction between 'mine' and 'thine', are well aware, at least intellectually, that their behaviour is 'wrong'. As for the postulated 'primitive' mental attitude to property, it is doubtful that it ever existed as a general attitude. Judging by the primitive societies now in existence, it is much more probable that several different ways of owning property co-existed at the same time and in the same group. Some kinds of property might have been pooled and shared, whereas others remained in exclusive personal possession, and its theft might have been punishable by expulsion, or even death.

Another attempt to explain criminality by hereditary factors was made by Professor J. Lange in his study of forty pairs of twins (37). In dissimilar twins, whose innate differences can be as great as between any pair of ordinary siblings, no close similarity in social development or subsequent careers was found between the members of a pair. In identical twins, however, only three pairs out of seventeen showed such divergencies, whereas in the remaining fourteen pairs both twins were criminal. In the three divergent pairs one member of a pair only was criminal, but in each case there were contributory physiological factors which could account for criminal behaviour, such as brain injury at an early age.

These findings led Lange to the conclusion that:

> 'Heredity plays a role of paramount importance in making the criminal; certainly a far greater role than many are prepared to admit' (37, p. 173).

Later, however, he adds that:

> 'Heredity alone is not exclusively a cause of criminality; one must allow a certain amount for environmental influences. Even our monozygotic pairs did not by any means show complete agreement in their attitude to crime' (37, p. 173).

He admits 'the possibility that both twins were subjected to similar mental influences in early childhood, which, according to their similar natures, determined their similar destinies' (37, pp. 179–80), but almost immediately he dismisses the crucial problem of early mental environment in the following sentence:

> 'But it is perhaps unnecessary to go closely into this matter, as according to the well-known theory, the influences in question appear to recede further and further back to the earliest and dimmest beginnings of childhood' (37, pp. 179–80).

This light-hearted dismissal of the 'well-known theory' (presumably Freud's) detracts from the value of Lange's investigation, for he seems to imply that the earliest influences in the child's life are the least important for the development of

character, and so can safely be ignored, whereas this is con-
tradicted by the evidence of all recent research (to say nothing
of a mass of evidence accumulated by individual analysts of
various schools), not the least being the study of the effects of
separation from the mother on infants under four years of age,
carried out by John Bowlby and his collaborators (5). It might,
of course, have been impossible to secure the required data, as
all the pairs of twins Lange studied were adults, but in any case
this did not justify his assumption that such data were not
worth investigating.

It should be clear that the relative importance of innate endowment and of early environment in the causation of both
delinquency and neurosis would never be decisively demonstrated unless several pairs of identical twins were separated at
birth and brought up in widely differing mental environment.
Nothing is proved by Lange's study, because none of the twins
he studied was separated before the age of seven, and the
majority remained in frequent contact and communication
with each other throughout their lives.

Perhaps a decisive blow to physiological theories of delinquency has been dealt by W. A. Willemse, who studied 200
youths in a reformatory school in South Africa (56). Using
Kretschmer's typology (35) to classify them, he found 'an
extreme diversity and complexity of type of criminal personalities' (56, p. 3). He also found that certain distinct types of
delinquent behaviour tended to be associated with distinct
types of constitution, but the same constitutional types were, of
course, common among the general population. Willemse, however, did not attempt to investigate the original causes of
criminal behaviour in his subjects. Therefore, his analysis,
though useful for prognosis in individual cases, contains little
that is of value for preventive work on delinquency, or for the
diagnosis of a pre-delinquent personality.

It is, perhaps, true to say that the tendency among medical
writers is to overstress the innate, physiological factors, such
as 'degeneracy', inborn 'perversity', the defects of the brain or
the glandular system, as probable causes of delinquent be-

haviour. Sociologists, on the other hand, over-emphasize the role of environment, and imply that an all-round improvement in living conditions would dispose of most crime. This is not improbable, for much juvenile delinquency may be regarded as sporadic and seasonal, due principally to external, rather than to inner causes. Lack of supervision, idleness, abundance and accessibility of food and toys in street markets or multiple stores, lands many a child in a Juvenile Court. Yet this observation, however correct, does not account for recidivism, for which sociological studies provide no adequate explanation.

Some environmental factors were known to be associated with delinquency as early as 1816 (10), and it is rather remarkable that the most recent sociological studies of delinquency represent little more than elaboration of the themes already outlined by the earliest. In 1816, 'broken homes, the improper conduct of parents, the want of education, the want of suitable employment, the violation of the Sabbath and the habit of gambling in public streets' were listed as the principal among the causes of 'crime among the young' (10). Recently, 'broken homes' figured prominently in J. H. Bagot's study of juvenile delinquents in Liverpool and the surrounding districts (3). He found that 69 per cent of the delinquents he studied were unemployed and that in about 80 per cent the home discipline was 'defective'. Cyril Burt (8) also puts 'defective discipline in the home' high on his list of factors which he regards as important in the causation of delinquency. Carr-Saunders, Mannheim and Rhodes (10) found that delinquents, on the average, do not have such good school records as nondelinquents, and that their average attendance at Sunday schools is lower than that of the latter. Thus, all the findings of 1816 are confirmed in 1940–42, with the exception of 'the habit of gambling in public streets', and it seems that in the last hundred years, sociologists have not made any startling discoveries in this particular field, even though they greatly widened the scope of their investigations.

Bagot concluded his investigation with a statement that 'environmental factors must be held to be the principal causes

37

of such delinquencies as appear in court' (3, p. 85), yet in another connection he admits that :

> 'Recidivism seems to occur in approximately equal proportions in all areas (of Liverpool and the surrounding districts), and *the problem is not confined to any one section of the population.* The reason for this is not clear' (3, pp. 46-7).

Significant also is his remark with regard to unemployment among delinquents:

> 'Unemployment, however, is *frequently a symptom of some other factor,* which may not always be very obvious, such as inability to hold a job' (3, p. 57).

The manner in which Bagot repeatedly approaches recognition of the importance of psychological factors in delinquency, and yet fails to draw the obvious inferences, is in itself a demonstration of the danger of separating the sociological and the psychological aspects of the problem. Clearly, it is recidivism, and not isolated delinquent acts, which constitute a social problem, and if sociologists are unable to account for it in terms of enviromental factors alone, they should recognize that material environment is important only in so far as it affects human, and especially family, relationships.

The especial value of Carr-Saunders, Mannheim and Rhodes's study of *Young Offenders* (10) lies in just this recognition of the importance of family relationships, and in their use of the control group technique. As we have seen, Bagot made no attempt to investigate whether the factors to which he attaches so much importance really were causes and not merely concomitant circumstances of delinquency. And moreover, his own remarks, quoted above, show that he could have noticed that. Carr-Saunders and his collaborators, on the other hand, showed how deceptive statistical methods can be, unless their data can be seen in a true perspective, by comparing them with the data for an unselected group belonging to the same strata of the population.

What Bagot had found, Carr-Saunders and his collaborators

confirmed: broken homes, irregularity of parental employment, relative lack of recreational facilities, etc., all these were present, *but* only slightly more frequent in the lives of the delinquents than in those of normal children living in the same neighbourhood. With regard to any of these factors, the quantitative data for the two groups were not significantly different. The only two significant differences were in the greater incidence of delinquency among the siblings of delinquent subjects, and in the type of family where the heads, not being the parents of the subject, were cohabiting. Out of 144 cases where there was previous delinquency in the home, 133 were themselves delinquent (10, p. 149). Of 47 homes where the adoptive parents were cohabiting, 43 had cases of delinquency (10, p. 150).

The inference which the authors drew from these findings was that:

> 'The chance of a delinquent coming from a home with an abnormal atmosphere is three or four times as great as the chance of a delinquent coming from a home with a normal atmosphere' (10, p. 159).

and they emphasize the important role of psychological factors by urging that research should be extended into the psychological realm, for the reason that:

> 'We shall not begin to know what to do with regard to susceptible types until progress has been made in this field, and unless we have well-founded lines of action with regard to susceptibility, we cannot make any attempt to cope with one half of the whole problem' (10, p. 149).

It seems as if, with this concept of 'susceptibility to delinquency', which Carr-Saunders and his collaborators explicitly postulate, the wheel has come full circle. From the periphery, the outward circumstances, we return to the centre, the delinquent himself. Is it not time that we studied him as a person? Have we not almost forgotten him in studying his environment, or rather come to regard him as an abstraction, something in the nature of the Economic Man? Are we not near to assuming that

39

he possesses certain characteristics common to the whole of his species and that he can be identified by these particular traits?

Among other questions, we wonder what this 'susceptibility' might be. Might it be, after all, some lack, or excess, of certain innate potentialities? The search for an answer, however, is now transferred from the physiological and sociological into the psychological sphere, and we find that psychologists have never quite lost sight of this particular possibility, for most of them are clearly aware of the intimate interaction between heredity and environment.

In 1912, Burt (8) looked into the histories of his delinquent subjects and found that in their families there was a much greater incidence of drunkenness, wandering, inability to hold a job, violent temper, etc. These, he thought, could be regarded as signs of general 'emotional instability', and there is not much doubt that emotional instability, in so far as it is related to temperament and the instinctual basis of personality, can be transmitted. Burt therefore concluded that:

> 'The share of innate constitution in the production of delinquency is beyond doubt considerable' (8, p. 605).

This, of course, does not mean that emotional instability is always transmitted, or that if it is transmitted, it inevitably leads to delinquency. It is possible that if the family background of these children was more favourable, their emotional instability would not have expressed itself in delinquent behaviour. Burt fully recognizes this when he emphasizes that:

> 'It would be a gross distortion, a mistake too commonly deduced from current fatalistic theories, to paint every criminal as the helpless victim of his inborn nature. There still remains a large balance of offenders (60 to 65 per cent) whose lawless actions have been precipitated primarily by the difficulties of their environment or by the events of their own past life' (8, p. 605).

As it happens, some of the specific characteristics of the delinquent, which Burt regarded as probably innate, such as over-potency of the sexual, acquisitive and combative drives, have been postulated by Freud as pre-requisites of neurotic maladjustment ('the innate strength of instincts'); whereas Henderson and Gillespie (28) found much evidence of emotional instability, or 'neuropathic constitution' in the families of their neurotic and psychotic patients.

In any case, whatever these innate factors may be, they appear to be of too general a nature, and difficult, if not impossible, to isolate. In Burt's words they are 'by their nature irremediable, apart from measures of eugenics' (8, p. 605). To advocate eugenic measures in order to deal with emotional instability in the present state of public—and specialist—opinion would be, to say the least, unrealistic. Public opinion is unanimously against such measures, whereas specialist opinion is divided. The whole matter of the inheritance of mental traits is too complex, and our knowledge of it too much in a state of flux, to allow a formulation of a definite policy, even of a *pia desiderata*. The popular belief that 'genius is akin to insanity' is, no doubt, a gross exaggeration of the known fact that some geniuses were unstable, while some became insane in later life. Nevertheless, such careful students of mental abnormality as Henderson and Gillespie (28) are against the sterilization of 'neuropaths' on the grounds that gifted individuals do emerge from such 'highly-strung' families, and that 'neuropathic heredity does not inevitably lead to deterioration of the stock, but sometimes improves with successive generations' (28, p. 39).

Therefore, even if we knew for certain what kind of innate traits are associated with delinquent behaviour, we would still hesitate to prevent such people from having children, for the children might not inherit these particular traits, nor, if the environment were controlled, need they inevitably become delinquent. In other words, the effects of emotional instability on the formation of character might be reduced by an appropriate modification of the environment.

Sociological studies of delinquency have shown clearly that the crucial part of environment consists of human relationships. Hence, it is principally with the study of the relationships between the delinquent and his family, and other persons important to him, that some of the recent psychological investigations have been concerned.

By concentrating on the psychological aspect of environment the psychologist does not imply that the material side is unimportant and could be neglected. Like the social reformer, he wishes for an all-round improvement in material conditions, both for humanitarian and for scientific reasons. He is well aware, with Julian Huxley (31), that gross inequalities in material environment obscure the very real differences existing among individuals in respect of their intellectual and emotional endowment. When material inequalities are eliminated, the effects of mental environment on the development of the child will appear undisguised, and the task of separating such effects from innate characteristics will become much easier.

Some very important findings emerged from recent psychological studies of delinquency, especially from those in which control groups were used. It is impossible to over-emphasize the importance of control groups' technique, for it must be obvious that not until we compare delinquent children with the non-delinquents of the same social and economic strata, and of approximately the same level of intelligence, can we be certain that what we learn about their environment, or their mental make-up, has any real relation to their delinquency.

In fairness to the pioneer investigation of Burt (8), we should admit that many of the factors associated with delinquency, 'discovered' by other investigators in the last twenty years, had been mentioned by him in his book, written in 1925. One such discovery was that a delinquent act frequently represented a reaction to an unconscious inner conflict, involving jealousy, fear, anger, or any other powerful emotion, and that sometimes it was a substitute for an action which the child regarded as more blameworthy than delinquency. Healy and Bronner amplified and confirmed this discovery in their study of *Mental Conflict and Misconduct* (26). In many of their cases, stealing was a substitute for masturbation or 'improper' thoughts about sex.

It would have been most instructive to have compared this group with another, of children who also had conflicts about sex, yet developed other symptoms, instead of resorting to delinquency. Neither Burt, nor Healy and Bronner, however, employed control groups in these studies, and so this particular question has remained unanswered so far.

Healy and Bronner corrected their deficiency of method in a later study (27), in which they posited a very pertinent question: why is it that in large families, from which delinquents usually come, not *all* the children are delinquent? It appeared as if neither defective discipline, nor the crowded home, poverty and unemployment of the parents, nor common heredity, nor even the example of the delinquent sibling were sufficient to induce delinquent behaviour in most of these children. What was it then that tipped the balance in the case of the delinquents? 'Their relationship with their family', was the answer given by Healy and Bronner.

Of the 153 delinquent children whom they studied 'not more than 20 per cent had reasonably satisfactory relationships with their families', and 'a major emotional disturbance was discovered to exist in 92 per cent of cases' (27, pp. 48–9). Almost a third of the cases 'felt rejected, unloved or insecure in emotional relationships' (27, pp. 48–9). The non-delinquent sibling, though living in the same, often unfavourable material environment, had, as a rule, the advantage of a more satisfactory relationship with one or both parents.

With regard to the personalities of the delinquents themselves, Healy and Bronner noted their hyperactivity. Delinquent children are usually very restless, and have a history of restlessness as infants. Healy and Bronner, however, doubt that it is a constitutional trait. They write:

> 'There is evidence that emotional thwartings and dissatisfactions, dating back to very early years, may be the exciting cause of hyperactivity. . . . It was discovered that the vast majority of our cases had highly disturbing emotional situations in family life' (27, p. 45).

43

Thus, both delinquency and hyperactivity may be the consequences of what the authors describe as 'highly disturbing emotional situations' occurring in 'very early years'.

The next step was, clearly, to try to ascertain the character of these emotional situations, and it was taken by Dr. John Bowlby in his study of 'Forty-four Juvenile Thieves' (6). Bowlby compared forty-four pilferers with the same number of emotionally disturbed, or neurotic, children who did not steal. He found that seventeen of his delinquent subjects (about 40 per cent) had been separated from their mothers at an early age, for periods of varying length. Of the forty-four controls only two (5 per cent) had suffered such a break. Twelve of the delinquent group, who had suffered early separation, developed a 'reactive character' which Bowlby describes as 'affectionless, shameless and irresponsible'. They 'displayed an inability to form emotional relationships, and a profound distrust of anyone who offers kindness and help'.

He concludes that:

> 'There can be little doubt that prolonged mother-child separations are associated to a high degree both with chronic delinquency in general and with certain types of chronic delinquent in particular' (6, p. 110).

Yet even this finding, however valuable and suggestive, does not explain why only *some* of the children who suffer early separation become delinquent. In my own psycho-therapeutic practice, I have had cases of children who had suffered separation from their mothers at the age of two to four years, the most critical time in Bowlby's opinion, and who developed severe mental illness, but were not delinquent. This sends us back to the study of the individual delinquent, not in isolation, but as a part of a total personal-social situation, of a particular interaction between the individual and his environment.

(b) The Individual Delinquent

Recent psychological studies have shown fairly conclusively that no single psychological type of delinquent exists, just as it had been shown earlier that 'criminals' are not distinguished by any one kind of physiological constitution. Individual differences among the delinquents may be as wide as in any other selected group of the general population (16). On the other hand, the very fact that they are delinquent and not merely neurotic or maladjusted, indicates that there must be something specific about their mental attitude which distinguishes them from the non-delinquent.

So far the search for the common factor, or factors, among the variety of psychological types forming the delinquent population, has not produced any conclusive results. In America, Stern (51) compared twenty delinquent children with twenty non-delinquent neurotics and found that the delinquents tended to be more active, energetic, outgoing, aggressive and physically healthier. The non-delinquent neurotics tended to be more introverted, solitary, submissive and unhealthy. In the family situation, parental rejection was found to be more common in the delinquent group, whereas over-protection and over-concern were prevalent in the non-delinquent. Unfortunately, the samples were too small to be anything more than suggestive of significant differences. Bowlby's study brought out one important character trait which 17 per cent of his cases had in common—their 'inability to form personal relationships' (6), but this trait is, of course, found in many schizoid neurotic or pre-psychotic personalities. 'Emotional instability', suggested by Burt, may be another characteristic trait, but this again the delinquents share with many maladjusted non-delinquents.

Some of the deeper studies of the individual delinquent include a psycho-analytical contribution by Dr. Kate Friedlander (17), who came to a conclusion that delinquency is preceded by the formation of an 'anti-social character', usually in the first five or six years of life. This character formation

'manifests itself in the inability to withstand a desire regardless of the results' (17, p. 94).

It is, perhaps, generally true of the delinquents that, in Dr. Friedlander's words:

45

'The gratification of their desires is more important to them than any object relationship' (17, p. 111).

In other words, delinquents do not seem to value the opinion which other people, be it their parents, teachers or neighbours, hold about them, and are not prepared to forgo immediate satisfactions because of parental or social disapproval. This, in Dr. Friedlander's view, constitutes the hall-mark of an anti-social character, and in this she is probably correct. What we all want to know, however, is the process by which this type of character is formed. Dr. Friedlander believes that three factors contribute to its formation:

'the strength of unmodified instinctive urges, the weakness of the Ego and the lack of independence of the Super-ego' (17, p. 94).

Translated into everyday language, this means more or less what a layman would describe as lack of self-control and the absence of properly assimilated moral standards, which, of course, has always been asserted about delinquents as a group. The knowledge that we need is exactly why the delinquents fail to acquire this self-control and to assimilate these moral standards, or, in psycho-analytical terms, why these 'instinctive urges' remain unmodified, why the Ego remains weak and the Super-Ego lacking in independence.

To this Dr. Friedlander replies by adducing the evidence of 'a disturbance in mother-child relationship'. She states that she

'has never found the same degree of inconsistency in the handling of primitive instinctive drives in the histories of neurotic patients as I invariably found in the histories of the delinquents' (17, p. 101).

Inconsistency in treatment has been noted also by Burt (8) when he listed 'defective' discipline as one of the most important among conditions associated with delinquent behaviour. He refers, however, to the 'inconsistent, alternately too harsh and too lenient' treatment of older children by their parents, whereas Dr. Friedlander is concerned with the early training of infants and toddlers.

Even so, she only claims to have found a relatively higher degree of inconsistency in the treatment of children who afterwards became delinquent, than in the histories of neurotic children. It can, thus, only be regarded as a contributory factor, but hardly as the one which determines the unconscious choice between delinquency and neurosis.

A welcome corrective to a temptation to generalize on a few cases is provided by several recent studies in which delinquents were classified into groups, according to the type of personality and of their social attitudes, with the circumstances and character of delinquent behaviour being taken into account.

Dr. G. W. Pailthorpe investigated 100 delinquent women and girls serving prison sentences in this country, and found that at least forty of them were suffering from some form of emotional maladjustment. Twenty-six of these provided clear evidence of mental conflict, which could be traced to some specific childhood experience, often to a 'fixation' on one of the parents. The delinquent behaviour in these cases appeared to be compensatory for early deprivation of security and affection. About 50 per cent of her cases, however, were 'contented and happy', and could be described as 'adapted to themselves', although not to society in general, or even to the group in which they found themselves (43). This may be the type which Dr. Friedlander would describe as due to 'anti-social character formation'.

Within the maladjusted group, Dr. Pailthorpe found some 5 per cent who, she thought, were 'suffering from defective sentiment development'. This may be the group whom Bowlby characterizes as 'affectionless, shameless and irresponsible'.

Perhaps the most valuable classification is the one made by Powdermaker (45), who studied 200 delinquent girls in a Home where conditions were especially favourable for treatment and observation. She distinguished three groups:

> '(1) Those whose early environment has been such that training in social living according to generally accepted standards had

been meagre or absent; (2) A group whose problems definitely involved psychopathology. Symptoms such as compulsions, conversions, depressions, and bizarre activities characteristic of schizophrenia were present; (3) An a-social but not a neurotic group, with whom no treatment methods were of any avail. The feature common to them all was their inability to make a real transference to any member of the staff. Some cases that might be ordinarily diagnosed as simple schizophrenia may well belong to this group' (45, pp. 61-2).

It is clear that the first group includes all cases of 'normal' delinquents, whose behaviour is determined principally by environmental conditions, and could be modified through improving these conditions and through educational measures. The second group includes neurotic and psychotic delinquents, such as constituted about 40 per cent of the group studied by Pailthorpe and more than 70 per cent of the group studied by Bowlby. The third group would probably include the 'affectionless, shameless and irresponsible' characters among Bowlby's pilferers, the anti-social characters as defined by Friedlander, and the large group in Pailthorpe's investigation whom she described as 'adapted to themselves' and 'contented and happy'. The smaller group (about 5 per cent), whom she described as 'suffering from defective sentiment development' may also belong here. All these have a common trait of 'inability to form a personal relationship', or 'to make a real transference' to any person in their environment.

Powdermaker notes that psychological treatment was rarely successful with the latter group. They certainly present the most arduous problem to the therapist, and society usually writes them off as beyond redemption. The hard core of prison population is probably recruited chiefly from them—the 50 per cent who are 'adapted to themselves' and appear 'contented and happy'. Yet failure in the treatment of such cases may only mean that it was not undertaken early enough, or not continued long enough. In this particular group, the emotional roots of delinquent behaviour probably go deeper and further into the individual's past, than in either of the other two.

48

That they go fairly deeply even in the usual population of Approved Schools has been shown clearly by the recent study of Stott (52). He found that among the 102 delinquent boys, aged between 15 and 18, whom he studied in one such school, there was not one case of simple 'wanting and taking' (52, p. 350), but a long history of thwarted emotional needs (52, p. 361). 'Every one of the boys found himself (at some time or other) in an emotionally intolerable situation' (52, p. 356).

In his analysis of the 'motives' of delinquent behaviour, which he classified into five groups: (i) avoidance-excitement, (ii) spite-retaliation, (iii) delinquent attention, (iv) wish to secure removal from home and (v) inferiority compensation (52, pp. 352 and 356-7), Stott emphasizes that all these reactions sprang from the unsatisfactory relationships between the delinquent and his parents.

This, of course, has been known for some time and was convincingly demonstrated by Healy and Bronner (27) in their comparative study of delinquents and their siblings. The problem which remains unsolved, as Stott himself recognizes, is the determination of the unconscious choice of delinquency as a way out of an 'intolerable situation', rather than any other form of 'breakdown'. Stott tends to dismiss this problem by indicating, quite correctly, that 'many formally non-delinquent breakdowns are delinquent in spirit, that is to say, are actuated by the same motives' (52, p. 363).

My own view for some time has been that both neurosis and delinquency are forms of 'negative' aggression, and that the principal external difference between them is that in delinquency aggression is transferred from the family to society at large, whereas in neurosis it is confined to the family group (33). Many neurotic symptoms have a strong aggressive component, and neurotic behaviour disrupts family life just as delinquent behaviour disrupts the life of a larger group.

For these reasons I chose to approach the problem of delinquency from the study of aggressive behaviour in general, rather than from the study of delinquent behaviour itself. And, as specific characteristics of behaviour in any creature, or

D   49

group, can only be made clear by comparing it with the behaviour of another creature or group, I undertook to study three groups of children—normal, neurotic and delinquent— in conditions where free expression of aggressive impulses and aggressive fantasies was possible and even encouraged.

Part II

Projection Studies of Aggression in Children

★

I. AGGRESSION AND FAMILY RELATIONSHIPS

The student of aggressive behaviour has, as a rule, more opportunity for studying negative forms of aggression than its positive forms, and there is always some danger that he will lose sight of its positive aspect in his absorption with the negative. I do not claim to have avoided this danger in my own investigations as much as I should like to have done. Negative forms of aggression, such as delinquent behaviour and a variety of neurotic symptoms, force themselves upon our attention, while society and our own humanity demand that they should be dealt with. A psychologist, who is also a psychotherapist, has greater opportunities for the study of deviations of the aggressive impulse than of its socially acceptable creative forms. It is not easy for him to remain a detached observer and experimenter, for he works with human beings whose suffering affects him. A great deal of his energy, skill and time is thus employed in relieving suffering, while knowledge of mental conditions necessary for healthy mental development remains largely limited to inferences drawn from the study of mental illness.

There is, besides, a considerable resistance on the part of parents, teachers, family doctors and educational authorities to psychological study of normal children—a superstitious fear that the psychologist may do something to 'upset' or disturb them. Yet, without a great deal of research into mental health, as well as mental illness, no preventive psychotherapy can be practised, nor could conditions indispensable for mental health become a matter of common knowledge.

It was largely this difficulty in studying the conditions of mental health in normal subjects which led me to adopt the projective method for the study of manifestations of the aggressive urge. This method opened up possibilities for quick diagnosis and comparison between groups of subjects in their emotional reactions to pictures, specially designed to investigate some aspect of their mentality. It could be used in many cases where the more penetrating but slow and cumbersome methods of mental analysis were out of the question.

(a) A Test of Sado-Masochistic Attitudes

The first impulse to the study of aggression was given me, as might be expected, by observing its unhealthy functioning in a group of girls at a Hostel for the Unbilletable, early in the last war. These girls, aged between 11 and 15, showed many symptoms of emotional maladjustment of varying degrees of severity, from bed-wetting and nail-biting to running away, truancy from school and sexual misdemeanour. Most of them pilfered from shops and from one another whenever they had the opportunity. The most striking trait of their behaviour, however, which they all had in common, was their intense eagerness to form a relationship with an adult, usually a member of the hostel staff, and to secure the adult's exclusive attention and affection. Yet, whenever such a relationship was on the way to being established, they displayed an utter inability to sustain it, and by renewed aggression and misbehaviour usually succeeded in wrecking it. Nor did they prove capable of harmonious relationships among themselves. They continually attacked, hurt, frustrated and annoyed one another, professing dislike or 'hatred' for each other, and only occasionally ganging together for a hostile demonstration against the hostel staff, or a pilfering expedition to the neighbouring stores.

The compulsive sado-masochistic character of this behaviour was clearly evident, for it injured the girls more than it did the

52

A TEST OF SADO-MASOCHISTIC ATTITUDES

staff by depriving them of privileges and of the very friendship and affection which they were seeking. The need for recognition and appreciation for one's own sake, which is a basic need of every human being, had taken negative forms in these girls, and it worked havoc with their social relationships. The mental processes behind their behaviour, however, were not clear, nor could they be studied by means of regular interviews, conversation and analysis for lack of time and opportunity. All I could do at the time was to find a means by which I could probe their aggressive emotions, and which could also be used to investigate similar emotions in a group of normal girls, with the aim of comparing them. I could think of no better method than that of pictorial projection.

The theories underlying the use of Pictorial Projection tests are too well known at present to require explanation or description. Their principal main assumptions, however, might as well be re-stated. Of those enumerated by W. E. Henry (29) the most important are: psychological determinism, the unconscious motivation of behaviour and the tendency of the individual to project himself into some character or characters represented in the picture. Much convincing evidence in favour of these assumptions has been provided since by the application of Murray's Thematic Apperception Test (41).

This test, however, was not suitable for the particular circumscribed study I wanted to make, and I found it necessary to design my own set of pictures which I called a 'Test of Sado-Masochistic Attitudes'. This set of six black-and-white drawings was done for me by an artist[1] to whom I explained my requirements, and represented a fairly close approximation to my conception. The pictures were intended to allow of at least two interpretations. In three of them a parent figure appears, who can be viewed as benevolent and protective or playful on the one hand, or as threatening or punishing, on the other. In each of the remaining three pictures a situation of suffering, cruelty or anguish is suggested, but not inevitably forced upon the onlooker. I showed these pictures to twenty

[1] Mrs. Kay Gardiner.

delinquent girls between 12 and 19 years of age, some of whom were the inmates of a Hostel for the Unbilletable while others came from a Home for Moral Welfare where they were placed by order of the Court. As a 'control' group I used twenty non-delinquent girls, members of various girls' clubs. All the girls with one exception in each group came from elementary schools, or had recently left such schools, and were employed in some unskilled or semi-skilled occupation. In each of the two groups there was one girl of border-line defective intelligence, and one of high average intelligence with an I.Q. of about 120.

They usually wanted to know the aim of the interview, and I explained that I was making a special study of people's ability to make up stories on pictures. They often appeared relieved to find that I did not come to preach good behaviour or ask them questions about their delinquencies. Many tackled the task with great gusto, and without apparent reserve or inhibition; some clearly enjoyed it. Others were reluctant, suspicious, almost frightened, yet unable to hold back the expression of feelings which the pictures aroused in them.

I showed them the pictures one by one with the following instructions:

> 'I am going to show you six pictures, one at a time. I want you to look at each picture carefully and make up a story about it. I don't want you to tell me exactly what you can see on the picture because, of course, I can see it myself. What I want you to do is to *make up* anything you like about it. I don't want you to make a long story because it would mean too much writing for me. I don't care about it being a "good story", but I want it to be *your own* story, not something you've read in a book or were told about. Well, here's the first picture. Start as soon as you are ready.'

If the girl, after having looked at the picture, hesitated and asked: 'What is it supposed to be?' I usually answered: 'Whatever you like to make it. It's up to you to tell me what you think it is.'

If the girl was particularly inhibited and seemed unable to make up a story at all, or if the story consisted of a bare, objective description, I prompted her with questions, using the same form of question in every case. For instance, I would ask about the picture (No. 1) representing a woman bending over a cradle: 'Do you think she is the baby's mother or a stranger? Or who else might she be? Can you tell me anything about the baby's father? Does he care for the baby? As much as the mother, or not so much? Is the baby a little girl or a little boy? Is he (or she) a good baby?' As a rule, no such detailed questioning was needed in connection with the other five pictures of the test, because the girls usually found more to say about them than about the first picture, which I came to regard rather as a shock-absorber. Yet its apparently neutral character proved to be far from neutral to some of the girls, whose responses to it were both varied and revealing.

After giving the test I usually had a short conversation with the girl, asking her about her family, in an attempt to find out her attitudes to her parents and siblings, her status in the family, and, whenever possible, the mental atmosphere of the home, as it was reflected in the girl's attitude to her companions, her work and life in general. In the case of the delinquent girls I was able to obtain much additional information from the superintendents of the home or hostel in which they lived. In a few cases I had the opportunity of seeing the girls several times and having long conversations with them. In every case there was evidence of a seriously disturbed relationship between the girl and one or both her parents.

This could be inferred from their stories, a number of which contained descriptions of maltreatment of children by adults. Pictures 3 and 6, which lend themselves most to such interpretation, produced a crop of stories of parental hatred and rejection. Even Picture 5, where only one human figure is represented, was interpreted by one delinquent girl as 'a man whipping a little boy who was a slave'. Of the possible forty stories on Pictures 3 and 6, the delinquent group produced sixteen stories of maltreatment, whereas the non-delinquent produced only seven such stories. This is clearly a highly significant difference.

On the other hand, the quantitative difference in the stories with *general* sado-masochistic content was not statistically significant for the two groups. It should, however, be made clear that in classifying these stories I used the term 'sado-masochistic' in a fairly wide sense. I included under this title all the stories which described a situation of suffering (maltreatment, punishment, pain, humiliation, rejection, threats) inflicted by one human being upon another, or by a human being upon an animal (e.g. 'He whips horses without mercy'). Stories describing attempts at suicide or suicidal wishes, cataclysms engulfing a number of human beings (earthquakes, floods), killing of human beings by animals and killing of animals by human beings were also included under this title. In so far as the term 'sado-masochistic' implies pleasure derived from inflicting and experiencing suffering, this was assumed to be implicit in the subjects' choice of theme. They would hardly have chosen such themes if they did not derive some satisfaction from them.

From the possible number of 120 for each group, the delinquent group composed sixty-six such stories, i.e. 3·3 per subject on the average, whereas the non-delinquent composed fifty-two, i.e. 2·6 per subject on the average. This difference is not statistically significant, and it means that in this unselected group of non-delinquent adolescent girls from working-class homes, sado-masochistic fantasies could be stimulated almost as easily as in a similar group of delinquent girls. The distribution of such stories per subject is shown in the following table.

TABLE I

Subjects	1	2	3	4	5	6	7	8	9	10	11	12	13	14	15	16	17	18	19	20	Total
							No. of sado-masochistic responses per subject														
Delinquents	3	3	4	3	3	4	3	5	4	3	3	4	3	2	3	1	1	5	5	4	66
Non-delinquents	2	1	1	4	1	2	2	2	4	4	1	4	3	5	4	3	4	2	2	1	52

This table shows that every subject in both groups produced at least one sado-masochistic story. It could not be said, therefore, that a few exceptionally sado-masochistic individuals were responsible for the bulk of such stories whereas the others were more or less free from them. There was, however, a greater saturation with sado-masochistic content in the stories of the delinquent group, as the following table shows.

TABLE 2

No. of sado-masochistic responses per subject

	5	4	3	2	1	0	Total
	No. of subjects giving the response						
Delinquents	3	5	9	1	2	–	20
Non-delinquents	1	6	2	6	5	–	20

Thus half of the non-delinquent subjects produced one or two sado-masochistic stories out of the possible six, whereas nearly half of the delinquents produced five or four out of six.

Frequency of sado-masochistic fantasies was, however, not the only and perhaps not the most important feature about these stories. A more detailed examination showed that a certain number of them had a 'happy ending'. The situation was represented as one of suffering or unhappiness, but the person or persons involved in it emerged safely out of their trials, or reconciliation took place, or compensation was provided. When I compared the stories of the two groups for this particular feature I obtained the following results:

TABLE 3

	Sad.-Mas. content unrelieved	Sad.-Mas. content corrected by 'happy ending'	Total
Group A (delinquent)	54	12	66
Group B (control)	20	32	52

These figures speak for themselves. The delinquents accept the sado-masochistic situation invented by themselves as one from which there is no escape, the non-delinquents emerge from a similar invented situation into a realistic world of ordinary happenings, a world in which many things that have 'gone wrong' are put right again.

Could the immediate environment and recent experiences of the girls account for this difference in their responses? Hardly so, for those who produced the unrelieved sado-masochistic responses were not at the time treated harshly or punished for their delinquencies. They lived under supervision but went out to work in a normal way and were allowed to mix with young people of both sexes. The discipline to which they had to submit was not very much more strict than that of ordinary hostels for young girls. They could go to a cinema or a dance once a week and to evening classes if they wanted to. If their sado-masochistic fantasies had a basis in reality, it must have been reality of an earlier date.

In any case, if reality was hard to bear, some compensatory fantasies could be expected. There was, however, an almost complete absence of these, as if suffering and cruelty depicted in these stories had in themselves a compensatory function and provided satisfaction for some, perhaps deeply unconscious, need. What, we might ask, determines the tendency of an individual, who is subjected to unpleasant, distressing or depressing experiences, to respond by producing compensatory, escapist fantasies, or pessimistic and sado-masochistic ones? The answer probably is that his responses are determined not by his immediate circumstances but by his innate temperament and his mental outlook, which is the outcome of his entire past. I feel therefore that it is justifiable to conclude that the content of the delinquent girls' fantasies was coloured so strongly with *inescapable* sado-masochism not because they happened to be delinquent, but because both their delinquency and their sado-masochism originated in some earlier experiences, of which their fantasies were a reflection.

(b) *Personal Histories of Two Delinquent Girls*

A confirmation of this was provided by the subjects' personal histories, whenever these could be obtained. The connection between these girls' stories and their grossly un-satisfactory family relationships can best be illustrated by the examination of a complete set of stories.

The girl Joan, aged 18 years 6 months, who was placed on probation for stealing and was living in the Home for Moral Welfare, produced the following stories. She was one of the first to whom the test was given, and the pictures were presented in the order shown in the record.

> *Picture* 1. A mother loves her baby and is working hard to make the baby happy.
>
> *Picture* 6. A father is bringing the baby up normal and healthy; he's bringing him up to face the hardships of life.
>
> *Picture* 5. He's ill-treating a child, being cruel to it.
>
> *Picture* 4. A native being punished for something he's done, and some cruel person tied him to a post to be eaten by vultures and to die helplessly.
>
> *Picture* 3. Husband and wife; the father has a grudge against the child for being a boy or a girl (opposite of what he wanted). He's wanting to kill or crush the baby.
>
> *Picture* 2. This woman set out on a journey to a desert; she finds she can't carry on much longer, and is begging and praying for help. There's a great deal of fear in her.

The first response is remarkable for its restraint, caution and brevity; it is indeed a 'screen' response, to avoid developing the dangerous theme of mother-baby relationship. The 'screen', however, is somewhat transparent, for the emphasis appears to be laid on 'hard work' rather than on love. No concrete example is given to illustrate how the mother's hard work contributes to the baby's happiness, as if Joan herself felt doubtful that it could do so.

The positive interpretation of the second response is obviously forced. There is nothing in Picture 6 to indicate that 'the father is bringing the baby up normal and healthy'. Joan's agitation, as she was faced with the picture, showed that her first thoughts about this picture were of a quite different

character; it probably aroused emotions which she was reluctant to express. It was most likely her awareness that she
herself was neither healthy, nor normal, which made her fly in
the face of the evidence and thus reveal her fears, and the
particular defence-mechanism she used in her personal relationships (as her history afterwards showed). This defence,
moreover, was as ineffective as her 'screening' device, for in the
second sentence of her story she gives away the secret of the
father's educational methods: '*He's bringing him up to face the
hardships of life.*'

As the test continued, the defensive attitude was gradually
abandoned and the inhibition partially overcome; the sado-
masochistic trends came to the fore. In the story on Picture 5,
also extremely brief, the man is said to 'maltreat a child' for no
particular reason. The man is swinging a long whip, but no
child is represented in the picture. In the story on Picture 4,
a 'native' is left 'to die helplessly' for some unspecified act; in
the story on Picture 3, the baby cannot please the father by
being either boy or girl; it is hated irrespective of sex, the father
wants 'to kill or crush it', and the mother apparently does not
object. In the story on Picture 2, the woman 'can't carry on
much longer, and is begging and praying for help' with 'a great
deal of fear'.

It looked as if Joan was identifying herself with the woman
in her last story, for she, too, was 'full of fear'. The very brevity
of her stories reflected her nervousness; she was afraid to
elaborate lest she should say too much and be obliged to reveal
something she preferred to conceal even from herself. She was
very nervous in the test situation, threw apprehensive glances
at me and twisted her handkerchief in her hands. She changed
colour and her voice trembled when she was shown Picture 6,
and had to make up her mind whether to speak her real
thoughts or to cover them up with some pleasanter invention.

I saw Joan several times after this and my conversations with
her brought out the following facts.

She was the younger of two children, her brother being
about two years older. Her father left her mother when Joan

was about four years old. Her mother then became a house-keeper to an elderly man and apparently cohabited with him, for Joan referred to this man as 'Daddy'. He died when Joan was sixteen, and her mother then obtained a post as a supervisor at a restaurant. Joan said that the post was a well-paid one, yet she claimed that it was necessary for her to help her mother financially because she had 'to pay off some debts'. Her brother used to help also, but, according to Joan, suddenly threw up the sponge; he went and married a girl of whom his mother disapproved, and since then had not visited the mother or sent her a penny of his wages.

Joan described her childhood as 'happy', although she said that her real parents before their separation 'were always at loggerheads'. Her foster-father 'gave her everything she wanted' and 'spoiled' her. On the other hand, her brother has always been her mother's favourite, 'her idol', in Joan's words. Joan, however, declared that she had the best of the bargain, as 'Daddy had more money than Mummy' and so could give her more and better presents than her mother could to the boy.

It was quite clear, however, that Joan had been extremely jealous of her brother. She had not a good word to say for him; he had been selfish, inconsiderate, heartless; he had deeply wounded his mother by his marriage and withdrawal; he had failed in his duty to her by cutting off financial help. Joan was sure that it must have hurt his mother all the more because 'he used to be so nice to her'. 'He has always been the one to show affection and to kiss mother', whereas Joan found it difficult to be demonstrative. He 'used to take mother to dances and cinemas and to spend money on her'. Yet Joan seemed to imply that he was not really sincere, for 'he could never talk to mother freely'. She claimed that, of the two, she was the one who could have 'heart-to-heart' talks with mother, and take care of her when she was ill or worried.

Joan's attitude towards her mother was clearly very ambivalent. Her hostility was evident from the exaggerated protestations of her concern about the mother's welfare and health. She declared that she was not interested in getting married, in having a home of her own. The only thing she wished to do after leaving the Home for Moral Welfare was to live with her mother and 'look after her'. 'I keep on dreaming about going travelling with mother—going abroad or somewhere . . . and of giving, giving to her all the time, sharing this and sharing that. . . .'

Nor was this 'need to give to the mother' confined to day-dreams alone; Joan, in fact, sent a pound to her mother out of her wages as a birthday present. Her anxiety about her mother's health was such that she threw up a job which she professed to like, and, without permission from the Warden of the Home, travelled to the town where her mother lived—just because she heard that her mother had had a fall and hurt her leg. Her mother, incidentally, was an able-bodied woman in her early forties, but Joan spoke of her as if she were an elderly invalid.

That Joan's unconscious hostility towards her mother was stronger than her conscious wish to help and to give, was shown by subsequent happenings. She was able to go back to her mother after she had left the home, but a few weeks later she wrote to the Superintendent asking if she could return to live in the town and whether she would be willing to help her to find a job. She could not get on with her mother and was soon 'in trouble' again.

The facts of Joan's childhood provide enough data to account for the sado-masochistic content of her fantasies. They originated, most likely, in the feelings of insecurity and of being rejected, which arose directly from parental quarrels, her father's desertion, and her mother's preference for the boy. As we know well from our own experience, being refused affection makes one feel inferior and unlovable. It also frequently arouses resentment and a wish to punish or hurt the rejecting person. We realize, however, that we are not likely to win love or recognition by these means, but on the contrary may antagonize this person further. Besides, our self-respect or pride often prevents us from fully admitting to ourselves the very fact of rejection or the feelings it has aroused in us. We can thus easily understand how intense, even if much less differentiated, such

62

experiences can be in the child, and how much more afraid he would be, by reason of his complete dependence, inexperience and youth, to express his hostility to the very person on whom he relies for love and protection. Nor is he less likely than we are, in similar circumstances, to feel guilty about his hostility and unwilling to admit it to himself or anybody else. He might then seek punishment by being 'naughty' which is less danger-ous than turning round and attacking the offending adult, and he will no doubt derive satisfaction from arousing emotion in the parent, even if it is the wrong kind of emotion. The maso-chism of later years, as Havelock Ellis has shown often derives from the emotional satisfaction obtained through being punished by an admired parent. On the other hand, the sadistic component of the complex emotion aroused by rejection might find expression in fantasies of power or in actual maltreatment of a weaker creature, such as a younger child or an animal.

In Joan, perhaps by reason of her instinctual endowment, the masochistic trend was noticeably stronger than the sadistic. In Irene, a twelve-year-old delinquent girl whom I tested at the Hostel for the Unbilletable, the sadistic trend was clearly predominant.

Irene's responses to the test were as follows:

Picture 1. Once upon a time there was a poor woman; she had seven sons and one baby girl. Her husband was dead, so her sons had to go out into the forest and earn money to keep them all. They often went to bed hungry, as they didn't earn much. The baby often cried because it was hungry, and the mother tried to comfort her.

Picture 6. There was once a husband and wife, who were very happy, but one day the husband was killed in a motor accident, so the wife married again. The second husband was a bully, who used to go out with other women and pretend he was not married. The wife had a little girl, Dora, and then the wife died, and the husband used to whip the little girl every day until she died, and then he was hung for cruelty.

Picture 4. Once upon a time in Egypt there was a man who's done wrong, so the King of Egypt had him put out on a desert, and tied to a post, and the birds came and ate him.

Picture 5. Tom was a very wealthy man who worked at a circus. He pretended he was poor, and worked at catching things up with a whip. He had taken a job away from a very poor man, so this poor man went to the police, and the police put the rich man in prison, and gave the poor man his job.

Picture 3. (When Irene was shown this picture she exclaimed: 'Ah! The one I did for No. 6 would have done for this one!') Then she proceeded. A lady had a little girl called Mary. Her mother is holding the little girl up. The father is playing with the baby and the baby has stopped crying.

Picture 1. A little boy has been wandering about the desert for a very long time and was very thirsty, and is jumping about for joy because he has found water.

No restraint is exercised over sado-masochistic fantasies in the first three of these stories. Everyone in the first story is unhappy: despite hard work, the sons of the widow 'often have to go hungry' and the baby 'often cried because it was hungry'. The mother merely 'tried' to comfort it, presumably without much success. There is a hopeless atmosphere about this story, as if it were assumed that whatever this family did, they could not escape their misery. The hunger from which all of them suffer is probably symbolic hunger—a craving for the affection of the mother, who 'tries' but does not succeed in giving them comfort.

The second story is quite remarkable in its concentration of sado-masochistic content. All the characters in it die, three of them a violent death. Irene, who chose to write her stories instead of saying them, had no hesitation in setting down this grim sequence of events: she wrote without stopping to consider, as if the story had been ready in her mind just waiting to be told.

The third story is a fairly objective description of the picture, significant chiefly by its matter-of-fact acceptance of the suitability of inhuman punishment for an unspecified 'wrong' action. In it, there is no sign of compassion, of any attempt to explain or justify the punishment which would indicate that its cruelty puzzled or disturbed. Irene appears to accept the situation with equanimity: there is philosophic calm, tinged with cannibalistic relish, in the concluding sentence of her story, 'And the birds came and ate him'.

When she was about to start on her fourth story, Irene was interrupted by other girls coming in and wanting to know what she was doing. This may have caused the change in the character of the three stories that followed. However, when Irene saw Picture 3, she exclaimed: 'Ah! The one I wrote for number 6 would have done for this one!' Clearly, the sado-masochistic fantasies were again stimulated, but she resisted them and produced an insipid little story instead.

As she wrote her last story, other girls were looking over her shoulder and she was anxious to finish and go off with them. The cowering posture of the figure in the picture could hardly suggest anything as boisterous as 'jumping for joy', and Irene's response to it was a mixture of impatience, mischievousness and defiance: here you are, take it or leave it, I'm not going to try any harder.

I got to know Irene fairly well during the few months I was in charge of 'the girls' half' of a Hostel for Unbilletable Children. She came to the hostel after she had been put on probation for stealing a bicycle and after two or three billet hostesses had refused to keep her because they found her unmanageable. She was a good-looking dark girl, well-grown, strong and mature for her age and, with an I.Q. of 125, well above the average in intelligence.

During her stay in the hostel her behaviour was characterized by an unusual blend of conformity and defiance. She could control herself well enough to avoid breaking the conditions of her probation, i.e. she refrained from stealing or running away. On the other hand, she often was extremely provocative and could not tolerate any preference being shown to other girls. If she thought this was happening, she voiced her accusations in the most vivid language and at once attacked 'the favourite' with her tongue and often with her fists. She persecuted two younger girls because she thought they were favoured by the staff. If one of them was reprimanded for something, Irene declared her indignation at the insufficiency of this 'punishment' and went around saying, 'I'll do the same as she's done. She doesn't get into trouble! I'll crack her head for her. I'll pull her eyes out!'

Whatever Irene's other defects, she certainly was no coward. She was ready to challenge and stand up to the biggest and strongest girl in the hostel. In this respect she was very different from Joan, six years her senior, who gave in to bullies and indulged her sadistic impulses only in fantasy. She was, in fact, a strong personality, determined and able to preserve calm and poise in a situation which would have flustered Joan.

Irene's background was, like Joan's, a broken home. She was the youngest in a family of four and had a brother and two sisters. She told me that her sisters tried to bully her when she was little, but 'they didn't like my teeth and nails'. Her mother died when she was three years old; her father did not want to re-marry, but kept the children, for his wife made him promise that he would not 'put them into a home'. He himself had been brought up in an institution and professed to believe that it was 'the best place for children to be brought up in'.

He cohabited with a woman whom Irene called 'Auntie' and who favoured her elder sister but treated Irene as an un-mitigated nuisance. Irene told me that once this woman was nagging her brother who suddenly lost patience and threw a chopper at her. The chopper missed 'Auntie', but struck Irene, then aged about five, on the wrist. Her father, who happened to come in at that moment, saw the child covered in blood, assumed that the woman was butchering her and 'went for Auntie'. From the way Irene gloated over this memory, which may not have been a genuine one, it was obvious how much satisfaction she had derived from this violent scene. She thought her father had threatened to turn 'Auntie' out of the house: for once he was taking notice of, and protecting her.

A social worker who had dealings with her father, described him as a morose, undemonstrative man who appeared to feel little affection for his children. During the two years Irene was away from home, he came to see her only once, when she was brought before the Juvenile Court, and he made no effort to see her after that. He never wrote to her and was persuaded only with difficulty to make her a small allowance of pocket money, although he was earning good wages and two of his elder children were in employment.

Irene had no recollection of her mother, but as far as her memories went, she had been deprived of affection from the age of three. No wonder she liked to dwell on the memory of the only occasion on which her father had stood up for her. That memory happened to be one of violence, pain and fear— but also of delight and triumph over her rival and persecutor, 'Auntie'. It provides a striking illustration of how pleasure can become attached to situations of suffering and fear. There is little doubt that Irene deeply resented not only her step-mother's preference for the elder sister, but also her father's unresponsiveness. It is not without significance that in two of her stories the father of the child dies; in her second story he dies a violent death twice over. It is permissible here to speak of unconscious guilt feelings which Irene had most likely, both on account of her mother's death and her father's rejection. The little girl Dora is whipped every day until she dies—is it for her hostile wishes against the parents and for their death that she is punished so ruthlessly? Perhaps, if she were given the choice, Irene, too, would rather have been whipped than completely neglected by her father. After all, when she 'got into trouble' through stealing, he came and saw her—even if only in court.

Although unconscious of its origin, Irene was well aware of the pleasure she found in sado-masochistic situations. Before a visit to a cinema, 'Oh, I hope it'll be a murder picture!' she exclaimed: 'I love a murder!' She saw murder where there was none. Gazing at a picture of a languid woman, she asked: 'Has she got a knife stuck into her?' As there was nothing even remotely resembling a knife in the woman's breast, and no other person in the picture, I asked: 'Who could stick a knife into her?' 'A man.' 'What sort of man?' 'A man in a pub throwing knives.'

Not long ago, she told me, she used to be afraid of the dark because she imagined that someone was following her. 'I used to run, I used to look at every gate I passed, thinking someone might jump out.'

'The man' in her fantasies was thus associated with brutality and danger, and, unconsciously, with punishment for both the possessiveness and the hostility she felt towards her father. On the other hand, her character showed many signs of identification with him, as if, in her longing for him, she had introjected some of his characteristics. She developed the traits of independence and self-assertion; like her father she was obsessional and somewhat paranoid, always complaining that she was unfairly discriminated against. She had an urge to dominate which extended to cruelty—bullying and frightening younger children.

When I pondered over the histories of these two girls and the significance of their behaviour at the time I met them, I came to the conclusion that despite all the differences in their personalities, the meaning of the 'negative' aggression which they displayed was essentially the same. It was a response to the lack of a good relationship with an adult from an early age, before either girl was five years old. The desertion of Joan's father and the death of Irene's mother were probably significant only in so far as these events had the effect of throwing the child back upon the remaining parent who was unresponsive, and with whom the child had formed no affectional bond. In other ways the histories of these two girls, and their identification with the unresponsive parent present a significant parallel.

Why they both should have chosen delinquency as a preferred symptom is another matter. The motivation of delinquent behaviour is complex and cannot be reduced to any simple formula. To seek solace for emotional deprivation in material possessions is common enough, and it is not only children who regard gifts as the most convincing proofs of love. Possessions might thus be treated as a substitute for love, and stealing as symbolic love-getting. We must remember that Joan stole ostensibly 'to help her mother'. In this case it was her mother who was the unresponsive parent. But her stealing was also damaging her mother by attracting disgrace and blame upon her and by removing Joan from home, so that, in her own words, she could not 'look after' her mother and 'share everything' with her.

Thus, a double purpose was achieved by delinquent behaviour: an ostensibly positive and an unconsciously negative aim. If her relationship with her mother had developed on positive lines, the positive aspect of the self-assertive urge might have become dominant: there would not have been need for Joan to try to 'help' her mother by stealing: she might have asserted herself, as well as helped her mother, by working hard and by being 'good'.

Similarly, Irene's stealing of a bicycle attained the double aim of hurting her father, who prided himself on his honesty, as well as forcing him to take notice of her—the nearest approximation to affection she could obtain from him. Since her mother's death she could only establish herself with her siblings by means of her 'teeth and nails', and her stepmother apparently gave her no encouragement in forming a tie of affection with her. No wonder that the negative way to self-realization was the only one Irene had learned: fighting, bullying and stealing became her natural mode of self-expression. If her father had been affectionate and kind, she would, most likely, have found a positive way of establishing her worth and earning his appreciation.

The crucial event in the lives of both these girls occurred well before their fifth year, and it is from that time onwards that the particular pattern of behaviour began to establish itself. This pattern could be represented schematically as follows: seeking of affection by the child: parental unresponsiveness: self-assertion through negative aggression: punishment or disapproval: guilt feelings and anxiety: more negative aggression to allay guilt: more punishment, all resulting in a vicious circle. If the second element in this scheme were a positive response from the parent, the whole pattern would, no doubt, have been quite different.

69

II. A COMPARATIVE STUDY OF THREE GROUPS

(a) A 'Test of Family Attitudes': description and examples of stories

These speculations led me to plan another study, which I hoped would throw more light on the connection between the child's early family relationships and the direction of his self-assertive drives. The first experiment was designed especially to investigate sado-masochistic fantasies, and, in the course of it, the connection of sado-masochism with early parent-child relationship was revealed. In the subsequent study I planned to explore the child's fantasies about parents and children, and by this means to track the beginnings of deviations of the self-assertive drive into negative channels, of destructiveness and hostility.

I decided to bring this study nearer in time to the beginning of these deviations by designing pictures which would appeal to younger children, approximately between the ages of 6 and 12. In this set, four of the six pictures carried no suggestion of hostility, whereas two, formerly used for the original study, were ambiguous in that, in Picture 4, the aggressive posture of the man was balanced by the carefree posture of the woman, whereas in Picture 5 the male figure could be seen as beckoning the child away from danger, or as threatening her. These were, in fact, the two principal ways in which, as I found later, Picture 5 was interpreted by different children.

In designing and using these particular pictures I hoped that they would touch off in the minds of the child-subjects emotions and ideas connected with the several most important aspects of parent-child relationship. Thus, Picture o, I thought, would induce the child to express his ideas on the relationship between a mother and her baby. The child might project on the woman the feelings and ideas he had of his own mother, and on the (invisible) baby in the cradle, his own infantile self. Or he might see the situation in terms of a relationship between his mother and his younger sibling.

Picture 1 was designed to suggest a situation when the parents appear absorbed in their own relationship, leaving the child out, and to introduce the idea of intrusion of another adult who might be felt to be helpful or threatening. As is well known, children, both boys and girls, often project their aggressive impulses on to a 'bad man', such as a burglar, who, they imagine, might be hiding behind a door or in a dark corner. I thought that delinquents especially might regard this 'man outside' as someone who comes to take them away.

The intention behind Picture 2 is probably obvious without comment: to probe the child's emotions towards a sibling and the particular ways in which the child deals with the situation of rivalry for parental affection. Picture 3 was designed to suggest isolation, following perhaps on transgression, or chosen for some reason by the child himself, and thus to explore the child's feelings and thoughts about misbehaviour, punishment, guilt, repentance and reconciliation. Picture 4 was to probe the child's fear of parental aggression, but as the mother was represented in a carefree posture and the child undismayed, several interpretations were possible. Finally, Picture 5 was meant to carry a suggestion of a forbidden satisfaction, and thus arouse the complex emotions centring round situations of this type, common in the life of every child.

In all pictures, except Picture 2, the child was drawn so that it could be taken for either boy or girl, and so the set could be used for testing children of both sexes. Of Picture 2, however, on which two children are represented, there were two versions. In one the older child was a boy, in the other, a girl. This was done to facilitate projection.

I did not, of course, assume that projection in every case, or even in the majority of cases, would be direct, simple and naïve, that what the children said about the persons in the pictures would be literally true about themselves and their parents. Nor did I expect all their stories to be an unconscious reflection of their repressed fears and wishes. I knew, however, from observing children in free play and from reading works on projection, that what they thought, felt, and imagined would transpire, perhaps disguised, in some at least of their spontaneous compositions. These compositions would require interpretation and would probably allow of two or more different ones. Which of these was the most correct would be ascertainable only by a further study of the child himself, and of his past history and family background. It was reasonable, however, to expect that the child's responses to the pictures would give a true general picture of his family relationships, as harmonious or disturbed, and that perhaps the seriousness of the disturbance could be judged from the responses.

As it happened, the very first experiment with these pictures produced an unusually revealing set of stories. They were by a boy aged 7, 6, with an I.Q. of 101. On this occasion I did not use Picture 0.

Stories by Michael, aged 7, 6; I.Q. 101

Picture 1. (Excitedly.) A man behind the door. A baby crawling. A man and a woman. ('Who are they?') The boy's father and mother. ('What is the man coming for?') He's coming for the baby. ('Why?') To adopt him. ('Do his father and mother mind?') They don't know. ('How is the man going to get the boy, then?') Going to snatch him.

Picture 2. This can be fixed with that other one. This is the boy they've adopted. ('What is he thinking?') He's thinking of getting away. ('Why?') He doesn't like it (points at the baby and mother). ('Why not? Is he jealous, or what?') Yes, he is. ('Does he think that these people don't like him, or what?') Yes, that's it.

Picture 3. It's the same boy. He's thinking how to get away.

Picture 4. He wants to kill the woman. ('Why?') Because she won't give him the baby. ('Why does he want the baby?') He wants to put him in the oven and cook it. ('Why?') He wants to have another wife and baby; he doesn't like these.

Picture 5. A man coming to thrash the child. He's going to put her in the fire and burn her. ('Is he her father?') Yes. ('Why does he want to do that to her?') Because he doesn't like her.

This boy was one of my own treatment cases and the connection between his responses to the pictures and his real

0

1

A TEST OF FAMILY ATTITUDES

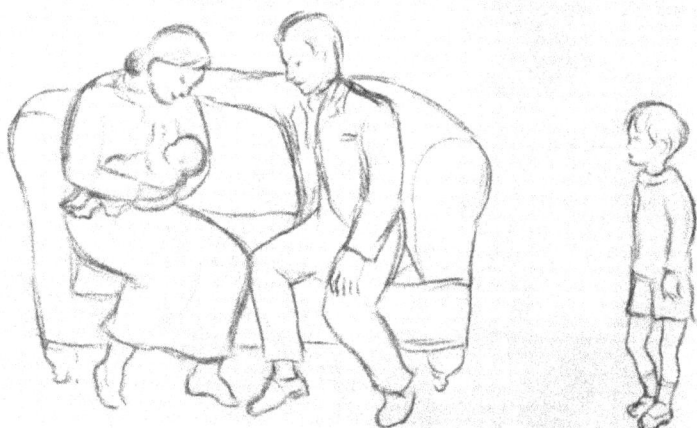

2

3

4

5

experiences could be verified by referring to his history and family background. He was brought for treatment because he was extremely restless, had screaming fits when thwarted, had compulsive movements of hands and fingers when excited, and was so unresponsive at school that his teachers thought he might be defective. He was the elder of two children; his sister was two-and-a-half years old when he was first seen by me. His mother appeared to be a rather ineffective person, who spoke of her husband almost with awe. One of her remarks was that there are 'many things about one's husband which take a lot of getting used to'. Her husband was a coalman, a large, brawny, primitive type of man, who could appear quite terrifying to a young child. She admitted that the boy's symptoms exasperated her, that she often slapped him and even tried to tie his hands when he had his 'turns'.

She dated the onset of the boy's symptoms from the accident he had when he was five years old. He fell into an unguarded fire and was badly burned about the hands. Soon after that his sister was born, and he was sent away for a fortnight. When he came back, he refused to speak, or to go to his mother.

It is clear from this boy's history that several of the most significant experiences of his life found expression in his responses to these pictures. The burning episode is referred to twice, in stories on Pictures 4 and 5. In both these stories the man is represented as the brutal, murderous father who wants to destroy the child just because he does not like it. In the story on Picture 1, the man outside is represented as a baby snatcher. This story may reproduce a distorted memory of being sent away, 'adopted' by people who were not his parents, when his sister was born. Hostility and jealousy towards her are reflected in the story on Picture 2. These emotions are so intolerable that in the story on Picture 3 the boy 'is thinking how to get away'.

In one only of the five stories (on Picture 4) is a parent, the mother, pictured as protecting the child. ('She won't give him the baby.') It was very clear that Michael felt extremely insecure in his relationship with his parents, and that his insecurity was due to both his parents' personalities and their treatment

73

of him. His mother hinted at feelings of fear and revulsion she had had for her husband: the son might have been aware of these feelings before he could speak. If he, too, felt afraid of, and hostile to, his father, the burning accident might have been experienced by him as punishment for these feelings, especially if he had been forbidden to go near the fire and had broken this prohibition. Nor had his mother proved to be a reliable and loving person. She produced a baby and had him sent away for a time. He resented it so deeply that he refused to speak or go near her on his return home. A secure and happy child might have dealt with the situation by making himself more lovable, but this boy's family background provided him with no means for positive assertion of his rights and claims as a personality. He fell back on the ways which were both negative and regressive: he asserted himself by screaming and waving of hands, and thus started the vicious circle of parental correction, leading to more negative aggression on his part, followed by more punishment, and so on. That he felt guilty and frightened about it all was clear also from his play during treatment interviews: he was full of fantasies about ghosts, burglars and murderers who came in the night, and at whom he fired many imaginary shots without ever killing them, for they came again and again.

Although this boy was evidently entangled in the contradictions of his hostile and fearful emotions, there was a saving feature in his fantasies: the woman in the story on Picture 4 refused to surrender the baby. Michael, therefore, still felt he was protected in some measure, though he feared betrayal and crushing retaliation.

Another little boy, whose symptom, significantly, was persistent pilfering, can be said to have had no such illusions. His stories run as follows:

Stories by Roy, aged 6, 10; *I.Q.* 90

Picture 0. This is a wicked old woman. She's going to steal this baby. No, not because she likes it, but because she goes about stealing things all the time. She's a thief. No, she's not going to be nice to him.

Picture 1. These are two bad people. They got in to steal the house. They are thinking what to do. Because the man is knocking on the door, and they are not going to open it. The little boy is going to scream. It is his daddy outside, and it is his house. These people are going to kill the little boy. And the boy's daddy is going to kill them.

Picture 2. This is a little boy and this is a big boy (pointing at the man on the sofa). The little boy is not allowed to come near the baby because he's always smacking it. The big brother and the mother went out and put the baby down. So the boy hit the baby hard and the baby cried out. It's a little brother. He's *not* naughty. The boy is a naughty boy. He lights fires in other people's houses. (Why is he so naughty?) Because there's a devil inside his mind.

Picture 3. This is the same boy. His mother put him in the bedroom and locked the door because he hit the baby. The boy is thinking, 'I'll get myself undone'. Yes, his hands are tied. He thinks, 'No, I won't because if I stay quiet, my mother might let me out.' But she won't. She's going to take him to a police station. She's sad. Because he's been very naughty. He killed the baby. Because his mummy would never let him come near the baby. Because he was angry with his mummy and the baby. He's very naughty. He mustn't do these things.

Picture 4. This is a kidnapper. He's going to kill the baby. It's a little boy. The kidnapper comes in and tells the mother to hold the baby up. The mother is crying. He wants to kill it because the lady's father told him to. The baby's granddad is a wicked man and he doesn't like babies.

Picture 5. This little boy . . . girl is very naughty. She's playing with the fire all the time. Her daddy is also a wicked man. He comes in and is going to smack her. . . . It is her big brother. He's going to hit her . . . not very hard . . . not kill her. He is going to kill her. His mother will come in, and she'll be very angry and take him to court. The court will do the same to him what he did to the little girl. (Kill him?) Yes. Because he shouldn't have done it. (Why did he do it?) I don't know. He's a good boy: he never hit anybody before; only when other boys hit him, he hit back. (Urged to give a reason.) Because the little devil inside him told him to.

Perhaps the most striking feature of this set of stories is the intense fascination which the theme of violence exercises on their young author. In the most unusually high proportion of the stories murder has been, or is going to be, committed. 'Killing' may well not mean the same to a boy of seven as it does to a maturer person, but it does mean a final disposal of someone by violent means, and the penalty for it, he feels, should be the same. In two of his stories the baby is killed by its brother, and the reasons for it are made quite clear: they are jealousy and resentment because of love and protection the mother gives to the baby.

Another striking feature is the mother's behaviour: she hands the boy over to the police in the story on P. 3 and she 'takes him to court' in the story on P. 5. This is the supreme betrayal of a child's life: his mother handing him over to his avengers, and thus giving him an impression of life as a trap. Anyway, the whole adult world, as reflected in these stories, is hostile and dangerous. In the story on P. o, the old woman is a thief, who steals the baby but 'is not going to be nice to him'; in the story on P. 1, the two grown-ups are 'bad' people who 'are going to kill the little boy'; in the story on P. 2, the mother and the big brother are represented as frustrating the boy; in the story on P. 3, the mother ties the boy's hands and locks him up, with the intention of later taking him to a police station; in the story on P. 4, the baby's grandfather hires a murderer to kill him, and the child's mother does not even put up a fight; in the story on P. 5, the little girl is going to be killed by her big brother, who then will be handed over to his executioners by his mother.

The boy, who invented these stories with great ease and spontaneity, was one of my treatment cases and was originally brought to the clinic on account of asthma. A fair-haired, blue-eyed ingenuous looking child, he was found to have a host of other symptoms besides. He was a persistent pilferer, and stole not only from his mother, but also from neighbours and other children. Thus, on two different occasions he stole a child's tricycle, afterwards abandoning it by the roadside. He truanted from school, and told lies both about his stealing and his truanting. He suffered from fits of ungovernable temper, and when in this state threw anything that came to hand, including knives, at whoever enraged him, especially his mother and his younger sister. He was in the habit of putting toys, books and clothes on the fire.

One may well wonder how a child so young could have come to such a pass without having been dealt with somehow, at an earlier stage. The explanation lies in the attitude of the parents, who were from the beginning divided on the question of having children. The father did not want them, and when they came, disclaimed all responsibility for their upbringing and took no interest in them. The mother had wanted them, but her relationship with them remained on the biological level. She treated them as extensions of her own personality and punished them especially severely for traits and tendencies she feared and hated in herself. She was a woman of excitable violent temperament, and in her anger must have been both terrifying and dangerous. In fact, she confessed to the fear of 'killing' Roy, when he drove her to exasperation, and she often caned him.

The boy's early history presented a most disturbed picture. When he was two years old, the house in which they lived was bombed, and the family were buried under masonry for several hours. Immediately after, they were evacuated, and no sooner had they got to their new destination, than Roy had fallen ill with pneumonia and had to be removed to hospital, where he stayed for some weeks. When he returned, his mother was unhappy in her lodgings and had to divide her attention between him and his baby sister. Roy was 'very difficult', developed some other illness, and had to go away again. It was during his second stay in hospital that he was found for the first time piling bedclothes on an open fire. The hospital authorities returned him to the mother forthwith.

When he started pilfering, his mother 'thrashed' him for it. When he truanted, she took him to school, brought him back and kept him in the house for the rest of the day. He was also confined to the house during the week-end. Thrashings and other punishment had no desirable effect: Roy did not even cry and carried on as before. When questioned about the motives of his behaviour, he put the blame on 'the little devil' who, he said, was 'inside him' and was 'telling him to do things'. (This may have been a crude reflection of the religious teaching he received at the Catholic school he was attending.) But from his idea of himself as possessed by 'the little devil', there was not a long stretch of imagination to another idea which he represented pictorially. It was a picture of a small house, and of a human figure standing outside. A long curved line, starting from the door, traversed the 'sky' and ended in a large, round, bursting object. Roy said that the human figure was 'the little devil'. His mother 'got angry with him and locked him out of the house'. The round object was a ball . . . no, 'a grenade', which she threw at him, but 'it missed him'.

Obviously, there is only a step from the idea of 'the little devil' to that of the 'devil's mother'. In this boy's imaginative experience, his mother's wickedness and his own were evenly matched. She feels she might 'kill him' when she thrashes him; in his stories, she hands the killing over to others, but not before he 'kills' the hated rival. Roy's hostility to his sister was intense: the two children were always quarrelling and fighting, and Roy, being older and stronger, usually won. On one occasion, when his sister blew out a match he had struck, he thrust the charred match into her eye and nearly blinded her. In school, he was always 'in trouble' for provoking and striking the other children.

One of his best planned exploits was forbidden visits to the local cinema. He got in by waiting near the back exit and slipping in when a crowd came out at the change of programme, a well-known dodge, but seldom practised by one so young. On one occasion he even managed to smuggle in his young sister, not so much to give her pleasure as to make her participate in his transgression and to share his punishment. This came swiftly enough in the form of a sound caning. When I asked him whether he had hoped to get away with it, he calmly replied that he had expected to be punished, but that the evening

78

at the pictures was worth the caning. The more severely he was punished, the more inventive he became in getting his own way. He could not be left alone in the house; no neighbour would take charge of him; so his mother had to take him about with her. If she left him outside a shop, he would disappear; if brought inside, he wanted nothing better, and missed no chance of helping himself to things from the counter while his mother was doing her shopping. Thus she was obliged to make herself virtually a prisoner in her own house, by acting as her son's jailer and guard. Her battles with him were wearing her out, and Roy seemed to be winning on all fronts.

Roy's is, no doubt, an appalling history, and it gives a portrait of a child quite impervious to punishment or persuasion. The personality of the child, however, must be judged in relation to the personality of his mother, for this child's behaviour represented his reactions to maternal treatment.

Roy's mother was an extremely impulsive woman, a non-stop talker, physically tall and strong, with a powerful voice. Her relationship with her husband was not a good one: they had frequent quarrels, usually about the children. She was unable to be consistent in any line of behaviour or attitude she took towards Roy's misdemeanours; her natural impulse was to punish him by beating and depriving him drastically of all pleasures and privileges. When she found this did not produce the desired effect, she left off thrashing for a time, but later, when her anger was aroused, caned him again. One of her educational methods was to try to 'cure' Roy's untidiness by putting his toys on the fire, if they were left scattered about the room. No wonder Roy imitated this by burning some of *hers*, and other people's, belongings.

She felt he was thoroughly wicked and could never improve. Secretly, she feared that it was something 'bad' in herself that he had inherited. She confessed that at times she hated him and wished he were dead. The social worker who saw her weekly over a period of several months gained the impression that she was temperamentally unstable and emotionally almost as immature as her seven-year-old son.

What he felt towards her is clear from his fantasies. She was 'the devil's mother' who was capable of throwing a 'grenade' at him. As she had handed him over to strangers twice in early childhood, soon after he had suffered the shock of bombing, and when he was in both physical and mental pain, so she might be expected to betray him again at any moment. He behaved as if he felt he had nothing to lose and that nothing worse could happen to him than had already happened—the break of his relationship with his mother. This relationship had never had the chance of becoming established because of the separation occurring at the very traumatic time, when the bombing accident, the birth of a sister and his illness became constellated. Even so, if on his return the mother had, lovingly and tactfully, wooed him back and drawn him into the circle of her benevolence and protection, tolerating his demands and resentments, Roy might have weathered the inner storm and started anew on the path of positive self-assertion. As it happened, the situation was woefully mishandled, and the child reacted to subsequent rejection and violence by more or less reproducing the pattern suggested by maternal behaviour.

(b) *Stories by the Normal, the Neurotic and the Delinquent Children compared and assessed*

However revealing were the responses of these two boys to my set of pictures, however closely linked to their actual experiences, they could be regarded as exceptional unless more examples were obtained, and unless they proved to be different from other responses given by children, who were neither neurotic, nor delinquent. I therefore proceeded to test all my young patients and to try to get access to schools where I should be able to test some 'normal' children. This proved to be almost the most difficult part of my task, for the educational authorities were most reluctant to grant facilities for 'private research', on the grounds that the parents might object to their children being 'tested with pictures' in school time, and that keeping them after school time would cause an even greater commotion. Then, a progressive School Medical Officer spoke privately about my research to the Education Officer of a small market town, and as a result of that conversation, the primary school of the town opened its doors to me. At first I was given a table in the assembly hall, but later the teachers turned out of their common room so that I could have more privacy. Since then, I have had access to other schools in the districts where I have been working as a psychotherapist, but I have kept a special feeling of gratitude for that rather grim and draughty assembly hall in which I interviewed my first 'normal' children.

The test was given to 110 children altogether, forty Normal, forty Neurotic and thirty Delinquent. Selection was exercised only in so far as it was necessary to match them with regard to age, sex and intelligence quotients. I had enough 'neurotics' among my clinic cases, but not quite enough delinquents, and delinquent girls under twelve were particularly difficult to find. For that reason there are only ten girls in my Delinquent group. Nearly half of them were tested at the psychiatric hostel where they lived.

The experimental procedure was simple. I usually asked the child whether he would like to look at some pictures and to try inventing stories about them. I explained that it was to help me in the study I was making of children's imagination, and that the story had to be their own. I usually tried to show the whole set in one interview, but sometimes, especially with the younger children, it was necessary to break off after only three pictures had been shown, because their interest flagged.

No length limit was set on the stories thus composed, but if the story showed signs of becoming too diffuse and confabulatory, I urged the child to keep to the main subject, or asked a standard question, such as: 'Tell me more about the boy (or girl). What is he like?' The length of the stories the children produced varied considerably with the personality and age of the child, approximately within the range of 20 to 300 words. In most cases I wrote the stories down as they were being narrated, but with particularly distrustful and nervous children, and with some of the younger ones, I found it more expedient to make notes immediately after the child had left the room.

I carefully guarded against asking leading or suggestive questions, and questioned the children usually only if their stories were exceptionally poor in content. The questions I asked were the following:

> *On Picture* 0. (i) Is the baby a little girl or a little boy? (ii) Is it a nice baby or a naughty one? (iii) Always nice (naughty) or not always? (iv) What does he (she) do when he is naughty? (v) What does his mother do when he is naughty?
>
> *On Picture* 1. (i) Is the little boy (girl) a good boy or a naughty one? (ii) Always good (naughty) or not always? (iii) What does he do when he is naughty? (iv) What does his mother or father do when he is naughty? (v) Do his father and mother like him very much or not very much? (vi) Always or not always? (vii) Does the little boy like his father and mother very much, or not very much? (viii) Always or not always? (ix) Does the man outside like the boy? (x) Does the boy like the man?
>
> *On Picture* 2. (i) What is the little boy (girl) thinking? (ii) What sort of a little boy (girl) is he? Good or naughty? (iii) Always good (naughty), or not always? (iv) What does he do when he is naughty? (v) What do his father and mother do then? (vi) Is the baby a little brother or a little sister (of the older child)? (vii) Who do they like best, the baby or the little boy (girl)?
>
> *On Picture* 3. (i) Why is the little boy sitting by himself? (ii) What is he thinking? (iii) Where are his father and mother? (iv) What is going to happen? (v) How long will he stay there? (vi) Is the door locked or just shut?
>
> *On Picture* 4. (i) Why is the mother holding the baby up? (ii) Does she mind the father playing with the baby in this way?
>
> *On Picture* 5. (i) Where is the child's mother? (ii) What will she say (or do) when she hears what has happened?

The purpose of these questions is self-evident. They were designed to induce the child to commit himself on the subject of parent-child relationship and to reveal his feelings and ideas about it. I did not, of course, expect such revelations to be naïve and straightforward, although in some cases they were both. I believed, however, that there was no such thing as 'pure fantasy' or 'pure invention' and that I might be able to pierce through the disguises and distortions to the underlying real experience. But my first aim was to compare the responses of the three groups as objectively as possible.

From my 110 subjects, I collected 652 stories. There should have been 660 stories, but in eight cases one of the pictures (usually P. o) was not shown. I analysed these stories into types of responses, all of which had a bearing on the relationships between children and adults in the pictures.

In stories on Picture o, nine types of responses were distinguished:

(1) Woman is baby's mother
(2) Woman is a stranger to the baby
(3) Baby is 'good' or 'nice'
(4) Baby is 'bad' or 'naughty'
(5) Woman is kind to baby
(6) Woman is unkind to baby
(7) Father of the baby is at home or at work
(8) Father is away or dead
(9) Mother is away or dead.

In stories on Picture 1, sixteen types:

(1) Child 'naughty'
(2) Child 'good' or 'nice'
(3) Child sometimes good, sometimes naughty
(4) Transgression serious
(5) Transgression minor
(6) Punishment severe
(7) Punishment mild
(8) No punishment
(9) Man outside dangerous
(10) Man outside relative or friend
(11) Parents ambivalent towards child
(12) Child ambivalent towards parents
(13) Parents reject child
(14) Parents are fond of child
(15) Child hostile to parents
(16) Child fond of parents.

In stories on Picture 2, twelve types:

(1) Older child rejects baby
(2) Older child likes baby
(3) Older child jealous of baby
(4) Older child accepts baby
(5) Older child is 'good' or 'nice'
(6) Older child is 'naughty' or 'bad'
(7) Older child is sometimes good, sometimes naughty
(8) Parents prefer baby
(9) Parents prefer older child
(10) Parents like both equally
(11) Older child rejects parents
(12) Parents reject older child.

In stories on Picture 3, twelve types:

(1) Transgression serious
(2) Transgression minor
(3) No transgression. Alone by choice
(4) Loneliness or bereavement
(5) Remorse or regret shown
(6) No remorse or regret shown
(7) Punishment severe
(8) Punishment light
(9) Parents away or dead
(10) Parents near
(11) Door locked
(12) Door unlocked or not mentioned.

In stories on Picture 4, nine types:

(1) Situation of danger
(2) Situation of play or co-operation
(3) Child 'naughty' or 'bad'
(4) Child 'good' or 'nice'
(5) Child rejected by *one* parent
(6) Child rejected by *both* parents
(7) Child accepted by both parents
(8) Child maltreated
(9) Child treated well.

In stories on Picture 5, ten types:

(1) Child 'naughty' or aggressive
(2) Child playing or industrious (helping parents)
(3) Parents punishing or forbidding
(4) Parents playful or protective
(5) Male figure—hostile sibling or stranger
(6) Male figure—friendly sibling or stranger
(7) Mother against child
(8) Mother on child's side
(9) Mother at home or near at hand
(10) Mother away or dead.

There were, of course, responses which did not fit into these 'types', and so could not be subjected to statistical treatment, for which this classification was intended. In any case they were not comparable, for they represented the original, imaginative touch, particular to the individual child. Such responses, however, were taken into account when the stories were compared for qualitative differences.

At first I expected to find differences between boys and girls in the number of certain types of responses, but after having tabulated them separately, I found that the numbers tended to be almost equal. Then, I added up the number of responses of the same type for each group as a whole and compared them, leaving out those which showed only slight differences. Where the differences were large, they were treated statistically, to see if they were significant.

The statistical method used was Fisher's chi-squared test (3). Chi-squared was calculated for each response in turn, assuming that the number of responses given by the Normal subjects represents the 'expected' possibility, and that the numbers given by the Neurotic and the Delinquent subjects are the 'observed' values. So used, the test provides at least some notion of the extreme nature of the latter subjects relative to a 'hypothetical' set of data, that is, such as is expected for a normal group of children.

The following may serve as an example of calculation. In the case of the first response to Picture 0 ('Woman is baby's mother'), thirty-eight Normal subjects gave the response, and only twenty-eight Neurotic subjects, out of forty in each case. Chi-squared for this response is thus $\dfrac{(38-28)^2}{38}=\dfrac{100}{38}=2.63$. The probability of a deviation greater than this is approximately 0.10, that is, the difference cannot be regarded as significant. A value of $P<0.01$ was taken as a criterion of significance. The account was taken, of course, of the fact that there were thirty Delinquent subjects, and not forty, as in each of the other two groups. Table 4 shows in columns (iv) and (v) whether the differences are significant or not.

I then examined the data of Table 4 in the following order:

(a) Types of response which showed significant differences for *both* the Neurotic and the Delinquent subjects relative to Normal group;

(b) those that showed significant differences *only* between the Normal and the Neurotic subjects;

(c) those that showed significant differences *only* between the Normal and the Delinquent subjects;

(d) those that showed such differences between the Neurotic and the Delinquent subjects, in so far as these differences have not been brought out by the examination of (b) and (c);

(e) those that showed *no* significant differences between the three groups.

I found that the following types of responses showed significant differences between the Normal group on the one hand, and the Neurotic and Delinquent groups, on the other:

| | Given |
| (a) Type of Response | by the Neurotic and Delinquent |

Picture 1

1. Child 'good' or 'nice' .. *Less* frequently than by the Normal
2. Punishment severe .. *More* ,, ,, ,, ,, ,,
3. Man outside dangerous .. *More* ,, ,, ,, ,, ,,
4. Parents reject child .. *More* ,, ,, ,, ,, ,,
5. Parents fond of child .. *Less* ,, ,, ,, ,, ,,
6. Child fond of parents .. *Less* ,, ,, ,, ,, ,,

86

Picture 2

7. Older child rejects baby .. *More* frequently than by the Normal
8. Parents reject older child.. *More* „   „   „ „   „
9. Older child is 'naughty' .. *More* „   „   „ „   „

Picture 3

10. No regret or remorse shown
     by child .. .. *More* „   „   „ „   „
11. Punishment severe .. *More* „   „   „ „   „

Picture 4

12. Situation of danger .. *More* „   „   „ „   „
13. Child 'good' or 'nice' .. *Less* „   „   „ „   „
14. Child rejected by both par-
     ents or parent-figures .. *More* „   „   „ „   „
15. Child accepted by both
     parents .. .. .. *Less* „   „   „ „   „

It is clear from these data that the Neurotic and Delinquent child subjects paint a predominantly negative picture of family relationships, whereas the Normal give a positive picture. There is little doubt that all subjects, to a varying extent, projected themselves, that is, ascribed their own emotions and thoughts to child characters in their stories. But, as is well known, different aspects of personality can be projected, and the child can project his standards of behaviour, or super-ego, as well as his instinctual needs and wishes, on to persons in the pictures. In his stories he thus may act as himself and as his own judge.

The Normal children show by this set of responses that they are fairly confident of their own 'goodness', and on the whole tend to regard other children, including their siblings, as 'nice' (items 1 and 13). They are obviously more certain of the children being accepted and loved by their parents than are the Neurotic or the Delinquent (items 5 and 15). They have fewer doubts that children love their parents in return (item 6).

The Neurotic and Delinquent subjects, on the other hand, show a tendency to feel rejected and unloved, or to wish that the child in the picture, who may stand for a sibling, should be

87

TABLE 4

Showing data for 40 Normal, 40 Neurotic and 30 Delinquent subjects: columns (i), (ii) and (iii) give the number of subjects whose responses were those on the left of the table: columns (iv) and (v) indicate whether the differences between (i) and (ii) or between (i) and (iii) are significant (X^2 test). A value $P < 0.01$ is considered highly significant: other values are not significant.

No. of Picture	No. of Item	Responses	No. of subjects giving the response			Significance	
			Normal	Neurotic	Delinquent		
			(i)	(ii)	(iii)	(iv)	(v)
0	1	Woman—baby's mother	38	28	24	—	—
0	2	Woman—a stranger	1	1	3	—	—
0	3	Baby 'good' or 'nice'	36	21	20	$P < 0.01$	—
0	4	Woman kind to baby	37	19	22	$P < 0.01$	—
1	5	Child 'naughty' or 'bad'	8	14	12	—	$P < 0.01$
1	6	Child 'good' or 'nice'	18	7	4	$P < 0.01$	$P < 0.01$
1	7	Punishment severe	2	8	9	$P < 0.01$	$P < 0.01$
1	8	No punishment	8	3	1	—	$P < 0.01$
1	9	Man outside dangerous	2	21	14	$P < 0.01$	$P < 0.01$
1	10	Man outside relative or friend	38	23	19	—	—
1	11	Parents ambivalent	17	10	12	—	—
1	12	Parents reject child	1	10	8	$P < 0.01$	$P < 0.01$
1	13	Parents are fond of child	32	13	9	$P < 0.01$	$P < 0.01$

TABLE 4 (continued)

No. of Picture	No. of Item	Responses	No. of subjects giving the response			Significance	
			Normal (i)	Neurotic (ii)	Delinquent (iii)	(iv)	(v)
1	14	Child hostile to parents	2	13	3	P<0·01	—
1	15	Child fond of parents	25	9	8	P<0·01	P<0·01
2	16	Older child jealous of baby	11	19	10	—	—
2	17	Older child likes the baby	30	13	14	P<0·01	—
2	18	Older child rejects the baby	6	14	10	P<0·01	P<0·01
2	19	Older child is 'good'	18	10	7	—	—
2	20	Older child is 'naughty'	3	13	10	P<0·01	P<0·01
2	21	Parents like both children equally	14	9	7	—	—
2	22	Older child rejects parents	4	13	7	P<0·01	—
2	23	Parents reject older child	5	11	12	P<0·01	P<0·01
3	24	Remorse or regret shown	16	9	9	—	—
3	25	No remorse or regret shown	7	22	17	P<0·01	P<0·01
3	26	Punishment severe	6	16	16	P<0·01	P<0·01
3	27	Punishment light	25	13	9	—	P<0·01
3	28	No transgression. Alone by choice	12	7	3	—	—
3	29	Parents far away or dead	5	17	10	P<0·01	—

TABLE 4 (continued)

No. of Picture	No. of Item	Responses	No. of subjects giving the response			Significance	
			Normal (i)	Neurotic (ii)	Delinquent (iii)	(iv)	(v)
3	30	Parents near	36	23	20	—	—
3	31	Door unlocked or not mentioned	35	26	14	—	P < 0.01
3	32	Door locked	7	14	16	—	P < 0.01
4	33	Situation of danger	12	31	19	P < 0.01	P < 0.01
4	34	Situation of play or co-operation	17	9	11	—	—
4	35	Child 'good' or 'nice' ..	32	12	5	P < 0.01	P < 0.01
4	36	Child rejected by both parents or parent figures	1	13	5	P < 0.01	P < 0.01
4	37	Child accepted by both parents	31	10	12	P < 0.01	P < 0.01
4	38	Child maltreated	6	24	13	P < 0.01	—
4	39	Child treated well	34	8	15	P < 0.01	—
5	40	Child playing or industrious ..	24	14	6	—	P < 0.01
5	41	Parent playful or protective ..	21	11	3	—	P < 0.01
5	42	Mother on child's side ..	11	4	7	—	—
5	43	Man in the picture hostile sibling or stranger ..	7	14	9	P < 0.01	—

rejected by the parents (items 4, 8 and 14). When they invent stories about 'a naughty child', they tend to decree that punishment must be severe, often quite out of proportion with the transgression (items 2 and 11). This points to feelings of guilt and a severe super-ego, from which the Normal, as a group, are relatively free.

There is clearly a connection between the feelings of rejection expressed by the Neurotic and the Delinquent, and their feeling of 'badness', for if they identify themselves with the child in the picture, they tend to see that child as 'naughty'. If, on the other hand, they see that child as a sibling or play companion, they project their 'naughtiness' on to him (item 9). At the same time, when the child is seen as having committed some transgression, he is more often than not viewed as unrepentant (item 10). The thoughts ascribed to him are often rebellious thoughts, such as 'He's thinking how to get out' (B.D., male, aged 6, 11, I.Q. 100); or 'He's thinking he's got a bad mother' (T.F., male, aged 9, 8, I.Q. 130). This 'naughty' child does not want a younger brother or sister (item 7). As might be expected, probably because of his hostility, his 'naughtiness' and his awareness of parental rejection, he is very insecure and views the ambiguous male figure in Pictures 1 and 4 as dangerous (items 3 and 12). On these figures he bestows his projected aggression, his expectation of punishment arising from his feeling of guilt, and his fear of the avenging parent.

Other types of responses showed significant differences between the Normal and the Neurotic groups, but not between the Normal and the Delinquent.

(b) Type of Response   Given by the Neurotic subjects

Picture 0
16. Woman kind to baby   .. *Less* frequently than by the Normal

Picture 1
17. Child hostile to parents .. *More*   ,,   ,,   ,, ,,   ,,

Picture 2

18. Older child likes baby   .. *Less* frequently than by the Normal
19. Older child rejects parents *More*   ,,   ,,   ,, ,,   ,,

Picture 3

20. Parents far away or dead .. *More*   ,,   ,,   ,, ,,   ,,

Picture 4

21. Child maltreated ..   .. *More*   ,,   ,,   ,, ,,   ,,
22. Child treated well   .. *Less*   ,,   ,,   ,, ,,   ,,

Picture 5

23. Man in the picture hostile
    sibling or stranger   .. *More*   ,,   ,,   ,, ,,   ,,

It appears from these data that, in addition to feeling rejected by their parents, the Neurotic children also tend to feel that they are maltreated, in so far as they identify themselves with the child in the pictures. The Normal, on the other hand, tend to feel that they are treated well (items 21 and 22 respectively). If the child stands for a sibling, the Neurotics' choice of this response is in line with the earlier indications of sibling jealousy and hostility towards the sibling. A confirmation of this is provided by item 18. Item 23 provides additional evidence of Neurotic children's insecurity, their expectation of aggression from others, whether strangers or siblings. Even the mother's relationship with her baby is not seen as very secure (item 16). If the baby stands for a younger sibling, the Neurotic children apparently prefer the mother not to be kind to it. Items 17 and 19 illustrate the projection by these children of their own hostility towards their parents on to the child in the picture. That they unconsciously expect to be punished for their hostility by parental desertion, or by the realization of their 'death wishes' is revealed by item 20.

It may be asked why the Delinquents, who share several other trends with the Neurotic subjects, do not significantly differ from the Normal in the trends just examined. In their stories they do not show as much hostility towards parents and siblings, as much anxiety or as much self-pity (item 21), as the Neurotics. This need not necessarily mean that the Delinquents are, in some respects, more like the Normal than the Neurotic children. It may mean, however, that the direction of their emotional drives is centrifugal rather than centripetal, away from the family, instead of towards the family, as is the case with the Neurotics. They show a greater detachment from the family. On the other hand, it is possible that this detachment is a form of defence and that hostile emotions are deeply repressed, which gives their responses a superficial similarity to the responses of the Normal. The relative infrequency of hostile, anxious and self-pitying responses in the stories of the Normal is less likely to be due to repression alone: items 16, 18 and 22, as well as several items in section (a), indicate better integration and overcoming of ambivalence by the Normal.

In some responses, however, the Delinquents and *not* the Neurotics differed significantly from the Normal. These were the following:

(c) Type of Response   Given by the Delinquent subjects

Picture 1

24. Child 'naughty' or 'bad' .. *More* frequently than by the Normal
25. No punishment .. .. *Less*   ,,   ,,   ,,   ,,   ,,

Picture 3

26. Punishment light .. .. *Less*   ,,   ,,   ,,   ,,   ,,
27. Door unlocked or not mentioned .. .. .. *Less*   ,,   ,,   ,,   ,,   ,,
28. Door locked .. .. *More*   ,,   ,,   ,,   ,,   ,,

Picture 5

29. Child playing or industrious *Less*   ,,   ,,   ,,   ,,   ,,
30. Parents playful or protective .. .. .. *Less*   ,,   ,,   ,,   ,,   ,,

In this set of responses the Delinquents show a pronounced trend towards 'bad identification', or, if the child in the picture stands for a sibling or play companion, they tend to project

93

their own feeling of 'badness' on to him. This child is apparently regarded as dangerous, hence the fantasy of his being in a
locked room (items 27 and 28). The Delinquents find it difficult to imagine such a child to be innocently playing or helping
someone (item 29), or to think that the parent might be playing
with, or protecting the child (item 30). They cannot imagine
this child being forgiven when it had been guilty of some
transgression (item 25) or of receiving light punishment in
such a case (item 26).

It is most probable that these responses reflect actual situations in the Delinquents' families. Delinquent children are
more liable to be scolded, punished and told they are 'bad' or
naughty than the Normal, or even the Neurotic children. They
are less likely than the latter to be forgiven or punished lightly
for their transgressions because their behaviour arouses more
alarm and hostility in the adult than the less anti-social transgressions of non-delinquent children. Their parents are less
likely to be companionable than those of the Normal or even
the Neurotic children because of a greater estrangement
between them. Delinquents are, without doubt, sometimes
threatened with 'locking up', even if the threat is rarely carried
out; and because their freedom is curtailed more often than
that of other children, they would tend to feel they are 'bad'
and 'dangerous'.

This set of responses, it seems to me, gives a picture of
greater estrangement between the Delinquents and their
families than do the responses of the Neurotics.

(d) The differences, however, between the responses of the
Neurotics, on the one hand, and the Delinquents, on the other,
are subtler and less easily definable than between these two
groups and the Normal. The Delinquents, on the whole, draw
a picture of a harsher family background than do the Neurotics. At the same time they appear to accept this situation with
greater equanimity, or at least with less overt resentment, as if
their sensibilities were less developed, or already blunted. The
Neurotics, on the other hand, give evidence of more intense
emotional reactions to the parents and siblings than the

94

Delinquents, which suggests that the emotional bonds tying them to their families are much closer.

It is true that both groups tend to feel rejected by their parents, but while the Neurotics react to this mainly by anxiety (i.e. fantasies of death of the parents or separation from them), the Delinquents seem to expect direct, concrete aggression in the form of punishment and isolation, as is shown by the last set of responses.

The similarities between the responses of the two groups were many, but this was to be expected, for the majority of the Delinquents in this group were clinical cases, that is, recognized as emotionally disturbed. Their delinquent behaviour was not an isolated symptom, but usually combined with several others which they had in common with the Neurotics.

(e) Some of the responses contained in Table 3 showed no significant differences between the groups. These belonged to one of the four following types: (i) stock responses, such as in stories on Picture 0: 'Baby's father is out at work'; (ii) unusual responses, so infrequent that they could not be grouped and compared quantitatively, such as in stories on Picture 2: 'Parents prefer the older child (to the baby)'; (iii) similar responses due to different motives, such as occurred in stories on Picture 3, when the Normal, the Delinquent and the Neurotic gave responses, describing a 'minor transgression' of the child in an almost equal proportion. This may have been a projection of real experience on the part of the Normal, whereas on the part of the Delinquent the response may have been motivated by a reluctance to mention their own, more serious transgressions; and on the part of the Neurotic—by the fear of their own aggression, leading them to minimize the child's guilt; and finally (iv) responses motivated by the suggestive influence of the picture, as in stories on Picture 5, where the majority of responses for all groups described the child as 'naughty' or aggressive—'doing something she was told not to'.

The absence of differences between the groups in some types of responses was, of course, to be expected in a test involving free composition, and with groups of subjects whose social background and ordinary everyday experiences could not but be very similar.

I also examined the stories for the recurrence of certain themes. Five themes appeared to be especially significant: (i) the Murder theme, (ii) the Violence theme, (iii) the 'Cruelty to Baby' theme, (iv) the Stealing theme and (v) the 'Being sent away from Home' theme. Some children ascribed murderous intentions to the 'man outside' in Picture 1, to the two male figures in Pictures 4 and 5, and even to the small boys in Pictures 2 and 3. Several neurotic and delinquent subjects invented stories about the boy murdering the baby. One neurotic boy described how the boy in Picture 3 killed his father.

Various scenes of violence, such as 'bombing', 'smashing up the home', 'thrashing', 'throwing things about', were frequently described. Some of the subjects described maltreatment of the baby by the elder child.

The number of times these themes recurred in the stories of the three groups of subjects are given in the table below.

TABLE 5

Subjects		Themes					Responses
		(i)	(ii)	(iii)	(iv)	(v)	(total)
Normal (40) ..	..	—	5	2	5	—	12
Neurotic (40) ..	..	30	18	4	5	4	61
Delinquent (30)	..	11	10	8	6	8	43

(The figures in columns (i), (ii), (iii), (iv), (v) show the number of times the theme designated by this number occurred in the stories by the subjects of each group.)

I believe it is most significant that the 'murder' and the 'being sent away from home' themes do not occur once in the stories by Normal children, notwithstanding the fact that they came from the same social milieu, and were, no doubt, seeing the same films and reading the same stories as the other two groups. I regard this as an indication of a solid sense of security, as well as a strong 'reality sense' which puts a brake on fantasies of danger to life and loss of parental protection. The 'violence theme' occurs only five times in the stories by the Normal, compared with the Neurotic subjects' eighteen and the Delinquents' ten. The 'cruelty to baby' theme occurs twice in their stories, whereas the stealing theme occurs five times, that is, as frequently as it does in the Neurotic group, and only once less than in the Delinquent group.

It is obvious why the Delinquents should try to avoid this theme, and why, on the other hand, the 'being sent away from home' theme should occur in their stories more frequently than in those of the Neurotic group. There is little doubt that they are often threatened with being 'put away' or 'sent away to a boarding school' by their exasperated parents, but it probably also indicates their genuine belief that the parents want to get rid of them. It may also be a pointer to their feelings of isolation and of being rejected.

This theme is much less prominent in the stories by the Neurotic group. On the other hand, the murder theme occurs in their stories with a remarkably high frequency. A murder fantasy can be a reflection of a sado-masochistic situation between two persons, or it may be an expression of anxiety and an expectation of punishment for 'naughtiness' or hostility. In Neurotic children it may be a blend of all these emotional attitudes, inherent in disturbed family relationships, with anxiety, perhaps, predominating. These feelings are expressed with great clarity and dramatic force by a neurotic boy, aged 6, 10, with an I.Q. of 131, suffering from fear of the dark and of burglars. He said about Picture 3:

> 'This story starts not about the picture. There was once a little boy. His Mummy told him, "Go down and get me some coal." He said, "No, I won't." "I do things for you, why shouldn't you do things for me?" "No, you don't." His Daddy then came in, and she told him, and he gave the little boy a *good* hiding (with gusto and much emphasis on "good"), and took him upstairs and put him in the nursery. He's sitting alone on a stool. Yes, the door is locked (with certainty, as if it were a matter of course). He's thinking, "I wish there were some real

magic, so that I could become a big prince and have a sword and kill her." (I asked: "Kill whom? Mummy?") This Mummy. And Daddy heard him. ("How?") He was listening through the keyhole. The boy was saying it quietly to himself, and his Daddy heard him. He came in and gave him a harder smack. His Mummy is in the kitchen. The little boy then made up his mind to run away. Yes, he ran away and bought himself a gun at a fair. He made himself a sword. He became a wicked man. He went back and told his Mummy, "See, now I can kill you." Then Daddy came in. The boy stood there, and he took his sword and killed his Daddy.'

This boy's mother was a neurotic woman, hostile to her children, rigid, yet inconsistent in her demands on them, expecting a degree of efficiency and responsibility from them quite out of proportion to their age. (The boy's sister was only two and a half years old.) The boy's relationship with the father had been good, but the father was away in the Forces, and the boy developed fears soon after he had left home. These fears were partly suggested by the mother, who confessed that she was afraid to sleep in the house alone with the children. Yet she regarded the boy's calling out at night as mere 'naughtiness' which he ought to be able to control, and she threatened him with caning if he persisted. She carried out her threat one night when he called her, and it had the desired effect. She had also told him that by making her get out of bed in the cold he would make her ill.

When I probed into the boy's fear of burglars, he at first declared that he really believed a burglar might come to his room at night 'to steal my toys'. When I pointed out that burglars were not interested in children's toys, but in money, or jewels, he replied: 'He might come for my jewels—the necklace I gave my sister.' When pressed, he, in the end, revealed the real cause of his fears: 'I think Mummy might send a man to kill me . . .' '*Kill* you? Whatever for?' 'For being naughty.'

That he was deeply aware of maternal hostility was evident from other stories besides the one quoted. Thus in the story on Picture 1, after describing the man outside as a burglar and a murderer, he suddenly pointed at him with a question: 'This is really a lady, isn't it?'

His own hostility towards the mother came out in every one of his six stories. In three of them the woman—the mother of the child—is murdered. In the one I quoted, the son threatens to kill the mother, but kills the father instead. In the story on Picture 2, he described the following incident:

> 'Mummy is holding a little baby and Daddy is looking at them. It's a little boy. Suddenly the baby is sick all over Mummy's *very best dress* (with a burst of laughter, gloating and triumphant. Repeats) Very best dress! The boy runs and brings a chamber, and then the baby is *not* sick any more. (Still gloating and delighting in the baby's "perversity").'

Although his early memories of his father were gay and tender, he was clearly apprehensive when his father was due to return home from abroad. He murmured something about his mother writing to his father to tell him how naughty he had been. As he played with the toy farm, he made the bull break into the enclosure containing a cow with her calf. A fight followed and the bull killed the calf.

A day or two after his father's arrival, he came to see me, a much happier and less anxious boy. I asked him what his father had said when he saw him. He replied delightedly: 'She forgot to tell him!' His mother must have threatened him often with 'telling the father', and the thought must have preyed on his mind, disturbing the genuine longing the boy felt for his father's return. ('His Daddy then came in, and she told him.') Hence the fantasy of paternal punishment in the story on Picture 3, and the subsequent duel between father and son.

This boy, despite his youth, was unusually reserved, and except for these stories and a few remarks quoted earlier, would not talk about his fears, or things which happened at home between him and his mother. Later it transpired that his mother had forbidden him to tell things to the therapist and ordered him 'to forget' his fears. Throughout the short period of the boy's attendance, she remained unco-operative, hostile to the clinic and unwilling or unable to modify her treatment of him. Under her influence, he was rapidly developing into an anxious, perfectionist, obsessional personality. She used her husband's return as a pretext for terminating the boy's treatment. She believed that 'strictness' and punishment were much more effective ways of dealing with his difficulties[1].

The boy's stories thus, unwittingly, gave a true picture of the emotional attitudes which maternal hostility and harshness had induced him to adopt. This attractive, intelligent, affectionate child with a strong self-assertive drive (his mother described him as 'stubborn') was in danger of transferring his negative emotional attitudes upon the world at large. In his story on Picture 2, the little boy 'when he is naughty' 'bashes up people who've done nothing to him'. In the story on Picture 3, the boy, treated unfairly by both parents, made 'himself a sword' and *became a wicked man*'. Here, adult 'wickedness' is seen, with remarkable insight, as a direct consequence of bad family relationships.

Thus, it appears that a child's *Weltanschauung*, in so far as it is inevitably determined by his early experiences within the family, is reflected with varying degrees of fullness, sometimes with great frankness, sometimes transparently disguised, in spontaneous compositions, stimulated by a set of specially designed pictures. Statistically treated, these compositions give, as might be expected, a very general picture of these children's attitudes to life and to other human beings. This general picture is, however, very different for the Normal group from those obtained from the Neurotic and the Delinquent groups. There general differences can be summarized as follows:

The normal children function more on the plane of reality than either the neurotic or the delinquent. They tend to think of others, both adults and children as 'good', rather than 'bad', but are realistic enough to admit that children are sometimes 'naughty' and are usually punished for their transgressions.

[1] The mother was visited by a P.S.W. five years later. She reported that the boy, despite his high intelligence, was not doing well at school and was 'nervous,' unco-operative and withdrawn.

This punishment, however, is rarely imagined by them as cruel or excessive. Although they tend to think of parents as ambivalent towards their children ('they like him when he's good, they don't like him when he's naughty'), they believe that most of the time the parents are fond of them and ready to give them help and protection. They freely admit sibling jealousy, but this does not lead to rejection of the sibling, and is overlaid by affection for it. They are sufficiently secure within their family to assume that outsiders are likely to be benevolent, and they do not suffer much, if at all, from fear and mistrust of strangers.

The neurotic children are much less realistic in their approach to family life situations than the normal. They believe that 'naughtiness' or 'badness' are much more commonly met with in children than 'goodness', and that it is likely to be punished with a severity disproportionate to its seriousness. Their jealousy of siblings is hardly moderated by a natural liking and leads to rejecting them, and to a fear of aggression from the older more powerful sibling. They tend to believe that parents reject and maltreat their children more often than they like and protect them, and that children react to such treatment with hostility and rejection of the parents. This belief appears to increase their feelings of insecurity, so that they are inclined to view every stranger as dangerous, and are apt to react with anxiety to any ambiguous situation.

The delinquent children share with the neurotic their unrealistic approach to life situations, but in some respects show themselves to be more 'conventional', or perhaps more reserved. Even more strongly than the neurotics they tend to believe that children are usually 'bad' and parents ever ready to deal out severe punishment. Similarly, they are aware of parental rejection, but are less ready to recognize or to admit that children, too, feel hostile towards, and reject parents. Nor do they show such recognition of hostility towards, and rejection of, a rival sibling. On the other hand, fantasies of being 'shut out', isolated, or sent away, are more common among them than among the neurotics. The delinquents are also somewhat more realistic in their attitude towards 'strangers' or outsiders: they view them as dangerous somewhat less frequently than the neurotics.

In general, emotional interplay between neurotic children and their families appears to be more lively and intense than between delinquents and their families, although these emotions are of a predominantly negative character. Delinquents seem to be more detached, less deeply involved in family loves and hatreds than are the neurotics. This may be due to the actual feeling of 'not belonging', as well as to a more thorough repression of both hostile and positive emotions.

These generalized outlines, however, hardly do justice to the highly individual ways in which these differences were expressed by some of the children. They, of necessity, leave out the personal touch, sometimes delightful, sometimes pathetic, or even tragic, which epitomizes the attitudes of the normal, the neurotic, or the delinquent towards persons and life in general.

No neurotic or delinquent child, for instance, provided such a spontaneous testimony of his belief in maternal reliability as the small boy, C.P., aged 7, 6, with an I.Q. of 116. He said about Picture o that the baby in the cot was a little boy. When I asked whether his mother liked him, he replied: 'Yes, the mother likes the little boy when he's nice.' Then he added immediately and with conviction: '*She still likes him when he's not very nice.*'

The same impression of emotional security and warm affection between parent and child is conveyed by the following remarks of a girl, M.S., aged 8, 4, with an I.Q. of 125. She said about the rather sinister male figure in Picture 5:

> 'The little girl liked her father very much because she thought he was very kind and lovely, and very gentle.'

The same little girl described the little boy in Picture 1, in the following delightful sentence:

> 'He was a very good-behaved little boy and he had lots of manners. His father and mother and his great big brother liked him a lot.'

The jealousy of a baby sibling of the opposite sex was expressed in a gentle and subtle way by the girl M.S., aged 7, 2, with an I.Q. of 120. When I asked whether the mother in Picture 0 liked her baby son, M.S. replied:

> 'Yes, she did like him. No, not very much because she wanted a little baby girl, really.'

Her own hankering after the lost privileges of babyhood was charmingly revealed in the following remarks about Picture 2:

> 'There was once a little boy and a little girl and the father and mother. And the baby loved father and mother and the little girl very much, as well. The little girl was very good always. *She's thinking how she would love to be a little baby again, because she likes the little baby so much.*'

What a contrast this presents with a barely disguised wish to get rid of the baby, expressed by a neurotic girl M.J., aged 7, with an I.Q. of 101, who was also very jealous of a young brother: She said about Picture 3:

> 'This little boy is naughty. He threw the baby out of the window. His father and mother went out and picked the baby up. The little boy will go to prison. His father and mother say: "Good!".'

An even cruder admission of hostility to the rival sibling was volunteered by a very disturbed boy, A.F., aged 8, 5, with an I.Q. of 93. He said about Picture 2:

> 'This is father, mother and a little baby. This is Mum, Dad and my brother John. And this is me. And I'm feeling a bit jealous because Mummy is cuddling John and not me. And I'm thinking how to get him and kill my brother.'

A detailed fantasy of attempting to destroy the rival sibling was produced by a neurotic boy, B.R., aged 12, with an I.Q. of 91. He was suffering from a variety of fears, was enuretic

and was very jealous of his sister six years younger than himself. He said about Picture 2:

> 'These people had at first one little boy, and then the mother
> had a baby—a little girl. This boy was a wicked one, and he did
> not like the baby; he was jealous because they made a fuss of
> her. He wanted to be petted. So he tried to get rid of her. On one
> occasion when his parents were at the pictures, he took the baby
> and put her on someone's doorstep. Then he went to the pictures.
> When the parents came home, they saw the baby wasn't there,
> and the boy was out, too. When the boy came back, the father
> thrashed him and sent him to bed. Then the neighbour, who
> knew the baby, saw her on the doorstep and brought her in. On
> another occasion, the boy decided to kill the baby. He carried
> her to a pond and wanted to throw her in. He thought the pond
> was shallow, but that the baby would be drowned in it because
> it was small. Neither of them could swim. But his father followed
> him, and as he came up from behind, the boy turned round and
> saw him. He dropped the baby on the ground, and fell himself
> into the pond and was drowned.'

Jealousy in this case had been successfully repressed, and
the boy himself said to me that he had wanted a baby sister.
His mother reported that 'he got very upset whenever she was
punished', which in itself might have been an indication of
sado-masochistic wishes on the boy's part. In the course of
treatment, his hostility towards her came to the surface, and
he began to 'lash out' at her when she interfered with whatever
he was doing. On the mother's admission, the parents used to
quarrel a great deal in the early years of their marriage, and it
is obvious that a young child would find a great difficulty in
asserting himself in such a family atmosphere. He managed
to some extent to dominate his mother by developing many
nervous fears and by remaining unhelpful and dependent on
her like a much younger child. These symptoms represented
passive forms of negative self-assertion, while the active energy
of this urge was released in play under treatment, in a wealth
of sado-masochistic fantasies, as well as in his responses to the
Family Attitudes Test. His spontaneous inventions in play

were always concerned with soldiers fighting, or bands of 'crooks' and policemen pursuing each other, and his favourite themes were tortures, executions, massacres, drownings, being sucked up by quicksands and falling over precipices. His mother reported that at the age of 12 he was still playing with ants, putting them into nut-shells, which he floated on the water, then pushed over in order to watch the ants drown. He himself described to me the pleasure he derived from crushing his lead soldiers in his hands or between two boards.

Several children in the Neurotic group showed a high degree of insight into their difficulties. Thus, a very individual way of describing neurotic anxiety was provided by B.R., a highly intelligent boy aged 8, 8, with an I.Q. of 138. He was brought for treatment because he was suffering from asthma, habit spasms, inability to mix with other children and a dislike and fear of school. This is what he said about Picture 3:

'This boy is very lonely, and he hates it, and he's afraid of being alone. He's sitting down and thinking, and thinking. (How did he happen to be there by himself?) He happened to walk into this room, and there was a great wind blowing, and it blew the door to. He didn't understand how to open it; he thought he couldn't, because there was something slippery about it, and he thought of the horrible things that might happen. (What sort of horrible things?) Oh, things that happen in old legends and stories. He is a boy with a great imagination and he imagines things. And he has dreams, some nice and some very horrible. He decided to wait until his mother comes back. He hates being alone, and he also hates being in a crowd, when he can't see his mother—when his mother walks off and he wants to get to her through the crowd, and they are all so big. He's day-dreaming—you can direct your dreams, can't you?—he's thinking of pleasant things, as if it were his birthday, or Christmas, and he was putting his stocking up. Oh, I don't know what he wants—a Meccano and a lot of other things. He goes on and on thinking, and forgets about the time—you can go on thinking without realizing how long you've been at it, can't you?—and then he suddenly remembers that he's alone. He hears a voice in his ears saying to him, "You're alone, alone!" Not a real voice, you know. And he's so frightened, he gets into such a state that he begins to scream. His mother hears him; she's come in. She screams, too, and she comes to him, and then he's all right. Then he's all right.'

The special interest of this case lies in the fact that the relationship between the parents, on the one hand, and between the parents and the children, on the other, was a good one. The family were united; the mother, a strong but gentle character, was devoted to her husband and children; the father was a good family man, although rather withdrawn and subject to moods of deep depression. Ronald, the patient, had never been separated from his parents, except for a minor operation, and had no special traumatic experiences in his early years. There seemed to be little reason for his developing such serious symptoms of anxiety.

There is, however, a type of parent who inhibits normal self-assertion in children by their very excess of goodness, which makes any sort of resistance to them appear to a highly-strung child almost as a sin against the Holy Ghost. Both parents in this case were very religious, very kindly and had very high standards. Their grave conscientiousness in dealing with childish jealousy, greed and tempers could easily make these 'failings' appear formidable to an imaginative child like Ronald, and to induce in him overwhelming feelings of guilt. Ronald's position in the family between a highly intelligent, perfectly behaved brother five years older than himself and a high spirited, attractive sister, four years younger, must have subjected him to many tensions from which the other two were relatively free. He dared not assert himself openly, hence his anxiety and the symptoms which allowed him to satisfy this urge in disguise, and at the same time to gain concern and sympathy from his mother. Significant and revealing is his description of the mother in the story answering the boy's scream by a scream, as she comes to free him from the empty room in which he had accidentally locked himself.

Some of the delinquent children, although rarely as imaginative as the neurotics, gave descriptions of their conflicts with a high degree of insight. One of the most striking examples came from a delinquent boy, aged ten, with an I.Q. of 128. He was so suspicious and inhibited that he would hardly allow himself to move a muscle, while his conversation with me for many weeks was limited to 'yes' or 'no' in answer to questions, or to stock replies, such as: 'I don't know' or 'I don't mind'. Persistent pilfering at home and at school was not his only symptom, he also truanted and wet his bed.

He preserved his mask-like facial expression as he made up the following story on Picture 2:

> 'A man and a lady sitting on a couch with a baby. The mother is holding the baby in her arms. There's a boy standing near the couch, and he doesn't look as if he liked the baby. He thinks that his mother cares for the baby more than she cares for him. They are not taking notice of the boy, they're just looking at the baby, and the baby's playing with buttons on the mother's dress. (And *do* they care for the baby more than for the boy?) They care for the boy as much as they do for the baby, but they are looking at the baby now to see what he looks like. He's a jealous boy. He always thinks that people should care for him and for nobody else. (Everybody or just his parents?) His relatives and his parents. He feels jealous and thinks he should do something to the other person, so that they like him. (What does he do?) He hits them and makes them go away, so that he is the only person there to be cared for. (What do his parents do then?) His parents hit him for doing it. (And what does he feel then?) He feels that he would like to hit that person again and make them go somewhere else where his father and mother wouldn't find out about it. (Are they nice people?) They are nice to the baby, but not nice to the boy when he hits the other people.'

This boy's mother left him in the care of a grandmother, and afterwards, of an aunt, from the age of eight months, while she went out to work. The boy spent the week in his aunt's house, and the week-end with his parents. When he was five, his sister was born, and his mother had to stop at home. She took the boy to live with her, and at the same time he started going to school. His pilfering began at that time and consisted chiefly in taking money from his mother's purse. By the time the parents decided to seek help, it had become an established habit.

The mother complained of having lost touch with the boy, but it seemed fairly clear from his history that she had never been really in touch with him. The shuttle-cock existence which he had led for the first five years of his life made it impossible for him to establish a secure relationship either with his mother or his aunt. The sudden change at the age of five must have produced a traumatic effect through the piling-up of security destroying experiences: the birth of a sibling, the beginning of schooling and the break with the aunt's household. A child as insecure as this boy could assert himself only in indirect ways, and the virtual absence of a relationship with an adult left him free to choose a symptom asocial in character.

His description in the story of the boy's reactions to parental punishment can be regarded as typical of a vicious circle situation which is created when a negative way of self-assertion is met with condemnation instead of understanding. 'They hit him for doing it', and he 'feels he would like to hit that person again and make them go somewhere else where his father and mother wouldn't find out about it.'

Another delinquent boy, Peter, aged 10, 7, with an I.Q. of 118, revealed his central conflict in two of his stories. He was a pilferer and a truant, liable to have severe temper outbursts during which he attacked his mother. This is what he said about Picture o:

> 'Once upon a time there was a lady who was ill after she had a baby. She had wanted a baby, but after she'd got it, she didn't like it. (Why not?) Because she wanted a different kind . . . a different type. . . . (What do you mean?) She wanted a girl and this was a boy. (Well, what did she do then?) She didn't want to sell it. (Why not?) Because she thought she might get to like it.'

The story on Picture 4 was a variation on the same theme:

> 'There was once a woman who had a baby, and she liked it very much. But the man didn't like it, and he puts his fists to its face. He doesn't like it, because he wanted a girl, and the baby is

108

a boy. So he tells the woman to get rid of him. If she doesn't, he won't give her any money—he won't go to work and won't earn any money. He won't give her any money because he knows that she would buy food for the baby and keep it alive. He likes her but he doesn't like the baby. So she gets rid of it. (After a pause he changed his mind and added): No, she goes away from him with the baby and gets a job.'

At the age of four this boy was evacuated to the country with his elder brother and was separated from his parents for four years, whereas his baby sister remained with the mother. The parents rarely visited the boys, and my patient asserted that he did not miss his own home, and, in fact, did not want to return to his parents at the end of the war. He liked country life, and the farmer used to take them shooting rabbits!

There is little doubt that in this case a prolonged separation from the mother when the boy was very young severed whatever bond may have existed between them. The mother was herself an insecure person, who stood in awe of her somewhat unreliable husband and clearly preferred her daughter to her sons. The boy's father was a former boxer, who ran a road-haulage service, and was away from home a great deal.

The boy told me that he believed both his parents favoured his sister and that girls, generally speaking, had a much better time than boys. He confessed that he had often wished he were born a girl because then his parents, especially his mother, would have liked him better. It became evident that he had not really accepted his masculinity, and that much of his tough-ness, violent temper and his delinquent behaviour were, at least in part, reaction-formations against the feminine aspect of his personality which he felt to be a weakness.

Peter's stories display a characteristic harshness and crudity, a lack of finer shades and of imaginative touch which are rather typical of the spontaneous inventions of delinquent boys. Despite his high average intelligence, this boy of ten-and-a-half talked of 'selling' babies, and of a father planning to starve his infant son. 'He won't give her any money because he knows that she would buy food for the baby and keep it alive.'

It is possible, indeed even likely, that the theme was un-wittingly borrowed from fairy-tales, but Peter showed that he believed such things possible, by giving his story a contemporary setting. On the other hand, the family relationships portrayed are primitive to a degree, which suggests that the boy lacked a sense of emotional realities. I believe that his early history justifies the assumption that he failed to portray the more usual relationships because he had not experienced such a relationship between himself and his mother.

Such qualitative differences in the conception of parent–child relationship are widely distributed through the stories by the normal, neurotic and delinquent children. In some cases, however, they were concentrated in a complete set of stories, and I believe it is worth while quoting the stories in full to illustrate the particular *Weltanschauung* which pervades them.

(c) *Qualitative Differences in the Stories of the Three Groups*

A normal girl, Jean, aged 11, 6, with an I.Q. of 132, composed the following stories on my set of pictures:

> *Picture* o. Mrs. Brown is a very poor lady. She was also very lonely because it was ten years since her husband had died, and often she wished that she had a baby for company. She would sit and look into the fire, and look, and wish. One day when the wind was howling round the house, there came a tap on the door, and upon the doorstep stood a weary traveller. 'Good Mistress, have you lodgings for the night?' he questioned. 'It's but a poor lonely house,' Mrs. Brown answered, 'but you're welcome to whatever there is.'
>
> She let the stranger in and gave him a seat by the fire. After he had something to eat, he asked for a bed. Mrs. Brown gave him her bed and slept by the fire all through the night. When she awoke in the morning, the traveller had gone, and Mrs. Brown thought no more of it. But a few days afterwards, when Mrs. Brown was cleaning the doorstep of her house, she found, wrapped in a silken coverlet, a tiny baby. Joyfully, she picked him up and carried him into the house and put him in a cradle she kept in case she did have a baby.

Now he has grown into a strong fine man, and though Mrs. Brown did not know, it was her kindness that led her to finding a baby.

Picture 1. It was quite an ordinary family that lived in a house in the suburbs of London: mother, father, baby John and his big brother Jack. Jack had sailed away to America, and nobody knew when he would come back, as nobody has heard from him for a long time. You couldn't call baby John a baby any longer, for he was growing fast. One day when father and mother were sitting by the fire, talking about Jack, and John was playing on the floor, came a knock on the door. It was rather strange that a knock should come on the door at that time of the evening, for having no relatives and few friends, visitors were rare. John looked up in sudden surprise. Mother and father looked at each other hopefully. 'Can it be? Is it?' asked mother hopefully. But no, only a late caller, asking his way to a small side-street. They were all very disappointed and took their seats again, looking sorrowfully into the fire. Seconds passed into minutes and minutes into hours, and mother said: 'Bed time, John.' John liked a bit of fun and wasn't spoiled. 'All right, Mummy,' he called. 'Bed time!' called a jovial voice from behind the door, and in walked a manly figure, who was instantly recognized as Jack, who had left long ago. And now in the house all four of them were happy, and so will for ever more.

Picture 2. In a small house in the country there lived father, mother and a little fair-haired girl called Susan. Nobody liked Susan because they said she was spoiled. Although she had no friends, she lived happily in the back garden, or roaming fields and hills. It was quite true to say that Susan was spoiled because she was an only child. Mother and father were very fond of her, and she did just as she liked.

One day a little baby brother came to live in the house with Susan. Mother and father were so busy looking after Brian, as the baby was called, they were not able to take much notice of Susan. She was aware of the fact that they were not taking much notice of her, and she began to plot in her mind that she would run away. She would go and live with her friend, the only one she had. She counted out her money and found that she had just enough to take her there. So on a bright September morning away she ran to the station. Arriving at her friend's house, her friend looked at her in great astonishment. 'Mummy, look at this, Susan is here, on the doorstep!' 'I've run away,' said Susan proudly. 'My dear child,' exclaimed Mrs. Walker, 'you must go back immediately', and she sent the wire off quickly, but wire came back saying that she was not wanted. That was a shock to Susan. For three weeks she stayed at her friend's house and did not enjoy it a bit. When she arrived home, her baby brother was growing fast. 'Served you right to be sent away', said her father sternly. 'Perhaps you will not be so jealous now.' And now Susan is the most popular girl at school and has many friends. Wasn't it a good job that Susan had a baby brother! ('Who did the parents really like best, the baby or the little girl?') They had to take care of the baby when he first came, but afterwards they did not like either of them better, they liked them equally.

Picture 3. There was no doubt about it, Colin was certainly a naughty boy. He would climb trees and tear his shirt, and trespass in Farmer Giles's fields. Mother and father could not do *anything* about it. One day his uncle and aunt decided to come over to look after Colin while his mother and father went for a holiday. Colin did not like the idea of this because both uncle and aunt had very sharp tongues. Uncle and aunt came over the day before mother and father went away, and Colin knew he was going to have a very bad time. But no, they took not the slightest notice of him when he climbed trees and tore his shirt; they just looked at it and said not a word. Colin thought that was good, but he soon found it wasn't because they did not give him his meals and did not make his bed. And then Colin sat down in his room and thought. He knew he was a naughty boy, and then he went to uncle and aunt and apologized for his behaviour, and was never a naughty boy again. What a surprise mother and father had when they came back and found him so good!

Picture 4. When father was a little boy he had been very fond of sport, and now he was grown-up, he has become a boxer and was married to a shy girl, called Violet. One day a baby was born, and much to father's delight it was a boy. 'I shall teach him to box', said father proudly. 'No, you won't, I shall not want him to be bruised before his life has hardly begun', said the mother. They quarrelled continuously over this matter. The boy was certainly strong. One day when father went out lumbering, he came back hungry and anxious to see the little boy, as he always was. Mother came out and held him in her arms, and much to their surprise, he clenched his fists just like father's. 'Looks as if he were going to be a boxer, too,' said father. 'Well, it looks like it,' said mother, 'and so, I suppose, you'll teach him.' And so he did. Now he has grown up to a fine lad of twenty or so, and can even beat his father in a ring. Although he was a strong man, he still remembers his mother, shy and delicate, and has a special love of spring flowers, especially violets.

Picture 5. In a small shack in the wood there lived a little girl and her father. Gill, as she was called, had a special love for Nature, especially birds. Father was just the opposite. The only thing of Nature he enjoyed was trees, because it was his job to cut them down. One day as they were sitting in their hut, watching the smoke curl upwards through the tall trees, a sparrow came through the door and looked round hopefully for some crumbs. In the winter months food was scarce. Seeing a lump of bread lying close to the fire, he hopped over to the fireside. He was about to peck it when father saw him and made a run at him, but Gill was too quick for him. The bird hopped into the leaping flames, and Gill caught hold of him. His feathers were scorched. Gill laid him on a bed of cotton wool and he soon recovered. During that time father had helped Gill and gave him crumbs from his hand, and so when the sparrow had gone, Gill questioned him. 'I thought you didn't like Nature,' she said. 'No, but I feel it was my fault that the sparrow was scorched,' he said, 'and I had resolved to like Nature as much as you do.' And so he does. And it was a pleasant sight to see Gill and her father sitting on the doorstep and all the birds hopping round them, feeding out of their hands. (Where was Gill's mother?) Her mother had died.

This girl's imaginative treatment of a variety of emotional situations between adults and children reveals fairly fully her own attitudes relating to the family.

Thus, in her story on Picture o, the baby is 'longed for' and is obtained as a reward for virtue, for the kindness shown to a stranger. The unconscious sexual symbolism of some details is irrelevant in this connection; what is important, I believe, is the assumption that a child is a precious gift to be bestowed on good women.

The theme of her second story is family affection. A close bond between parents and children is described: the parents miss the son who has been away a long time; they are overjoyed when he arrives home. The relationship between the younger son and the parents is also represented as an easy and affectionate one. The family is seen as a closely knit unit.

Her third story is concerned with a family disagreement and subsequent reconciliation. The problem of sibling jealousy is tackled courageously and adequately. The little girl is described as 'spoilt' because she is allowed to do 'just as she likes'. But the parents condemn her jealousy of the baby-brother and punish her by a temporary rejection. She learns her lesson, and on her return home, becomes 'the most popular girl at school, and has many friends', whereas before this incident she had only one. Thus, the salutary effects of an unpleasant experience on the development of character are recognized. The parents are represented as sensible and fair—'They did not like either of them better, they liked them equally'.

In her fourth story the parents are unable to control their naughty son, but a couple of parent-substitutes step in to prove to him that naughty behaviour does not pay. He accepts his defeat with good grace. Thus, reality principle is again triumphant.

Both these stories illustrate the adoption of adult standards by Jean, the operation of a reasonably mild and realistic 'super-ego'. Punishment is seen as a consequence of the child's own actions rather than as an act of personal vindictiveness on the part of an adult, and the result of punishment is the reformation of the transgressor, not his annihilation.

The theme of Jean's fifth story is a disagreement between husband and wife which is settled by the child they both love. This picture, which suggested stories of violence and cruelty to so many children in the Neurotic and the Delinquent groups, merely prompted her into representing the parents as contrasting in temperament. The husband is a 'boxer', the wife 'a shy girl'. Both parents are positive in their attitude towards the child: the father in trying to bring him on, the mother in protecting him. Parents are seen as entirely bene-volent: the 'bad parent' fantasy is completely suppressed.

In her sixth story, Gill, the girl, is represented as more humane and spiritually more developed than her father, of whom Jean says rather sardonically: 'The only thing of Nature he en-joyed was trees because it was his job to cut them down.' She is, thus, not uncritical of adults, which may be taken as a sign of a degree of independence from the parents. The daughter in the story makes the father see the error of his ways and helps him to learn compassion. No doubt, in this story Jean reveals a certain amount of priggish self-satisfaction, for the nature-loving heroine is most likely a self-portrait. Yet one can hardly quarrel with an ego-ideal which gives such prominence to kindness. The child in Picture 5, reaching out for something, was seen by so many neurotic and delinquent children as 'doing something she is not supposed to'. Jean made her reach out for a sparrow and save it from being burned. She went further: she made her heroine give an object lesson in kindness to her father, who profits by it. Adult standards are thus not only accepted but are shown to work.

Jean was a tall, slender girl, nice-looking and pleasant-mannered, but by no means a personification of stolid 'normal-ity'. Her manner and the way she talked revealed considerable drive and a desire for achievement. She told me she had a sister aged seven, but rarely played with her because she preferred to play with her own friends. She was not keen on having any more children in the family. These remarks and the content of her stories suggested that she had been jealous, but had suc-ceeded in overcoming it. That her early years had not been free from stress was indicated by her class teacher who told me that now her behaviour was excellent, although she had been 'somewhat difficult' in the past. The headmistress added that Jean's mother gave an impression of a smart and rather shallow person, showing little affection for her children. Interestingly enough, it is the father who plays a more active part in Jean's stories than the mother. But it was, perhaps, the mother whom Jean wished to emulate when she told me that she would like to go on the stage when she grew up. At school she was made a prefect, and declared that she liked the responsibility.

Unfortunately, I could obtain no more information about Jean's parents. But judging by the portraits of sensible, friendly and not over-indulgent adults she drew in her stories, they must have at least satisfied her need for emotional security and had not blocked her way to self-realization. Her stories show no signs of compensatory trends, although her self-assertive drive is evident in the adventurous or didactic qualities with which she endows some of her child characters (Susan in P. 2 story, Colin in P. 3, Gill in P. 5), as well as in her achievements at school and ambitious plans for the future. She allows them a measure of imperfection—another indication of emotional security and of a mild 'super-ego'. There is a predominance of pleasant themes in her stories, obtained chiefly by means of a 'happy ending', but unpleasant themes are not avoided. In this way, a realistic balance between 'good' and 'bad' is achieved, which can be regarded as characteristic of 'normality', or inner balance. With this goes the realistic content of the stories, none of which are fantastic, although the first one (P. o) is obviously based on a well-known fairy-tale theme: wishing for a child and obtaining it in a miraculous way. In brief, the attitude of mind which is reflected in these stories is characterized by objectivity; an acceptance of reality-principle; a belief in parental affection and protection; a relative independence from the parents and an ability to judge them fairly; a balanced moral judgment. The self-assertive urge of this child assumed positive forms presumably because her relationship with her parents was as satisfactory as the one she described in her stories.

Of a very different type are the stories by a neurotic girl, Helen, aged 11, 1, with an I.Q. of 102.

> *Picture* o. There was once a lady named Mrs. Jones who had a little girl. She was only about four months old and was in her cradle. The baby was rather big and had blue eyes. It was a good girl, but sometimes cried. Mrs. Jones didn't use to smack the

baby when it cried, but just used to say, 'You naughty girl!' and the baby used to stop. Her father was an engineer and thought the baby was ugly because they had another little boy whom he liked best. Mrs. Jones did not take much notice of what the father thought, but did everything she could for the baby.

Picture 1. Mr. and Mrs. Smith were once sitting round the fire, and the little boy John was playing with some bricks. John wasn't a bad boy, but he would play for hours with his bricks when he had the patience. When he hadn't, he was a very naughty boy. He would run upstairs and hide in his father's and mother's wardrobe and make them hunt for him. And when it was time to go to bed, his mother and father would give up looking for him after an hour or so, and he would play upstairs until it was time for his mother and father to come up to bed. And then he would rush into bed before his mother would know where he was. And when his mother went to see if he were in bed, he would be fast asleep. His father and mother were good people. They liked the little boy. He liked them—sometimes. His uncle sometimes came to see them and always brought him something.

Picture 2. One day when Jean Brown came home from school she saw her father and mother sitting on the couch. Her mother was nursing a little baby just been born. She went over to look at it and found that it was her little brother that she'd been promised. Jean wondered why her mother had been away for two weeks and found that she'd been in hospital with baby. Jean thought he was a pretty little boy and very bonny. ('What sort of girl was Jean?') Jean was sometimes very naughty and used to play tricks on people—grown-up people. She used to hide behind the corner and jump out on people, and gave them a fright. Father and mother used to smack her sometimes and send her to bed when they found out what she had done. And then she would stop for a fortnight, and then do it again. Then they said they wouldn't let her have the baby, so Jean promised that she would be good. ('Whom did they like best, the baby or Jean?') Mother and father liked them both the same. Yes, Jean kept her promise.

Picture 3. Jack was a very naughty little boy and one day played truant from school. His mother and father did not find out the first time, so Jack thought, 'I'll do it again tomorrow.'

The next day he did the same. When he got home his mother asked him if he'd been to school. Jack said to her 'Yes', telling a lie. And his mother said: 'Why have I had the school board round here, then?' So Jack said: 'I don't know, Mother,' telling another lie. So his mother said: 'Oh, I'll better take you to school tomorrow to see why they came round.' Jack, being a very naughty boy, said that he wasn't well the next day. So his mother said: 'I'll better go to see your teacher by myself.' Jack said: 'Oh, Mother, stop with me, you know that I'm not well.' But his mother said: 'I won't be long.' So she went up the school and asked the teacher. So the teacher said: 'He's been away for two days, didn't you know?' His mother said: 'No, I didn't know. I sent him to school, and he said he wasn't well today.' So his mother went straight home, took Jack out of bed and said: 'Oh, you naughty boy,' and gave him a whipping, and made him sit in a corner all day, with nothing to eat but dry bread and water. ('Did she lock the door or just shut it?') She locked him in so that he didn't get out. He's thinking: 'I am a naughty boy, I won't do it again,' and he was a good boy after that. ('What about his father?') His father didn't punish him because he's been punished.

Picture 4. Shirley was only four years old and was soon going to school. Her father was a boxer and he said when she got older, he would try on her. Shirley was a good little girl really, and her mother was fond of her, and would not let any harm come to her. She told her mother what her father had said, and the mother said, 'You'd better go away. I'll pack your things up in the loft, so that your father doesn't see.' While Shirley's mother went up into the loft to pack up her things, Shirley's father came in and asked where her mother was. Shirley accidentally said, 'In the loft.' Her father said: 'Whatever is she doing up there?' So she said: 'Packing', not remembering that her father was going to hurt her when she got older. ('Why did he want to hurt her?') He wanted to hurt her because he didn't like Shirley, and he wanted his wife to have another baby, not Shirley. Her father went up in the loft and found his wife there. He asked: 'What are you doing up here?' So his wife says: 'Who told you I was up here?' So he says: 'Shirley.' So she said: 'Shirley is a naughty girl, I think I will let you box her.' Her father was just going to do it when her mother said: 'Oh, no, I think we'll better put her in a Home than let you box her and kill her.' So Shirley was put in a Home.

Picture 5. Joan was once in a garden trying to catch some butterflies, and her father came out and said: 'You naughty girl! I'll hit you next time I see you trying to catch this kind of butterfly.' Joan was asked to tea by her friend Mary, and they were both very fond of catching butterflies. Well, when Joan and Mary had their tea, they went out in the garden to play. Mary asked Joan if she would like to catch butterflies with her butterfly net, so Joan, not thinking, said: 'Yes.' When it was time to go home, Joan had caught about twelve butterflies, and they were all in the net. Joan asked Mary if she could take them home with her in a jar, so Mary said: 'Yes.' Just as Mary was going to get the jars, Joan's father came for her, as she was trying to catch another butterfly. So her father said: 'Oh, I told you I was going to smack you, and when you get in, I will.' Joan left her butterflies with Mary and was soon indoors and in bed, crying. This learnt Joan a lesson and she did not ever catch butterflies again. ('What about her mother?') Her mother was very wild with her and hit her as well, and said: 'You can't go to any party you was asked to for a month.'

It is evident at once that the emotional climate of the families described by Helen is very different from that in the stories by Jean. In the story on Picture o, the father has no use for his baby daughter: he likes his son better. A lack of harmony between the parents is suggested by the remark: 'Mrs. Jones did not take much notice of what the father thought.' The mother is seen as a stern person whose mere words: 'You naughty girl!' suffice to silence the crying baby. It is significant that Helen considers 'smacking' as a possible remedy against crying, even with a baby four months old. There are indications that she is projecting something of herself into this baby, for she was 'big for her age' and had 'blue eyes'. Her father, too, had an elder son by his first wife, of whom Helen was very jealous and whom, she might have thought, her father preferred.

In the stories on Pictures 1 and 2 there is a great deal of emphasis on the 'naughtiness' of the children. There is a state of conflict between them and the parents, and an atmosphere of mutual hostility which spreads to other adults. 'John' tantalizes his parents by hiding from them, whereas 'Jean' 'gives frights' to grown-ups by 'jumping out on them from behind a corner'. Punishment does not deter these children: John is never caught at his pranks, whereas Jean 'stops for a fortnight' and 'then does it again'. The parents finally win by means of a threat to withhold the baby brother. They are represented in these stories principally as prohibiting and punishing agents. These parental functions are brought out with an astonishing degree of ruthlessness in the stories on Pictures 3, 4 and 5.

In the story on Picture 3 Jack's mother takes a sadistic pleasure in tracking him down and exposing his lies and truancy. He is punished with an unusual severity: dragged out of bed, whipped, and kept on bread and water the whole day in a locked room where he is made to sit in a corner.

Shirley's father, in the story on Picture 4, is also sadistic towards her. He threatens to 'box her' simply because he does not like her and would like his wife to have another baby. The mother is said to be fond of Shirley and determined not to 'let any harm come to her'. Yet, the almost indecent haste with which she decides that the child must go away, instead of intervening before the father on her behalf, is a doubtful proof of fondness. Most remarkable also is the suddenness with which this mother turns against her daughter and decides to let the father 'box her and kill her'. True, she changes her mind 'just as he was going to do it', but the alternative punishment is still a drastic one: Shirley is going to be 'sent away to a Home'. Thus is a child of four punished by its parents for having, quite innocently and to her own disadvantage, told the truth about something her mother wanted to conceal. The child is represented as hardly aware of her parents' dreadful unreliability, and nothing is said about her feelings towards them. This detail is characteristic of Helen's own tendency to dissociate the hostility she herself was feeling and to substitute hysterical symptoms for it.

The girl Joan, in the story on Picture 5, also suffers punishment disproportionate to her guilt. Her father issues an arbitrary prohibition: 'You mustn't catch *this* kind of butterfly.' But it is just what Joan loves doing, and on joining her friend Mary, who has a butterfly net, she promptly forgets her father's prohibition. For this she is spanked and sent to bed. As if this were not enough, her mother 'is wild with her' and declares that she would not allow her to go to any party she is invited to, for a month.

Whereas in the two earlier stories the children are mischievous, in the last two they are merely forgetful and could be easily forgiven for their minor lapses. Helen, however, says nothing about their reactions to punishment: they submit to it meekly, as if they felt it to be deserved. The phrase: 'You naughty girl!' occurs in four of her stories; in the other two, children are described as 'naughty'. One wonders if the parents' hostility to the children is accepted as deserved because of the children's unspecified and unmentionable hostility towards the parents.

Vindictive, rejecting parents, forgetful, absent-minded little girls—innocent victims of parental hostility—how does this picture fit in with Helen's own early experiences and family background?

She was an illegitimate child born to a married woman, who subsequently left her husband while the baby was only a few months old. The husband accepted the child as his own, knowing that she was not, but could not look after her himself and had to place her with a foster-mother. From babyhood till the age of four, Helen was with this woman, who was said to have drilled her to sit still for long stretches of time, and of whom the child was so afraid that she dared not touch anything or speak when she was taken visiting. At four she was placed with another foster-mother who was kind to her, and stayed with her until her father married again and took her to live with him. Helen was ten years old at the time, and her symptoms first appeared then.

She developed 'fits', during which she was said to 'turn blue in the face', stare wildly, choke, grow rigid and cry out that she was going to die. She had screaming attacks whenever thwarted; was afraid of going upstairs alone; was generally 'difficult' and disobedient with her stepmother; had moments of 'absent-mindedness' during which she endangered the safety of the home by actions such as raking out burning coals on to the floor of the living-room, or leaving the front door open as she went out, knowing that there was no one in the house except herself.

Helen's father was a kindly man, genuinely fond of her, but when she started having her 'fits', he was advised by the neighbours to 'thrash' her, and threatened to do so. Although this threat was never carried out, Helen took it seriously. Her stepmother was a bigoted woman of very limited intelligence, indulgent in some ways, yet pettily vindictive at times, and easily shocked or hurt by any expression of hostility or 'ingratitude' on Helen's part.

As had already been mentioned, Helen's father had a son by a previous marriage, who was not living at home and whom she hardly knew. When, however, he came home for a holiday, she was said to be particularly troublesome.

It is not difficult to see how the extreme insecurity of this girl's early years found expression in her spontaneous fantasies. Deserted by her mother in babyhood, she was handed over to a foster-mother whose 'strictness', applied to a child of Helen's age, must have amounted to cruelty. A child of four who 'sits still and dares not touch anything', could not have had normal opportunities for self-assertion or self-realization. She appeared to have been utterly squashed and cowed at that age, and whatever resentment she might have felt was either repressed or dissociated. Dissociation was the defence mechanism she used in developing her own symptoms; it was also the one used by the girls in her last two stories, who break parental prohibitions in a moment of forgetfulness.

With her second foster-mother Helen was said to have been happy, but from her, too, she was somewhat arbitrarily removed. In the ten years of her life she had had to adjust herself to three 'mothers' and with this third 'mother' she had to share her father's affection. It is hardly surprising that she was impelled to assert herself at this stage, and that she could only use negative ways of doing so, for the outgoing aspect of her personality had been suppressed in her earliest years.

A girl with a history like Helen's could have easily become a delinquent. The redeeming influence in her case must have been her father's sincere affection for her. Although he could not have her with him until he re-married, he visited her regularly when she lived with her foster-mothers and thus kept the bond of affection between them unbroken. Besides, Helen knew of her mother's desertion. She told me: 'My mother ran away with a man when I was a baby.' This knowledge must have saved her the profoundly disturbing uncertainty concerning her parentage, which is so often associated with delinquent behaviour in adopted and institutionalized children.

A year after she had acquired a new 'mother' and a permanent home, she was still extremely insecure and perhaps wondering whether she would be sent away again if she were 'naughty', like 'Shirley' in one of her stories. Her symptoms were no doubt, in one of their several aspects, a way of testing her parents' affection. They were also a disguised expression of hostility towards her stepmother, which she transferred on to me during treatment. When I spoke to her about jealousy, she accused me of being 'nasty' and threatened to tell her stepmother about it. 'Then don't be surprised if you don't see me here next week!'

One of the significant things she did during treatment interviews was to speak in a lisping baby language, as if she were re-living, in the presence of a sympathetic mother-figure, the early years of her life. She also became able to express her hostility, once with a considerable force after she had been kept waiting by me. When I pointed out the connection between her anger and the anxiety re-awakened by my apparent rejection of her, she admitted sulkily that she had thought I 'did it on purpose'.

Her responses to the pictures demonstrate how lasting are the early impressions of family relationships. The adults were

AGGRESSION AND ITS INTERPRETATION

unreliable and threatening in those days; they made her feel she was a 'naughty girl'; they inflicted punishment and thus appeared hostile and dangerous, but they also made her feel that the punishment was deserved. When Helen composed these stories, her picture of family relationships was unrealistic, nor was it very accurate as far as the facts of her past were concerned. Yet it was how she felt it to be. Her emotional attitudes were characteristic of a neurotic child: insecure, aware of her own hostility towards adults and therefore guilty; sado-masochistic because of her hostility and guilt; expecting harsh retaliation equivalent to murder for her 'badness'; lacking in reality sense and in objectivity.

Emotional attitudes characteristic of delinquent children are illustrated by the following set of stories composed by a boy aged 12, 6, with an I.Q. of 87. (This I.Q. was obtained on a group test given in school, and so probably was an underestimation).

> *Picture* 0. Once upon a time there was a middle-aged woman nursing a baby in a lone cottage in the country. This woman is quite a stranger to the baby, and his father and mother just gone and left it. They really left it to die, not thinking that this woman would find it. Her husband made a small cradle for it in which it slept. The baby is a boy, but being only eighteen months old, he hasn't been christened yet. She likes the baby very much and does not want to lose it. ('Why did the parents leave the child?') They really wanted a baby girl, and had been expecting a baby girl quite a long time, and were disappointed at having a boy.

> *Picture* 1. I'm going to carry on with the story. The old lady being quite feeble was singing to the baby when her husband came home. She left the baby and they sat down by the fire, discussing things, not knowing that there was someone outside the door, listening to them all the time. This man was a relative to the boy and was trying to get him away from those two people. The boy, having no toys or anything to do, used to just sit idle on the floor. This man was jealous of the two people having the baby. He was not a very good man, he was just an uncle to the boy. He just wanted to get him away and get rid of him.

Picture 2. This is going to be a different story. Once upon a time in a town up in the North country lived a young lady and a man who only had one child which was a boy five years old. The two parents were longing for a baby girl and they had one adopted to them. The baby girl was quite a pretty little thing, but the boy didn't like it at all. When the parents made a fuss, the boy felt very jealous and whenever he had a chance, he used to hurt her. When the baby girl was grown up, she left home, and the parents were very sad. In the end they lost the boy. He got so jealous of them having that girl, he couldn't bear it any longer, so he left home.

Picture 3. I'm going to carry on with the same story. When the boy was quite young, his parents used to forget about him and used to go out and lock the door behind them. The boy, feeling very sad, used to try and wreck the home for them. The parents feeling very hurt at this, tried to get rid of the boy. Knowing he had nowhere else to go, he used to go against their will and stay behind.

Picture 4. This is going to be a different story. Out in the country on a moor used to live two people, quite lonely without a child, until one day they had a little baby girl. One day the girl did something wrong and her father began to hit her. The woman did not know what to do, so she picked the baby up and tried to take it away. This the father didn't like, and so he left home, until one day he came back again when the child was grown up. The child didn't know who it was at first until it was told. When the child found out, she didn't like it at all, and left home that night. ('What was it she didn't like?') When she found out what her father had done when she was small.

Picture 5. One day there was a man and a little girl out on the allotments part of which he made into a flower-bed, and the little girl went round pulling flowers out of the ground. She didn't know what she was doing. The man began to hit him . . . her, when she ran away and told her mother what he'd done. The mother didn't like this, and so she took the child and went to live with her mother. ('Who was the man?') He was just a father to the child. When the child has grown up and the mother quite old, the girl went down to the allotments and was walking round when a man came up and asked what she wanted. She was with another girl, and the man chased them off and saw where they went. Then he suddenly realized that it was his own child. ('And what did he feel about it all?') He felt very sorry for what he'd done.

The picture of family relationships which emerges from these stories is unrealistic and unnatural as far as ordinary families are concerned, but the boy describes these unnatural happenings in the most matter-of-fact way. In his first story the parents desert their child, hoping that it will die, and they do it for the only reason that the baby happens to be of the wrong sex—a male, like the author of the story.

The theme of the parents' preference for a 'baby girl' and their dislike and rejection of the son runs through two other stories. Even when the boy is adopted by kind people, he has a pretty miserable time (' has no toys or anything to do'), and is threatened by a malevolent uncle who wants to 'get him away and get rid of him'.

In two of the stories the mother stands up for the child, who happens to be a girl, and it is the father who is hostile towards it, and leaves home rather than curb his animosity.

The children vie with the parents in demonstrations of hostility. In the story on Picture 3, the parents neglect the boy, and he responds by trying 'to wreck the home for them'. When they want to get rid of him, he stays with them in order to spite them. But, in the story on Picture 2, he leaves them *after* they had lost their favourite, the girl, obviously with the intention of adding to their distress.

These two stories might represent, in a condensed form, the conflict in the delinquent's mind, when he appears to be saying to his parents: 'I know you don't want me, but I will stay with you just to spite you. By behaving as I do, I will wreck your home.' The later stage is the feeling of cutting adrift, emotionally: 'Now I'll leave you.'

In each of the six stories, the family is broken up: either the children, or the parents leave home in consequence of intolerable emotional situations. Even the best loved child, as in stories on Pictures 4 and 5, divides, instead of uniting, the parents. It seems as if the parents and children are bound to part in anger.

The personal history of this boy, Terence, who was not one of my patients, contained much of what he projected into his stories. His parents did not get on together and his mother deserted his father when Terence was eight years old. She remarried, and at the time of testing, Terence had a half-sister, aged three. Since his mother's re-marriage, he has become difficult and has taken to pilfering, so she arranged for him to go away to a boarding school where such cases were accepted. He remained, however, the bone of contention between his parents, for his father was trying, through the Court, to obtain the custody of him. It was not, I was told, because he was fond of Terence, but merely because he wanted 'to spite' his wife.

This epitomizes the atmosphere in which Terence must have spent his early years. Parental quarrels, by dividing the child's loyalties, can prevent the child from forming a firm emotional bond with either of the parents. A premature emotional detachment may result, which is characteristic of many persistent delinquents. It is significant that the rejected boy in Terence's story makes no attempt at reconciliation with his parents: he cannot tolerate rivalry, so 'he leaves them'. Significant, too, is the casual way in which Terence refers to the *'status parentis'*. 'He was *just an uncle* to the boy.' 'He was *just a father* to the child.'

Terence himself was quite a likeable youngster, superficially friendly and at ease during the interview. Yet he was described by his teachers as 'remaining aloof' although he had been at the school for a year, as having no special friend, and as 'bullying on the sly'.

It was this quality of detachment and an atmosphere of hopelessness which made this boy's stories different from the stories invented by Helen, and by other neurotic, but non-delinquent children. There are several features their stories have in common: Helen's stories also were unrealistic in their cruelty and sado-masochism. She, too, dwelt on the hostility and unfairness of parents towards children. The children, however, were not utterly rejected: even by punishing them the parents showed some concern for them. Terence's stories, on the other hand, reflect complete estrangement of children from parents. Such estrangement, for whatever reasons it occurs, may be the most important condition predisposing the child to delinquency.

Unfortunately, I had no comparable set of stories by a delinquent girl, which was partly due to the smallness of the group tested (ten subjects), and partly to the fact that the girls' stories did not show the characteristics described with the same degree of concentration. The theme of parental rejection or desertion, however, recurred in them, though in a milder form. Moreover, it appeared from their social histories that the father's absence from home, which would prevent the formation of an emotional bond with him, might be conducive to delinquency in girls. In this group of ten delinquent girls, seven were temporarily or permanently fatherless—illegitimate, orphaned, or separated from the father for long periods during which the girl's delinquency started.

Sado-masochistic fantasies were less frequent and less intense in the stories by this group of girls than in the stories by the delinquent boys, which confirms the general observation that violent forms of delinquency are common among boys but rare among girls. On the other hand, compensatory fantasies of material affluence and social prestige occurred in the girls' stories, whereas they were absent in the stories by boys.

(d) A Group Test of Family Attitudes

I have given examples of complete sets of stories not only to illustrate the difference in the emotional atmosphere characteristic of the spontaneous inventions produced by different groups of subjects, but also to demonstrate my methods of interpretation. It should be clear from this that I was not following closely the system of interpretation of any particular school but was guided by widely accepted principles of psychology and mental analysis applied in clinical practice. The interpretation, however, was my own, and this leaves the possibility that it was coloured by subjective factors. To eliminate bias as far as possible I made a more strictly controlled experiment the results of which have largely confirmed the conclusions resulting from my individual interpretations.

The point on which there could be no doubt was that the picture of family relationships given by the emotionally disturbed children was, in a significant number of cases, very different from that given by the normal children, in spite of the efforts some of the disturbed children made to compensate for, or to conceal their real feelings. The phrases used by the normal and the emotionally disturbed to describe the parent-child relationship, and especially some of their answers to standard questions, suggested the method by which my interpretations could be verified. It was the employment of a group test of the same nature, but so designed that it would need the minimum of interpretation, and so would attain the maximum of objectivity.

I fully realized that a complete verification was scarcely likely even by this method, for there is indeed no evidence that projection tests in the selective form are necessarily comparable with the test in the individual, free-expression form. Thus, the attempt to give the Rorschach Test in a selective form (25) has not been very successful. What may be gained by the use of large numbers is likely to be small in comparison with the loss of sensitivity involved in giving the test a selective form with its inevitable restrictions. Nevertheless, driven by curiosity, I designed the Group Test of Family Attitudes, using configurations of items which I found recurring in the responses to the Individual Form of the test.

The same six pictures were employed, but instead of asking the subjects to do a free verbal composition, each picture was provided with a set of uncompleted sentences, which the child was asked to complete by marking off one of the three further sentences. The instructions printed on the front page read:

'If you were to make a story about this picture, which of the following sentences would you choose? Read (a), (b) and (c), and put a tick against your choice. Only *one* out of the three (*a*), or (*b*), or (*c*), is to be ticked off.'

The sentences which I selected for this Group Test were characteristic of four types of attitudes. The first type could be described as 'seeing the family through rose-coloured spectacles'. Thus, the child in the picture was 'always good'; he 'liked the baby very much'; was 'very sorry' if he had been naughty; was alone in the room 'because he liked it'; while his parents 'liked him better than the baby'; 'forgave him' if he were naughty, and 'were very sorry if he had to go away'. It was the configuration of such responses which produced a rather unreal picture of a perfectly harmonious family. Single responses of this type were frequently given by the normal children, but also by some of the older delinquents, and by a few neurotics with a tendency to dissociation. If given consistently throughout the test, they could represent 'screen' responses, a defence against their own impulses, or against the exploration of the highly disturbing emotional attitudes. For the convenience of marking, I designated such responses by the figure 'o'.

The second type of attitude revealed in these responses was more realistic, if not more conventional. The picture of the family was less rosy; they were merely getting on reasonably well together. The child was no longer a paragon; he was 'sometimes good, sometimes naughty'. His parents usually punished him for naughtiness, but not harshly. They liked the baby and the older child equally well. The examples of the sentences reflecting this state of affairs are: 'When the child is naughty, the parents punish him lightly'; 'If the man is cross he will . . . just smack the child'; 'If the child is naughty, he will have to stay there (alone in the room) for an hour.' This was the type of response most frequently given by normal children, and for the convenience of marking I designated it by the figure '1'.

The third type of attitude could be described as negative towards the family, with a component of revolt against parental authority. The child was definitely 'naughty'; he was the subject of complaints from other adults, but was not repentant; he had no great liking for his parents, or for the baby sibling; and the parents had no great liking for him. The baby was preferred to the older child. The examples of the sentences in which such attitudes were expressed are: 'If the man takes the child away, his parents will not be very sorry'; 'If the child has been naughty, he is not very sorry about it'; 'If the child has been punished, he is to stay there (alone in the room) till bedtime'; 'The child is doing something she has been told not to.' These responses were designated in scoring by the figure '2'.

The fourth type of attitude was strongly negative and frequently sado-masochistic. The child's parents were dead, or handed him over to strangers who maltreated him. If he was living with his own parents, they severely chastised him for misdemeanour, and he took his revenge on the baby by maltreating it. He showed no compunction about his 'naughtiness' but only thought how to escape from its consequences. This type of response was expressed in sentences like the following: 'The man and the woman are strangers to the child'; 'The man outside is coming to take the child away'; 'If the man takes the child away, his parents would be glad to let him go'; 'When the older child is naughty, he hurts the baby'; 'If the child has been naughty, he wishes he could do it again.' These responses were designated in scoring by the figure '3'.

The sentences were not designed to make a logically consistent story, but to provide an opportunity for expressing attitudes which might vary from being emotionally logical to being emotionally contradictory or ambivalent, even when related to the same picture. The language used was very simple, for the sentences were intended to be read and understood by children aged from 8 to 12, whose Intelligence Quotients ranged from 80 to 130, or more.

My expectations were that the children who were well adjusted socially and emotionally would tend to give the majority of '1' responses (realistic, on the positive side), with the '0' responses (very positive) as a close runner-up. The neurotics, on the other hand, and perhaps the delinquents of the less sophisticated and guarded type, would, I thought, mark more

'2's (realistic on the negative side) and '3's (strongly negative). I also thought it probable that the delinquent children who had learned to mistrust the adult, and the neurotics of a certain type (perhaps the hysteric and the very anxious) might choose a disproportionately larger number of 'o' responses, consciously or unconsciously using them to conceal their true attitudes and feelings.

The total number of sentences from which the children could choose was 111. Of these, twenty-one were 'o' responses, twenty-seven '1' responses, thirty-one '2' responses and thirty-two '3' responses. The balance was, thus, somewhat tilted in favour of negative, though realistic, and of strongly negative types of response. The total number of responses for each subject, if the instructions were followed and one sentence in each set of three were marked, would be thirty-seven.

The last page of the test paper was reserved for questions and answers concerning the subject's age, the constitution of his family, whether the home was broken by death or absence of one of the parents, whether the child lived with his parents, and, if it were an only child, whether he wished to have siblings or not. I thought that this information would be valuable in correlating the subject's responses with the family background and his own position in the family.

On the last page space was provided also for the use of the tester, where the subject's I.Q. could be entered, as well as whether he was 'normal', 'delinquent', or 'emotionally disturbed', with any additional remarks the tester wished to make.

This group test was given to 600 boys and girls in 'elementary' schools, not known to be neurotic or delinquent; to 172 delinquent boys and girls in 'approved' schools, and to 108 boys and girls suffering from various neurotic symptoms. Their ages ranged between 8 and 12, their I.Q.'s between 80 and 140. In the 'Normal' group the proportion of sexes was equal and the age groups were matched, that is, to 150 boys between the ages of 8 and 10 there was an equal number of girls of the same age group. The same applied to the age groups between 10 and 12.

This matching, however, proved impossible with the Delinquent and the Neurotic groups. I was able to get in touch with only six delinquent girls under the age of 12, whereas the number of boys tested was 166. Also the majority of these children belonged to the higher age group: the six girls were all between the ages of 10 and 12; of the boys, 138 were aged from 10 to 12 and only twenty-eight from 8 to 10.

In the Neurotic group the proportion of sexes was somewhat less in favour of boys: there were seventy-five boys and thirty-three girls. Of the boys forty-five were aged between 10 and 12, and thirty between 8 and 10. Of the girls fifteen were aged between 10 and 12 and eighteen between 8 and 10.

I had a very great difficulty in getting access to the children I wanted to test. Neither the Local Authorities, nor the Home Office were willing to give me permission to visit their schools or remand homes for the purpose. It was only through the courtesy of a private organization (The National Children's Homes) that I was able to have the boys and girls in the approved schools tested. The headmasters and staff of these schools were most helpful; some of them have had psychological training, and to them the administration of the test was entrusted, with appropriate instructions. These were mostly to make sure that the children could read the more difficult words occurring in the text, such as 'severely', 'threaten', 'altogether'.

The Neurotic group were reached through schools for maladjusted children, and through Child Guidance clinics. The co-operation of two such schools was secured, and the test was given by the staff. To many of the neurotic children the test had to be given individually, as it was not practical to combine them into groups.

The permission to test normal children was finally obtained from a local authority, through the intermediary of the Educational Psychologist working in schools. It was administered by class teachers, who referred to the psychologist for advice.

When I received the completed papers with the chosen sentences marked off by the child, I referred to my scale of responses: '0', '1', '2' and '3', and counted the number of times these occurred in each paper. I then examined the data obtained for the Normal group, first of all, to discover the frequency with which these children gave the four different types of response, then, in order to see whether there were any differences in this respect between the different age groups, the two sexes, the different position in the family, and the different levels of intelligence.

The complete tables of these responses are given in the appendix. Here I will describe only the general results and the conclusions which I think can be drawn from them.

Of the large group (600) of normal boys and girls between the ages of 8 and 12, who gave 22,200 responses in all, just over 82 per cent of the responses were positive (marked '1') or very positive (marked '0'), whereas only just under 18 per cent were negative (marked '2') or very negative (marked '3'). In other words, the type of phrase which was spontaneously used by the members of the small 'Normal' group tested individually, to describe family relationships, was also chosen in an overwhelming majority of cases by the large group of normal children in this selective form of group test. On the other hand, the type of phrase spontaneously used by the members of the small groups of neurotic and delinquent children tested individually, was chosen by this large group of normal children only to the extent of 17 per cent of the total.

One may ask why did these normal children choose any of the less realistic, harsh responses at all. The answer should, perhaps, be that the capacity for choosing a certain number of such responses may be the measure of their acceptance of the 'reality principle'. Reality is harsh to most individuals at times, and the fact that these children do not turn away from unpleasant facts, or close their eyes to the harsh aspects of life and human relationships may indicate that they are indeed 'normal'.

The comparison of the responses of 300 girls with those of 300 boys, all aged between 8 and 12, showed that although the run of the results was the same for boys and girls, rather more boys tended to give '2' and '3' responses, whereas rather more girls tended to give '1' and '0' responses. This seems to be a reflection of the different standards applied in the upbringing of the two sexes. There is little doubt that in our culture, the upbringing of boys tends to present them with a harsher view of reality than that obtained by girls, and thus, perhaps, stimulates the choice of more aggressive, less pleasant responses.

The comparison of the responses of two different age groups, from 8 to 10 and from 10 to 12, both groups including boys and girls, showed that the younger children tended to select the 'o' responses more frequently than the older; the older ones, the '2' responses. This is an interesting point, especially as it contradicts Jean Piaget's (44) findings. The 'o' responses are strongly positive, and, if selected in preference to any other response in the test, would give a picture of reality seen through rose-coloured spectacles. These responses include 'mild punishment' for transgression, whereas the '2' responses, realistic, but on the harsh side, include punishment proportionate to transgression. Jean Piaget's research, on the other hand, revealed the reverse tendency among the children he studied: it was the younger children who tended to decree the severer punishment for childish transgressions whereas the older ones decreed a milder punishment. Piaget's technique, however, was not selective: he described some childish transgression to his subjects and then asked them what punishment they thought the culprit deserved. In my study the children's freedom of choice was limited by three possible responses, only one of which was sometimes harsh. It is very likely that the younger child tended to choose the pleasantest of the three because he found it harder to face the less pleasant alternatives: he was, in Freudian terms, more under the influence of the 'pleasure principle' than the older child. The older children, on the other hand, were more 'realistic' in their choice, for the response '2' takes account of the harsher aspects of reality.

In order to see whether the level of intelligence influenced the type of response, the 600 boys and girls were assessed for intelligence on three levels as 'A' (bright), 'B' (average) and 'C' (dull). The data were treated statistically, and no significant relation was found between the level of intelligence and the giving of responses '1', '2' and '3' by the 'bright' and the 'average' groups respectively. They gave these responses in about the same proportion. On the other hand, the bright children as a group tended to give significantly more 'o' responses than either the dull or the average, whereas the dull gave significantly fewer '1' (realistic) responses and significantly more '3' (unrealistically harsh) responses than either the average or the bright.

This last finding is, perhaps, explicable by the fact that the majority of dull children have also dull parents who lack imagination, and so are apt, often unwittingly, to inflict upon their children unnecessary frustrations and disappointments, sometimes through sheer inability to be consistent in their treatment of them.

Finally, the groups of children were compared to see whether their choice of responses was affected by their position in the family. No significant differences were found between the 'eldest', the 'middle', the 'youngest' and the 'only' children, but the 'only' children showed a tendency to select the '2' responses somewhat more frequently than did the other groups. This, I believe, might be explained by the fact that the 'only' children who in their families are thrown more into adult society, tend to adopt adult standards before they are emotionally mature enough to assimilate them, and thus are inclined to assume a somewhat censorious, and therefore harsher attitude towards 'naughty' children in test pictures. It may mean that 'only' children, as a group, tend to have a somewhat harsher 'super-ego' than children who have siblings. As the studies of 'depth' psychologists have shown, a harsh super-ego is not incompatible with the experience of being 'spoilt' or indulged. 'Spoiling' frequently conceals the lack of real affection on the parent's part. Besides, indulgent parents, though they provide no obvious grounds for the child's antagonism, are yet bound to arouse some hostility at times, and thus stimulate feelings of guilt, which are reflected in a harsh condemnation by the child of any lapse on his part.

These results thus show that differences in age, sex, intelligence and position in the family are without any marked effect on the choice of responses in the Group Test of Family Attitudes.

A very different picture emerges from the comparison of responses of the normal, the neurotic and the delinquent children. When responses given by the Normal group were taken as 'norms', the following results have emerged:

The Neurotic group gave 13·7 per cent fewer 'o' and '1' responses than the Normal and 70·8 per cent more '2' and '3' responses than the Normal, whereas the Delinquent group gave 3 per cent fewer 'o' and '1' responses than the Normal, and 17·5 per cent more '2' and '3' responses than the Normal.

It is clear from these figures that the responses of the Delinquent, although significantly different from those of the Normal subjects, are more like those of the Normal than are the responses of the Neurotic subjects.

These results are, therefore, essentially in agreement with the results of the Individual Test of Family Attitudes. In individual testing the Delinquents showed themselves more 'conventional', as well as more detached, than the Neurotics. They were found less ready than the Neurotics to recognize, or to admit that children feel hostile to, or reject, their parents or their rival siblings. The Group Test was designed to probe into precisely these emotions of hostility, jealousy and affection, and it is probable that the same mental mechanism—of deeper repression of hostility—influenced the responses of the Delinquent subjects in their choice of response. The interesting trend in this group of Delinquents to give 'o' (strongly positive) responses is characteristic of a need to comepnsate for emotional deprivation, to picture the absent family in idealized colours, and perhaps to conceal from oneself and others how really unsatisfactory it has been.

What I believe emerges from this study in projection is the close connection between these children's self-assertive manifestations, as revealed in their spontaneous fantasies, and their relationships with their families. Moreover, it is revealed indirectly, and therefore more convincingly. The child's most fundamental needs are the need for a good personal relationship with its parents and the need for self-realization. Everything which obstructs the satisfaction of these needs, such as parental non-acceptance or downright rejection, unreliability or ambivalence, favouritism or clumsy handling of sibling jealousy, vindictiveness or unfairness, is liable to cause the deviation of the child's self-assertive urge into disruptive and destructive activities and attitudes, and to the conversion of the neutral, potentially constructive energy into the energy of negative aggression.

That this energy is potentially creative and that the main determinant in its deviation is an early disturbance in personal relationships is revealed also through the experience in psychotherapy, when, by establishing a good personal relationship with the therapist, the neurotic or delinquent child becomes capable of positive aggression and of employing his energies constructively.

This 'transformation' of destructive into constructive behaviour is the subject of the following section.

Part III

Clinical Studies of Aggression in Children

★

I. NEGATIVE AGGRESSION IN NEUROTIC CHILDREN

The nature of childhood's aggressive self-assertion and its rootedness in the parent-child relationship is brought out with a dramatic vividness in the therapy of emotionally disturbed children. In the course of treatment interviews, such children are not only allowed but encouraged to express their hostile and destructive urges, both verbally and in active play. Restraint is exercised by the therapist only if real harm can result to the child or the adult involved, or if the destruction of objects threatens to become so serious, as to produce a reaction of excessive guilt in the child himself.

Clinical studies have also the advantage of regular interviews with the mother, which provide the history of the child's early development and of his relationships with the parents and siblings, as well as the records of changes in these relationships as they occur during treatment. Thus the understanding of the child's behaviour in treatment interviews can be increased and clarified by relating it to his previous experiences and behaviour.

The equipment of the child psychotherapist's room is probably too well known to need detailed description. It usually includes sand-and-water trays, paints and paint brushes and a variety of simple toys: a dolls' house and a family of dolls, large baby dolls, toy pistols and guns, building bricks, saw, hammer and nails; none of them too good for it to matter if they are broken or soiled. Gradually, it is made known to the child that he can do almost anything he likes except breaking windows or hurting himself or the therapist. Messiness and noise are looked upon by the latter with equanimity.

The therapist assumes for most of the time an attitude of passivity and permissiveness, leaving the choice of play or occupation to the child, and falling in with the child's suggestions. This setting and the technique of the interviews aim at creating an environment in which the child can regain a relative freedom of asserting himself in any chosen way, and so enable the therapist to observe and comment on this behaviour in relation to himself, as a parent-figure. I am not assuming, of course, that the child behaves towards the therapist as if he were the real parent, but there is little doubt that in treatment the therapist does assume in the eyes of the child at least some of the parental attributes, and that some of the demands, expectations, fears and resentments experienced towards the parent, are transferred to the therapist. A relationship thus becomes established for which Freud has coined the term 'transference'.

I am not sure that the meaning now widely given to this term justifies its application to a relationship so fluid, yet so real, as the one which is built up during the course of treatment of an emotionally disturbed child. This, however, is a matter to be examined in another context.[1] What I am concerned with here is the process by which hostile and destructive behaviour of such children becomes gradually transformed into co-operative and constructive activities and attitudes. This process can, perhaps, be understood best through examples of the actual cases.

I will begin with children who showed sufficiently serious distortions of character and behaviour to be considered as 'neurotic' in the clinical sense. Their characters were different, their symptoms varied, but each in his own way succeeded in creating enough disturbance in his immediate environment for his parents and teachers to seek psychological help.

[1] Pp. 201–207.

(a) Martin

MARTIN, aged seven-and-a-half, has had periods of treatment at various clinics from the age of three, when he was referred for backwardness in speech. When I first saw him several more symptoms had been added to the original one: all-round backwardness in school subjects, bed-wetting, excessive timidity, inability to mix with other children, general tendency to withdraw, sit in a corner and brood.

The remarkable feature of this case was that this child, who, by all accounts, could not say 'boo' to a goose, from the first interview behaved towards me with an open and violent hostility. He was a puny, unattractive little boy, with large brown eyes and a wet, babyish mouth. Yet he glared at me out of his small, contorted face with an expression which was a mixture of terror and hatred. Planted in the middle of the room and looking defiant, he tore a cardboard box containing a bar of plasticine, and then proceeded to pull it to pieces, flinging it on to the floor, piece by piece. From this he turned to a sash window, leapt on to the sill, and pulled the window up and down with a bang several times. Jumping off, he seized an ancient meat-mincer which served as a toy, filled it with wet sand, and ground it furiously, scattering most of the sand over the floor. After several minutes of this, he dashed out of the room and started pulling the cord of a blind covering a sky-light with such force that he nearly broke it. Here, I had to intervene and induce him to return to my room. His way of escape barred, he crouched beside a large box full of bricks, some of them of stone, and proceeded to fling them across the room, towards the window. He did not stop until the box was emptied, and was clearly hoping that he might strike the window pane, although he dared not aim at it openly. He did not speak at all during this interview, except to shout: 'Open it!' when he found that another box containing bricks was locked.

For many subsequent interviews destructiveness alternated with persistent abuse and attempts to bully me. If he spoke to me at all, he shouted and gave me orders, usually setting me impossible tasks, such as making a number of wild animals out of a small bar of plasticine. He insisted that I should sit as far away from him as possible, on a baby chair, while he barricaded himself with furniture at the opposite end of the room, having piled up all the toys and books he could find within his enclosure.

The destructive phase culminated in the smashing of a dilapidated doll with a china head. He was engaged in throwing toys out of a cupboard as he came upon it. I was watching him, and he gave me a glance of defiance and fear before he started tearing it limb from limb, with deliberate savagery. His excitement and tension mounted as he went on; he flung the body on to the floor, shattering the china head, then picked up a large wooden brick and battered the body until it was completely broken. He then dashed out of the room and locked himself up in the cloakroom. When I persuaded him to come out and showed him some plasticine figures which I called 'Mummy' and 'Daddy', he snatched them out of my hands, crumpled them up and threw them into a bucket of water. I rescued them, and he repeated his action again, shouting: 'Leave them there!'

The bullying and abusive phase continued much longer. He turned me into a stupid, contemptible pupil who could do nothing right. As teacher, he shouted, scolded, and 'caned' me on the hand with a hard roll of cardboard. I was surprised to find how much force there was in the blows of these matchstick-thin, childish arms. His eyes glowed with fierce pleasure as he was maltreating me. I accepted all this, restraining him only from doing damage to the building and from running away.

Weeks passed, and his behaviour began to alter: he began to initiate different games. He was no longer a harsh, bullying teacher, but a kindly shopkeeper, who sold me a lot of toys and 'food' at a very low price. I was supposed to buy them for 'my children'. Then he became 'Father Christmas', and I the child, who received from him large boxes full of presents, and was expected to show delight and gratitude. In the last phase of his treatment the game we played together was 'Mothers and

Fathers'. Martin's family history will show the full significance of his assigning me the role of 'Father' in this game. He himself was quite devoted as 'Mother', and we had several children, a motley collection of dolls.

By this time he has matured sufficiently to be able to profit by remedial teaching, which was given him by a member of the clinic staff. He made rapid progress in learning to read and write. His speech has also become almost normal for his age.

Some regression set in when he found that his mother was going to have another baby: he clung to the idea that the baby was going to be bought in a shop rather than accept the fact that it grew inside the mother; and he could not tolerate the suggestion that it might be a brother. However, when a brother was born, Martin was confirmed in his newly attained maturity, instead of regressing again. No trace was now left of his babyish speech and babyish ways: he looked and behaved like an ordinary rather 'cheeky' urchin of eight, instead of a tongue-tied toddler. His mother reported that he was no longer afraid of running errands for her and that he occasionally 'answered her back'. Thus, the infantile forms of negative aggression (destroying objects and attacking persons physically) were replaced by more mature and milder forms ('answering back', 'cheeking'), and a considerable amount of self-assertive energy was directed on to mastering school tasks. Martin now was really determined to learn.

How did he come to behave, initially, in such a hostile and destructive way? His family setting, I believe, provides an answer. His parents were on the worst possible terms with one another. The mother 'hated' sexual intercourse with the father, but has had four children by him and was expecting a fifth. The father was inconsiderate and selfish, short-tempered with his family, jealous of, and cruel towards, his eldest son. He never took his family out, but had friendships with other women. The parents were frequently not on speaking terms. Martin's mother told her children to ignore their father because of his disloyalty to her.

Martin was the third of four children, with an elder and a

younger sister. The younger sister was born when he was three. It was at that time that his babyish speech began to worry his mother. During the subsequent four-and-a-half years he made hardly any progress, despite attending a speech therapist for long periods.

Careful studies of neurosis have shown that every symptom has 'aims' as well as 'causes'. One of the causes of Martin's refusal to learn normal speech was undoubtedly a deep anxiety arising from the family atmosphere. One of its aims, however, was the need to assert himself and obtain the attention which otherwise might not have been given him.

His early history provided plenty of 'justifications' for the means he had unconsciously selected. He was not a wanted baby. His mother confessed that she had not wanted any of her children: their conception was associated with a repugnant intimacy; their arrival brought no change for the better in her relations with her husband. She had, however, accepted them after they had arrived and gave them all the affection she had to give—too much, perhaps, as she expended none on her husband. Observation of disturbed children has shown that excess of affection given to children in an atmosphere of emotional insecurity is liable to increase their anxiety, rather than allay it. It is difficult to avoid the conclusion that Martin felt insecure from infancy and that he realized, intuitively, the advantages of remaining a baby. His ways of asserting himself were, therefore, infantile, for in his emotional development he had not yet reached a stage when he could do so constructively.

His feelings of insecurity must have been increased by the birth of his younger sister, for a refusal to grow up became evident from then onwards. This was carried over to school, where an unsympathetic headmistress believed that the only way of dealing with Martin's babyishness was to 'shame' him in front of the class, and to cane him on the hand for making a mess of his writing. At $7\frac{1}{2}$, she transferred him back to the Infants' class, after having tried him for a short time in the Juniors'. His younger sister's brightness at school added to his humiliation.

This boy thus found himself in a position, both at home and in school, where constructive ways to self-assertion were blocked externally as well as inwardly. He has 'chosen' to remain infantile, and so could not find an outlet in constructive activities on the level of his age. On the other hand, strong negative emotions of fear and anger were being frequently aroused in him by parental quarrels and his headmistress's treatment of him. These he dared not express, and the way of regression seemed to be the only one open to him. It represented a compromise between two fundamental human needs: in his case, between the need to be on good terms with his mother, to keep her affection, and the need to assert himself as an individual. But this compromise was not working very well: both school and home were trying to force his defences, and, in desperation, he began to fight in the first place where he felt his aggression would be tolerated—that is, in the playroom of a Child Guidance clinic.

Why did he not continue indefinitely being destructive and hostile when his hostility and destructiveness were met with friendliness and tolerant humour? Why, after having called the clinic 'this vile place' and told me he 'wasn't coming back again', did he develop an attitude so positive that he resisted termination of the interviews, and caused his mother to remark on his 'loving to come'?

I believe it is because for the first time in his life he was treated with respect due to every human being and was accepted as such, despite his unpleasant behaviour. He was met more than half-way in his clumsy and ineffective efforts towards establishing a positive relationship. I believe that the urge behind his efforts was a positive one—the urge to achieve a personal status as a human being and to enter into a good relationship with other human beings, and that this 'good' energy happened to become misdirected into 'bad' channels. Once 'good' channels were provided—and that means not merely a variety of toys, occupations, recreation facilities, youth clubs, or what not—but a 'good' personal relationship—the urge revealed itself to be constructive, not destructive, in essence.

The need for brevity may make this explanation appear over-simplified and perhaps even naïve. I do not, of course, imply that all that is needed to 'cure' neuroses or behaviour disorders in childhood is to become good friends with the child, and the rest will inevitably follow. Many more things must happen, both in the treatment of the child and in the family setting, before any lasting 'cure' in serious cases can be expected. What, however, I firmly believe and want to emphasize is, that a good relationship between the child and an adult is an indispensable basis of all real 'improvement' in the child's personality, and that without it, a person's mental development and full creative functioning is bound to be impaired. I am quite aware that suffering and unhappiness have provided stimuli for great art and for individual efforts in all fields of personal and social achievement; that genius has triumphed over many inner and external obstacles. What I am *not* certain of is, among other things, that Byron would not have been as good a poet if he had had a satisfactory mother, or that many gifted people would not have been even more creative, each in his own way, if they had enjoyed greater emotional security in childhood. Unhappiness and suffering usually come to all in the course of their adult life, but I believe their power to stimulate effort and to give greater depth to character is likely to be greater if the inner resources of the person had not been depleted by the denial of the basic emotional needs in childhood.

It is reasonable to suppose that the longer the period during which negative ways of self-assertion have been employed, the more difficult it is likely to be to 'switch over' to positive ways. Habits will have to be unlearned and long-standing emotional attitudes modified. The most important of all, perhaps, especially with younger children—parental feelings and values— themselves the outcome of *their* early experiences of home life —will have to be altered sufficiently to offer support, rather than discouragement, to new, more mature forms of self-assertion, some of which will be shown in a greater independence of the child from the family. Parents, who have suffered enough from the child's symptoms, welcome the social 'improvement', but are not alway willing or able to accept the corresponding measure of freedom for the child to change in other respects. It is especially difficult for them to believe that reconciliation is likely to be much more solid and permanent if it is preceded by a phase of open revolt.

The age of the child, therefore, and the relative rigidity or plasticity of his family setting, determine to a considerable degree the completeness of the change over from negative to positive ways of self-assertion.

(b) Bernard

The case of BERNARD can, perhaps, serve as an example of a partial achievement of this result. He was 11 years 5 months old when I first saw him, a gentle, tall, willowy boy, with expressive eyes and a pleasant manner. His I.Q. was given as 91 on the Stanford-Binet scale. His symptoms were numerous and of long standing: they included enuresis, nightmares, disturbed sleep, poor appetite, backwardness in school subjects, excessive timidity, inability to make friends, and a variety of fears: of the dark, of going upstairs, of pulling the lavatory chain, of water in general. He showed no interest in games usual at his age, but still played with his lead soldiers. His other favourite pastime was to catch ants and place them in paper boats or nut shells, which he then sailed in the bath, overturning them and watching the insects drown. Sometimes he was seen to put them between boards and squash them, as he also did with his lead soldiers.

During treatment, he was never aggressive towards me personally, but his play throughout many interviews was extremely sado-masochistic. He usually had two groups of toy people facing one another in deadly enmity: soldiers of different nationalities, or cowboys and Indians, or policemen and 'crooks', or two rival gangs of crooks. They fought, as a rule, to the finish, until one or the other side were exterminated to a man. As Bernard let himself go, horrors multiplied. There was hardly a danger or a torture of which Bernard had not thought in the course of his play: shipwrecks at sea, with 'all hands going down'; falling over a precipice; sinking in quicksands and swamps; dying from starvation; bridges collapsing under fighting men; trains running over them; men being poisoned by injections in prison camps; men being shot or hanged, or put into gas chambers; men being tortured by tying them under rafts and dragging them through water, and so on, *ad nauseam*. It seemed as if Bernard had filled his mind with all the horrors he had read about in newspapers and boys' magazines, and was irresistibly impelled to act them out in play.

It might, of course, be said that this was not very surprising, for at that time we had only just emerged from a total war, and the stories of 'atrocities' were still fresh in people's minds. But there was little doubt that Bernard enjoyed enacting these horrors, and that the zest and persistence with which he did it were quite exceptional. Among the two hundred odd children I have had for psychological treatment in the last ten years, I have not met another quite so obsessed with horrors and so ingenious in inventing, or so good at remembering all their varieties.

Why should it have been so? Bernard's family setting was not unlike that of Martin's, except that his insecurity was further stimulated by his mother's morbid fears. She admitted to having a fear of death and of going into 'strange' houses, as well as an undefinable kind of terror which 'just came over her' at times. Her method of training her children was by stimulating their fears. Thus, she tried to 'cure' her younger daughter's bed-wetting by telling her that 'black beetles would come out of her mattress and bite her' unless she stopped.

In this family, too, there were violent parental quarrels in the early years of marriage, when father and mother 'did not speak to each other for days'. But whereas the parents could be violent, young Bernard was expected to be 'good', and to welcome the arrival of a baby sister, after he had been the 'baby' for seven years. Thus, there was no normal opportunity for any form of self-assertion, and the only outlet for both constructive and destructive urges was provided in fantasy. In his play, Bernard decided the fate of imaginary armies and obtained a deep satisfaction from the fantasy of his courage and power. His fantasies could have been benevolent, instead of being sado-masochistic, but the early thwarting of his self-assertive urge produced the distortion, just as surely as a stone placed on the top of a young shoot would produce contortions in the growing stem, as it circumvents the obstacle.

My acceptance of Bernard's negative self-assertion and the discussion of the emotions by which they were stimulated —his feelings of inferiority, of resentment, of jealousy—gave him just that amount of security which he needed to express them within the circle of his family. He voiced his protests against the favouritism shown to his younger sister and stood up to his mother in various minor ways. Towards the end of his treatment, he acquired friends of his own age with whom he went boating and cycling. In the treatment interviews he stopped playing sado-masochistic games, and asked me to play draughts and other competitive games with him. Soon after the termination of his treatment he left school and obtained employment in a railway office. A report a year later showed that he had kept up his improvement and, though still rather timid, had no disabling fears and was enjoying his job.

Although this boy was helped to greater maturity through his relationship with me, I did not feel that the change in his personality was in any sense fundamental. More time was needed to effect this, but in Child Guidance practice expediency often has to come before thoroughness. Many parents will not allow deep or prolonged treatment, and the waiting list with urgent cases on it has to be considered, as well.

In Bernard's case his mother's attitude remained practically unchanged, and so the boy had little support from her in his somewhat fitful struggle for independence. Nor was his father of much help, as he had always taken a contemptuous attitude towards the boy on account of his timidity and childishness.

(c) Geoffrey

A somewhat different variation on the same theme—parental mishandling of the child's self-assertive urge—was provided by GEOFFREY's early history and symptoms. He was 9 years 6 months old when he was brought to the clinic on account of a severe stammer. Speech training lasting nine months brought no appreciable alleviation of the symptom. It was not the only one, for Geoffrey also suffered from travel sickness and from violent temper outbursts during which he threw over or kicked any object which happened to be in his way.

He was a short, well-set small boy, with somewhat mongoloid features, brown eyes and hair, and a ready smile. His I.Q. was given as 111 on Stanford-Binet scale. He was very quickly at ease with me and at once showed his preferences for train sets and ball games. When he discovered that I could kick a ball, he came to expect a game of football every time he attended for treatment. For some weeks he remained relatively well-controlled, prepared to credit me with doubtful points and ready to accept his failures along with his successes. But as time went on, he seemed to find each game more exciting than the one before it. He danced about and rushed at the ball so wildly that he frequently missed it altogether and wasted his chance of scoring a goal. If beaten, he would throw himself on the floor and lay panting, as if exhausted. He did not seem to resent his defeats, but seemed compelled to pit his skill against mine, week after week, for several months.

All my attempts to divert him to some other activity were only partially successful. He would politely agree to draw, or talk, or try to remember his dreams, but his attention would soon wander, and he would ask with an apologetic smile if he could *now* have a game of football with me. The only alternative which he found equally satisfying was the 'British Bulldog' game; needless to say, I found it even more exhausting.

Only on a few occasions did his self-assertion assume a negative form towards me, and even then it was expressed playfully. He used his hands to keep me away from the ball, and when he failed, chased me round the room, aiming the ball at my head. In a game of Ludo, which I was winning, he told me with a smile:'I don't like you', and at once added, significantly:'I always say that to my mother when I play with her and she wins'.

After more than twelve months' weekly attendance, Geoffrey's speech had improved considerably, but he still stammered slightly when he was excited or self-conscious. He no longer suffered from travel sickness or from temper outbursts, and—one of the most significant changes—he became good friends with his mother.

I had little doubt, when I heard his history, that it was an early disturbance of this basic relationship which was responsible for Geoffrey's symptoms. He was an only child, his twin brother having died at birth. His mother was told that Geoffrey might not survive, which had the effect of inhibiting her affection for him, for fear that she might lose him and suffer too much. This was the mother's version of the story, but further exploration showed that she was, in fact, rather repelled by Geoffrey, who was extremely ugly as a baby (described 'Query cretin' in a children's hospital), so that she dreaded the neighbours having a peep at him as he lay in his pram. He was so sickly as an infant that he had to spend the first few months of his life in hospital. At the age of 8 months, however, he was 'a thriving baby'.

Then, at the age of two, he developed a hernia and had to be rushed off to hospital. He stayed in for eight days, and on his return home would not go to his mother, and screamed, and scratched her when she tried to pick him up. At the same time he relapsed into soiling and wetting, although previously clean habits had been practically established. The mother, quick-tempered and excitable, could not control her disappointment and vexation, and reacted to his lapses by slapping and scolding. Geoffrey responded by temper-tantrums, while soiling and wetting continued.

He started stammering at the age of three, when one morning his mother lifted him from his wet bed. Stammering, as is well known, is frequently a compromise symptom of a conflict between fear and anger, and Geoffrey had many reasons to be both anxious and afraid. He had had a great deal of hospital treatment in infancy and not quite enough maternal affection to reassure him. Then at the age of two to three, he passed through some extremely disturbing experiences the meaning of which he was too young to understand. His mother handed him over to strangers, who kept him away from her for what must have seemed to him a very long time, and subjected him to an unintelligible and painful régime. His behaviour on returning home showed that he had interpreted her action as a betrayal. Two to three is, in many respects, a critical age, a self-assertive age *par excellence*, for it is just then that the child begins to realize his individuality and to speak of himself as 'I'. Speech development, especially, passes through a decisive phase: a new synthesis between complex thoughts and sentences is being achieved, superseding an earlier synthesis between the thought and the single word serving as a sentence. The shock of illness and separation could not have come at a worse stage.

Geoffrey's mother realized that he was rejecting her, but failed to understand the motives of this rejection, and reacted by treating him more harshly than she had done hitherto. Harsh treatment, however, does not bring forth constructive, co-operative or truly social responses from a young child. It might coerce him into conformity, but just as often it forces him into the negative ways of self-assertion which we see so often in both children and adults, not all of whom are recognized as 'difficult'.

In this case, Geoffrey and his mother joined battle and carried on until she nearly had a nervous breakdown. What she found particularly exasperating was that her husband could not believe Geoffrey to be so difficult, because the boy was always delightfully amenable and affectionate with him. But it was the father's gentle personality which saved the situation. He was a good cricketer and football player, and the boy, as he grew older, tried to model himself on him. Thus, much of his self-assertive energy was utilized in mastering games.

Geoffrey's relationship with his father has always been excellent, but he needed a tolerant and benevolent mother figure—in this case myself—before he could become fully co-operative and constructive with his own mother. He was a keen, happy and hard-working youngster when I saw him four years after the termination of treatment. A slight stammer was the only trace of his former difficulties.

(d) Margaret

The case of MARGARET, aged 9 years 1 month, can serve as another example of a child reacting violently to parental mishandling. She was brought to the clinic on account of spitefulness to children and adults, screaming fits, defiance, disobedience and bed-wetting. Her I.Q., on the Stanford-Binet scale, was given as 101.

Margaret's way of asserting herself with me was to be destructive and messy in minor ways, as a child of three or four might be. If she came upon a fresh box of crayons, she would break each one in two or three pieces. She would ostensibly start making something with scissors, paper and glue, but would finish by cutting her work into tiny pieces, or by smearing it with glue and paint on both sides and turning it into an unidentifiable sticky object, which she alone was prepared to handle.

She then developed a passion for mixing powder paints, especially yellow paint. She never got to the stage of using them to paint a picture or a toy, but increased the quantity as she went on, and insisted on mixing them on my table. Invariably, she used too much water, so that it overflowed and made yellow pools on the table and on the floor. Sometimes, as if by accident, she upset the pot and flooded the table. This was accompanied by a defiant question and a threat: 'Do you like yellow? If you don't, I'll drown you'! She would also tell me: 'You clear that up. Go on'!

I interpreted this to her as infantile aggression against the mother transferred on to me, and after many weeks of hostile messiness Margaret began to clear up the messes herself. Gradually, constructiveness began to emerge from destructive beginnings. She managed to make boxes and 'books' instead of merely cutting up paper or smearing it with glue. She actually made some dolls' clothes, whereas before she never got beyond the stage of cutting up the material. Her continuous grumbling, complaining, and accusing everybody of hostility and unfair discrimination towards herself gave place to more pleasant subjects of conversation.

Margaret had plenty of reasons to feel disgruntled, for the atmosphere of her family would have been unsettling to any child. Her parents did not get on at all well together: her mother described her husband as 'spoilt, vain and selfish', 'behaving badly' in the presence of the children, refusing food his wife had cooked for him, jumping up from the table and 'walking out on her'; withholding money for necessary expenses, yet spending freely on himself; threatening Margaret that he would leave home if she did not behave better; calling her 'a dirty cat' because of her bed-wetting, and generally behaving more like an overgrown adolescent than the father of a family. The mother was a harassed, querulous, nagging woman, who had not wanted Margaret, but adored her younger son. She showed her hostility to Margaret quite openly in my presence, was impatient with her and always criticized her in her hearing.

A child of such parents could, of course, have inherited a temperament which would account, at least in part, for her difficult behaviour. Yet to blame heredity where the environment is so patently unfavourable, is too much like invoking an 'act of God' to justify human improvidence. Margaret, in fact, had a very raw deal. When we imagine her parents quarrelling in her hearing when she was a toddler, and the emotions of fear, insecurity and anger which this must have aroused in her, we can understand why creative self-realization had become impossible for her. When she followed parental example by indulging in tantrums and spitefulness, she was punished and scolded. Later on, the birth of a brother, who was so blatantly favoured by the mother, intensified the conflict between the hostility she felt towards her mother and the fear of losing whatever affection she could glean from her. An additional obstacle on the way to growing up was erected. Growing up includes gradual conversion of infantile messiness and destructiveness which in themselves have no hostile meaning but are due to immaturity, into constructive forms of self-realization and self-assertion. Of this Margaret was incapable at the age of nine. She was full of hostility and her characteristic remarks were professions of hatred. She said about her young brother: 'I hate him. I told Mummy I did. He thinks I love him, but I hate him. He wants me to love him, but I won't. I'd like to take him to school and make him go without his tea. I'd like to smack him hard.' About her mother she said: 'She's cruel. She doesn't look it, but she is: she smacks me hard on the face.'

A vicious circle of mutual hostility had become established in that family, from which the little boy seemed alone to be excluded. The more Margaret felt rejected by her parents, the more she was impelled to 'pester' them, as she herself expressed it, for tangible marks of favour. Once she brought a cheap fountain pen to show me, and told me how she worried her father for one until 'he said he'd throw it at me'. And when at last she got it, it would not write! And yet, instead of throwing it away in a fury of frustration, she nursed it as if it were a talisman. She also seemed to cherish various small valueless objects which she begged from me and was allowed to take away. The significance of this is self-evident and hardly needs stressing.

My first point in describing these four cases in some detail was to emphasize the link between these children's early emotional experiences with their parents and the forms their self-assertive urge assumed somewhat later on. If I am told that Martin, Bernard, Geoffrey and Margaret would have grown to be what they were even if they had wise and kindly parents, I should challenge my critics to produce a child of such parents, who would consistently behave as these children have done.

My second point was to show that through a personal relationship with me—and it could have been any other adult whose temperament and training qualified him for this role—these children became capable in varying degrees of positive self-realization. My contention is that this capability was not the result of any conversion or transformation of one kind of energy into another, or was newly created, or released from some inner storehouse. I see no reason for believing that a special kind of energy called 'aggression' was employed in destructive activities by these children, and that an entirely different kind of energy was the driving force behind their creative activity. I claim that it is a more economical and objective proposition to postulate that this energy was neutral from the start, and only assumed negative forms because the young child's attempts at self-realization were clumsily and unsympathetically handled and I believe that this claim has a broader foundation in the observed facts of child development than many another theory.

II. NEGATIVE AGGRESSION IN DELINQUENT CHILDREN

From the clinical point of view there is no clear-cut distinction between neurosis and delinquency in children, for the so-called 'behaviour disorders' are only another kind of symptom in a child who is emotionally disturbed. Delinquent children, as a rule, suffer from a number of associated symptoms: enuresis, compulsions, hysterical dissociation, inability to mix, temper outbursts and many others. The usefulness of treating them as a special group has sometimes been questioned. Yet, although careful study supports the view that there is no such thing as a single 'delinquent type', my experience of delinquent children suggests that, as a group, they have certain traits in common which distinguish them from other emotionally disturbed children, and which are probably linked with their delinquency. I also believe that these distinguishing traits derive from the same source—the family atmosphere and the parent-child relationship.

Some examples of treatment and histories of delinquent children will make the meaning of my remarks clearer.

(a) Robert

ROBERT'S delinquent behaviour certainly could not be explained by economic or sociological causes. He came from a well-to-do family and lived on a farm where he could run wild. He went to a progressive school with small classes where teaching was good. He was six when I first saw him, and his I.Q. was given as 115. From the first interview his behaviour was a blend of 'showing off' and doing his best to provoke and annoy me.

He first announced that he was seven, which was not true, then showed me how high he could build with bricks and how easily he could knock the tower down with 'bullets' from his gun. He attacked me directly from the start by squirting water at me, dubbing my clothes, face and hands with paint, throwing sand at my head and 'shooting' me with sticks from his gun. When he discovered that there were a few things which I did not want him to do, such as throwing heavy toys out of the windows on to the children's playground below, he employed a variety of dodges to circumvent these prohibitions, and would, slyly and triumphantly, giggle and dance when he had his way.

He appeared happy enough at this game, although guilty as well, for he ran and ducked when I came near him. At other times he had phases of rage and depression when he destroyed toys by trampling on them, or scribbled over and tore up his own drawings. His usual comment on his constructive efforts, such as painting or cutting out, was: 'It's no good. I can't do it', and then he would destroy it.

He seemed to bear no personal ill-will towards me, nor did he show any positive feeling, except that once he hugged me for having made him a paper aeroplane. As a rule, he treated me as a kind of target at which he aimed a variety of 'shots'—many small acts of provocation and mischief.

He sustained this throughout the twelve sessions I had with him. By the end of three months his mother decided that he was not improving quickly enough and carried out her original intention of sending him away to a boarding school. His treatment was, thus, abruptly terminated.

It was sufficiently long, however, to suggest that even at the age of six negative forms of self-realization are much more firmly established in the delinquent child than they are in the neurotic. Robert's pattern of behaviour did not change during the three months of treatment, whereas the neurotic children showed within a comparable period an increase and then a lessening of hostility and destructiveness. Why it should be so is a point for discussion in another context.[1]

In Robert's case, destructiveness and pilfering were the predominant symptoms. The list of his depredations was long: he stripped his bedroom of wall paper, poked holes in the plaster and brought it down; smashed expensive flower vases; whipped

[1] Pp. 177 and 198–200.

off the heads of a whole bed of geraniums in front of the house; dug up a patch of freshly laid concrete in the stable yard. He urinated on the carpet in his bedroom; he broke his toys almost as soon as he was given them.

At school, he took money from his teacher's desk, bought sweets and distributed them to his classmates. He also stole a fountain pen, some books and a number of small objects from the boys' desks. This brought the whole thing to a head. The headmaster threatened expulsion; Robert's father thrashed him and kept him at home for a few days. Pilfering stopped for a time, but destructiveness continued. It was on the advice of the headmaster that Robert was brought for psychological examination, and afterwards for a period of treatment.

His mother, however, was unable to see that something in her feeling towards Robert might have been partly responsible for his behaviour. She was an immature woman lacking in warmth, who was horrified and disgusted by what she saw as a sudden transformation of 'a sweet and happy baby' into 'a horrid, dirty little boy'. He 'did nothing that he was asked to do' and 'everything that he was forbidden'. She confessed that whatever he did appeared to her 'naughty' and that she wanted all the time to issue prohibitions and to punish him. Yet punishment had no effect on him; even when thrashed, he would cry bitterly, then 'begin all over again' with the same apparent zest.

He resisted her in every way. He would not dress or undress himself, nor would he eat the food he was given, except after a great deal of argument and fuss. He was 'horrid' to his brothers: he broke their toys, knocked them about, tried to urinate and defaecate on them. His mother saw no reason whatever why he should behave in this way, except for his inherent 'badness'. Yet she confessed having been so jealous of her younger sister that she once tried to push her into the fire. It became evident from conversations with her that her own guilty feelings about this jealousy made her particularly intolerant of its manifestations in Robert. He reacted by regressive behaviour to the birth of his brother when he was two, indicating that he still needed to be treated as a baby. This was dealt with as 'naughty' behaviour by his mother, and produced further regression and revolt. The birth of another brother two years later did not improve matters. Robert found himself completely pushed out of the picture, and evidently felt that the only certain way of creating concern for himself was by means of outrageous behaviour. His father, unfortunately, was too busy a man to find time for a closer relationship with Robert: he often had to be away from home and left the up-bringing of children entirely in his wife's hands. What she made of it as far as Robert was concerned, we already know.

That he felt himself completely at odds with the whole of his family was revealed in his spontaneous remarks. As I drew the 'portraits' of his parents and brothers on a slate, he at once scribbled them out, shouting: 'Good-bye, Daddy. Good-bye, Mummy. Here goes Hugh!' Then with an onrush of emotion, he added: 'They make me feel so angry . . . they make me feel mad! They all do!' Intense hostility was in his voice when he drew a 'portrait' of his grandfather and spoke of his 'great big hands'. But feelings of guilt on account of his own hostility and 'badness' were also evident when he said that he was 'fed up with himself'.

As might be expected, the boarding school did not work the miracle Robert's mother was hoping for. She was asked to take him back after two terms. It was difficult to escape the conclusion that it was her own hostility towards the boy, the rigidity of her handling him from an early age and her inability to modify her feelings towards him which had established and sustained the pattern of his behaviour.

(b) Hazel

Despite the very different external circumstances, HAZEL'S behaviour towards adults had many points in common with Robert's. She, too, behaved as if she were irresistibly impelled to test adult forbearance by means of 'naughtiness'.

She was a little girl of eight, with an I.Q. of 101, a most

engaging, rather elfin-looking child, with light brown hair and large brown eyes, which watched mistrustfully, but could suddenly light up with gaiety and mischief. She revealed her nervousness by refusing to follow me to my room and by making attempts to escape from it before the end of the session. Yet during the very first session she threw a large ball and a doll's blanket at my head. In the fourth session she asked me to pretend to be a witch while she pretended to be the child captured by her and due to be baked in the oven and eaten. She entered so much into the spirit of this game that she struggled and screamed when I pretended to take her to the 'oven'. She shouted that I was 'silly' and that she 'hated' me. Suddenly she said: 'You'll be my mother. I'll run away from the witch and get home.' But she remained as mistrustful of me in my role of 'mother' as she had been when I was acting the witch. This game was repeated in the two following sessions, then Hazel decided she did not want to play it any more. It seemed as if the tension she experienced in the acting out of her hostility and fear was more than she could tolerate.

She never resumed this game, but during many subsequent sessions spread over twelve months of weekly attendance, she remained consistent in her wayward, defiant and provocative behaviour towards me. If we played ball, she would choose a hard ball to throw at me and aimed at my head, calling out: 'You wait, I'm going to hurt you.' Frequently she would give me a sudden hard slap with her hand or a large wooden spoon, used for digging sand. On one occasion she dipped the spoon into the coal-scuttle and tried to wipe it on my clothes. She would throw sand in my face, saying: 'I'm going to blind you.' She would scatter boxfuls of beads and small toys about the room with the comment: 'Now you'll have to pick them all up!' She would try to cut furniture and window-sills with a saw, remarking as she did so: 'They (she meant my superiors) can't tell me off for this, but they can tell *you* off!'

Other items from her repertoire were: taking off her shoes and paddling in the water tray; smearing the floor of the room with soap and trying to skate on it; strewing sand over the floor; putting the saw in wet sand 'to make it rusty'; splashing water all over the room; pouring paint into my water glass and trying to make me drink it 'to poison' me.

She also drew many pictures of me, wearing a witch's pointed hat, with the word 'DAFT' in huge letters written across it. She told me I was 'balmy', 'silly' and 'nasty' and that she 'hated' me. Sometimes, she would slyly pretend to be affectionate, then strike out at me.

When this hostile and provocative behaviour began to alternate with attempts to seek favour with me, and with requests for small gifts, I thought for a time that a change in her attitude was about to take place. But these beginnings of a positive relationship failed to develop: in subsequent interviews Hazel reverted to the earlier pattern. With the exception of her paintings—caricatures of myself and her school teachers—she never did anything constructive during her sessions with me. Her treatment had to be discontinued because both her parents resisted it. Hazel herself, sensing this, declared that she did not like coming and would not come again. They often missed an appointment, so that a weekly interview tended to become a fortnightly one.

Hazel's poor response to treatment may have been partly due to my initial mistake in interpreting her play of witch and child too early in our relationship, or perhaps to the fact that her mother got to know about this game. I have little doubt, however, that in this case the personality of the mother was the chief determinant in Hazel's difficulties.

Hazel was brought for psychological examination because she had been pilfering—money and small objects, toys and cheap jewellery—principally from her parents, but also from other children at school. She always denied her thefts, invented stories to explain the objects found in her possession and was generally given to 'romancing'. Another of her 'habits' was hiding food which she did not want to eat: numerous pieces of bread-and-butter, of pease-pudding and of toasted cheese were found behind her bed and under her mattress after an illness. This occurred at home and also at the hospital where

Hazel went to have her tonsils removed. She bit her nails severely, and occasionally, when thwarted, had temper outbursts during which she told her mother that she hated her and wished she would die.

Her mother was an inhibited frigid woman with thin, angular features and wisps of wild hair, rather witch-like in appearance. She was married to an easy-going man, whom she described as being 'fond of a joke'. She feared and loathed sexual intercourse, and confessed that she often felt she 'could strangle' her husband when he lay, fast asleep, beside her, after having had his urge satisfied.

Hazel's birth was a 'freak', as the mother became pregnant without losing her virginity. As might be expected, pregnancy was painful and confinement very difficult and prolonged. The child was born eight years after marriage, and the mother declared that she 'could never stand another', so Hazel remained an only child. The extent of her mother's inability to show affection was exceptional even among neurotic mothers. She had never cuddled Hazel who would sometimes go up to her and say: 'Let me be the dog, Mother, so that you can pat me.'

From her earliest years there were battles between the child and mother. Hazel was expected to eat up everything that was put on her plate, so even as a toddler she would 'scrape up food and put it into a dirty linen basket'. At the age of three she was punished for 'telling lies'. Later, the mother 'tried everything: smacking it out of her, shaming her in front of people, docking her sweets as a punishment'. None of this was of any avail, so obviously the child 'had been born wicked'—an idea which Hazel seemed to accept, for she told me in the first interview that she has 'always been naughty', even as a baby. 'I used to throw all Mummie's shopping out of my pram. And I always kicked my covers off. I'm not "a nice little girl", I'm daft.'

One of her memories—or fantasies—was of being 'smacked with a toasting fork when I was little—before I was five'.

The idea Hazel had of her mother was clearly patterned on the latter's righteous moral attitude towards the child's 'perversity'. 'My mother never tells a lie', Hazel announced to me. 'My mother never jokes.'

The mother told us that she had never got on well with her own mother and that they had frequent 'arguments' when the old woman came to stay in her daughter's house. Hazel was well aware of that, for once she asked me: 'Did you like your mother?' I tried to convey to her in as simple language as possible the ambivalence of the mother-child relationship, to which she replied with a sigh: 'People never like their mothers!' She told me that 'Grannie' was 'spiteful' to her, and had once knocked her head against a wall.

In this case the mother was unable to modify her attitude towards the child, probably because of her own feelings of guilt on account of her bad relationship with her own mother. The father disapproved of the clinic from the beginning and when Hazel began to show the effects of treatment in more open 'naughtiness', instead of her former sly, furtive ways, he came down heavily on the side of the critical neighbours, who held the view that Hazel ought to be disciplined, not treated. Her attendance became more erratic after her mother had taken on a job. This was used as a pretext to discontinue treatment, and unfortunately this happened very soon after Hazel had been frightened by a man whom she met picking blackberries and who tried to interfere with her.

Three years later we heard that Hazel's mother produced another child—a boy—and that Hazel had a bad relapse—pilfering, truanting and lying.

I have little doubt that the failure of treatment in this case was due principally to the virtual absence of an affectional bond between the mother and child, the mother rejecting the child because of her rejection of sex and her guilt in relation to her own mother. She saw the child as innately wicked, needing punishment, not to be indulged on any account, whereas the child saw the mother as a rejecting and condemning person, and in fantasy, as a terrifying witch. This image, with the accompanying fear, mistrust, hostility and a certain amount of fascination, she projected on me, and I did not succeed in building up a positive relationship with her on the basis of the insight into her real feelings which I tried to give her. If she had never had the experience of a close emotional relationship with her mother, a much longer period of treatment would be necessary to help her develop this capacity.

(c) Gerald

GERALD was a persistent pilferer from the age of five. He came to me when he was ten years old. His I.Q. was given as 128, but he was not doing well at school. He truanted, wet his trousers occasionally during the day, wet his bed every night and was subject to sudden and violent outbursts of temper. On such occasions he usually turned against his mother, punching, kicking and throwing things at her.

At the beginning of the treatment his hostility was expressed principally in an almost complete lack of responsiveness. His face was like a mask; he hardly moved his eyes; he would not allow himself to smile. He had been given seven weekly interviews before he was able to assert himself more actively in opposition to me. We were sailing small boats with paper sails in the water tray, and made them move by blowing on their sails. The idea was to have a race, but when Gerald saw that my boat was winning, he blew at it so hard that it sank, time after time. He looked guilty, but giggled and obviously enjoyed it.

Not until his sixteenth interview did Gerald show how violent he could be when he relinquished control over his need for self-assertion. I offered to play cricket with him; and in the relatively constricted space of my room, he bowled so wildly and with such force that the ball really hurt when it struck me, which happened quite often. I commented on it; Gerald giggled nervously, but carried on as before.

This behaviour recurred every time we had a game of cricket. On the other hand, a great many sessions were spent in a quieter kind of competitive games in which Gerald did his best to beat me. Ludo, snakes and ladders, draughts, shooting at a target, doing a simple jig-saw in record time by a stop-watch—all these pursuits seemed to give him pleasure only in so far as he could make sure of winning more often than I did. I could not let him win every time, for he might have seen through my tactics. On the days I won more games he would take his leave of me with the words: 'I've got to beat you next time.' His need to win was so great that at the threat of losing he became excessively agitated and prejudiced his chances by trying to work too fast, by making too many unnecessary jerky movements, or by drawing my attention to his mistakes by gasping or starting. Such behaviour suggested a defeatist tendency, almost a secret wish to lose, which conflicted with his overt struggle to win, but was in keeping with the character of his delinquency. Although he showed unusual inventiveness in the ways he used to cover up his thefts, he nearly always left a 'clue' which led to their discovery.

As a small boy of five or six, he buried the stolen money in flower pots in the house, or in flower beds in the front garden, but left the tell-tale traces of freshly dug-up earth. As a boy of ten while under treatment, he somehow got hold of a packet of pound notes saved for his grandmother's trip overseas. He drew attention to himself by shutting himself up in the lavatory where he was found with the notes spread in front of him on the floor, like cards in a game of patience. On another occasion he stole a book of savings stamps from a master's desk, and on the way to a post office where he cashed some of them, told a schoolmate about it. The boy at once went and reported him to the master. Immediately after this had been discovered and before the storm had blown over, Gerald was sent to fetch something from a school stores' cupboard, and stole a bunch of keys and a scrubbing brush. He could give no reason for these thefts except that he thought the brush 'might come in handy'. In short, his stealing bore all the marks of a compulsion in which the objects taken were a substitute for something he felt he had not been receiving from an early age.

He was the elder of two children, his sister being five years younger than he. His parents, respectable working class people, were not intelligent, the mother, on the whole, capable of better insight, but more anxious and fussy than the father, and inclined to nag. Her husband implied as much when he was seen by us, and betrayed the character of their relationship by begging us not to tell her what he had said about her. One of his phrases was that she 'had given Gerald a persecution complex'.

On the other hand, his wife, although she did not complain about him, could not have had an easy time with him. She conveyed to us that at the beginning of their married life, his earnings were so poor that she had to go out to work. Gerald, however, was wanted and was 'a lovely baby'. For the first eight months of his life he was cared for by his mother, then she took a job and left him in the care of his paternal grandmother. This grandmother, by all accounts, was an unstable, disagreeable woman, and disagreements about Gerald's management occurred from the beginning. It appears she was neglectful and impatient with the baby to the point of cruelty.

When Gerald was eleven months old his parents moved house, partly to escape from the grandmother's neighbourhood. The care of Gerald was then taken over by the mother's sister, who had a little girl of her own about the same age. The mother told us that she took Gerald to his aunt's house every morning before she went to work, and fetched him home every evening, but Gerald himself said that he slept at his aunt's and went home for week-ends. Whichever version happens to be true, the fact remains that for the first five years of his life he had two mothers, who passed him back and forth like a shuttlecock, so that he had no chance of establishing a deep relationship with either of them. His aunt had probably become a more important person to him than his mother, but at the age of five he was suddenly transferred to his parents' home where he found his mother installed with his new baby sister.

The demands for adjustment this situation made upon him were increased by his starting school at the same time. He began stealing, chiefly money from his mother, which he spent on toys and sweets, frequently giving them away to his school fellows. The mother was not very well after the birth of the

baby and could not give Gerald much attention. Later, however, she made many efforts to pin him down, for he would
never admit his thefts. She clearly derived pleasure from these
detective activities: searching through his socks and shoes after
he had gone to bed, looking under his mattress and through
his books after he had left for school, to discover whether and
where he had hidden stolen money or objects. He, on his part,
delighted in putting her off the scent by planting the stolen
things on his sister, who remained innocent and unsuspecting.

This sister was often the cause of his outbursts of violence:
on two occasions he threw a pair of scissors at her, wounding
her on the arm and forehead. She was a quiet, gentle child, who
was said to worship him. While he was under treatment with me,
she developed epileptic fits and had to be dosed with pheno-
barbitone. A bottle of these tablets disappeared, and the
mother found some under Gerald's pillow. Clearly, he had to
have everything his sister was given, and it was his intense
jealousy of her on account of the affection she received from
both parents which determined to a large extent Gerald's behaviour towards the members of his family, and towards me,
as a mother figure. He described his feelings with a high degree
of insight in a story on Picture 2 of my Family Attitudes Test,
which was quoted in Part II of this book.

I am not sure how much he was aware that in this story he
was describing his own situation, but he brought out both the
superficial bid for attention and the deeper need for affection,
characteristic of the delinquent. A profound insecurity was also
evident, for the boy who could not tolerate 'his relatives and his
parents' caring for anybody but himself must have felt particularly vulnerable.

His strong feelings of inferiority were revealed in some remarks he made during treatment. In my attempts to build up
his sense of personal value, I told him that newly married
couples usually wanted their first child to be a boy. He thought
that it was because they wanted 'to carry on the family name'. I
then commented on the fact that childless couples, on the other
hand, preferred to adopt a girl, and asked Gerald why he

thought it was so. He hedged, as usual, then said: 'Perhaps when they've had a boy and saw what it was like, they wanted a girl'. I pressed him to explain, and he added: 'Perhaps they think a boy would turn out vicious and that a girl would do as she was told'.

Once, telling me of his visit to Madame Tussaud's, he commented on his reluctance to descend into the Chamber of Horrors: 'I thought they might keep *me* there'. But the most pathetic example of his self-depreciation was the little poem he wrote to the girl he admired, and which his father somehow secured and brought to show us.

> Daphne is my lover,
> Daphne's my sweetheart,
> Daphne's face is beautiful
>   and mine's like the back of a door.
> Daphne always laughing
> But I'm always dull.
> Daphne so romantic
> While I look very poor.

In fact, he was a very good-looking boy, with regular features, large blue eyes, black eyebrows and fair hair, but in his efforts to remain inscrutable he kept his face so rigid that it could be fairly compared to 'the back of a door'. One of the changes the treatment produced in him was a change in facial expression: his features became relaxed and mobile, he laughed much more often and grew more spontaneous in general.

I think that after eighteen months' weekly attendance Gerald was persuaded that what was done for him by me and the other members of the staff was done for his own sake and not for any ulterior motives. The situation at home, however, was very disturbed by the illness of the little girl and the amount of the additional care and supervision she needed from the mother. Whenever his sister was ill enough to be in bed, Gerald, his mother said, was 'very sweet' to her, but at other times was still liable to hit out at her wildly. He continued pilfering money from his parents, but now, if questioned, admitted having done so and sometimes repaid it from his pocket money. Violent outbursts of temper still occurred when his mother interfered with something he was doing. On the other hand he developed some strong positive interests, normal at his age, in such things as electrical apparatus, small film projectors, etc., and was able to sustain these interests over the best part of a year. His school work also improved to such an extent that he was able to pass the scholarship tests and was admitted to a grammar school.

This was used by his parents as a pretext for stopping his attendance for treatment. They thought it might prejudice his chances at the new school, and there was no alternative for us except to agree and to keep in touch with the boy and his parents. Gerald found the grammar school rather a strain, for he was not academically minded and the conditions at home were not favourable for study in the evenings. He often had to do his homework with the family sitting around and the wireless on, as there was no fire in his bedroom. Once, he told me, as he was writing an essay, he found he had written a sentence from a broadcast instead of one he intended to write.

As he was very keen on practical pursuits and found grammar school work rather difficult, we advised the parents to transfer him to a technical school. This was also Gerald's wish, but his father dissuaded him by asserting that he would have a better choice of jobs if he stayed on at the grammar school. His mother meanwhile has had another baby, a little girl, of whom Gerald became very fond. Yet, at the same time there was an increase in pilfering from the parents and of temper outbursts against the mother and the sister. He then stole a bicycle wheel, taking it off a schoolmate's bicycle. No legal action was taken and Gerald escaped with the headmaster's reprimand and a scene at home.

When I saw him a few months later, he talked of the new bicycle he was going to make for himself out of parts he was going to buy separately because 'it was more fun to make than to buy one'. He admitted to the theft of the wheel without hedging and explained that he 'just wanted it'. He

170

clearly did not like admitting it, but was neither sullen, nor defiant.

The determination of this boy's persistent delinquency was undoubtedly complex. The experiences of the first five years of his life would have made him feel utterly rejected by his mother and therefore unlovable and inferior. The stealing, which in the beginning might have been a substitute for maternal affection, has acquired a double significance in later years— that of a solace and of a weapon of revenge upon the mother. Gerald's resentment against her was not entirely unjustifiable, for she clearly preferred his sister, and she admitted to 'hating' him when he was 'cruel' to the little girl. The impulsiveness and apparent 'stupidity' of his stealing even suggests that it might have been an epileptic equivalent. Yet, it is clear to me that the decisive element in the case was the absence of a strong bond between the mother and son, of a deep relationship which can only grow through a constant communion in the first years of the child's life.

(d) Barry

In BARRY'S case it was not the actual physical separation which prevented the formation of this bond, but the abnormal incapacity of his mother to feel affection for anybody.

When I first saw him, Barry was 11 years 9 months old, a tall, willowy boy, delicate looking, with clear skin, grey eyes and red wavy hair. His I.Q. was given as 78. He had just been 'in trouble', and was extremely restless and easily distracted. When after a few interviews he was able to settle down, he wanted to make some dolls, similar to those he had found in my dolls' house. He was, however, too critical of his efforts, and whenever he thought he had gone 'wrong' in some small detail, he would crumple up the doll and throw it into the fire.

This destructive trend was evident in most of his pursuits. He could draw and paint well and liked doing it, but would go on trying to improve his drawing, then suddenly declare that it was 'no good', and tear it up or scribble over it. Sometimes he would decide to 'make something', look round for material, and proceed to break up a toy, such as a wooden aeroplane, in order to make a boat. After the toy had been broken, he would declare that he 'couldn't do it', after all, and would resist the suggestion that he might at least try. Once he painted the dolls' house with white paint, doing it very carefully and spending a considerable time over it. Then, without a word of warning, he seized a brush and put large dabs of brown paint all over the white. He would mix paints of all colours, producing a dirty grey, and would smear it over the inside of a white wash-basin.

He showed no open hostility towards me until I had seen him about twenty times. I gave him an opportunity by offering a game of ball. Without a word, he seized the ball and threw it at my head. Before I had time to pick it up, he got hold of more balls and pelted me with them, throwing hard and aiming at my head and face. He said: 'I'd like to have a hard ball to throw at you.' These attacks he repeated during several of the subsequent interviews, and every time, despite my reminders to 'aim low', aimed at my head.

The phase of direct hostility towards me was short, but outbursts of destructiveness continued until his treatment was stopped, after he had had about fifty interviews.

From his history given to us by his parents, and from our acquaintance with them, it became clear that Barry had had a loveless childhood. He was conceived before marriage, after his mother and father had been 'walking out' together for seven years, and this fact decided his mother to marry his father. The sexual side of marriage repelled her, and she would have been quite content to remain engaged indefinitely. As a wife, she was frigid, obsessional and nagging, putting the order and cleanliness of her house before her family. She had been for years a chamber-maid in a big house, and her standards of housekeeping were taken over from there. Her husband was a successful business man on a small scale, intelligent but lacking in warmth and sincerity. There was no real affection between the parents, and the father's way of dealing with the boy's delinquencies suggested a strong sadistic streak in him. When stealing occurred, he insisted that the boy should admit to it, and pursued him with questions until he reduced him to tears. He had taken him to a police station 'to frighten him'. He told us that he had thrashed the boy 'for not telling the truth' and not for stealing.

Both parents wanted the boy to be sent away, the mother because he was 'a disgrace', the father, ostensibly, because he upset his wife. 'If he is not sent away, it'll kill her', he told us. On another occasion he hinted that, when the boy had been disposed of, he might leave the country and try to make a new life without his wife. He complained that she would quarrel with him about Barry after they had gone to bed, and, if he refused to answer, would pull the bedclothes off him and so drive him out of bed.

As an infant, Barry was brought up on the Truby King's method and was dry and clean very early. He was difficult to feed and later developed many food fads. He had always been delicate and had had most of the childish illnesses in his early years. At six, he spent several weeks in hospital under observation for T.B. He was said to have been 'naughty' there. At seven his parents decided to send him to his grandparents' farm because of the dangers of bombing. It was there that his stealing began. Barry took a pound note from his own money-box, which he prized open, and spent five shillings on sweets and cheap toys which he distributed among the neighbours' children. Later, his aunt's gold watch disappeared, and Barry was suspected, but his guilt remained unproved.

He was brought home after seven or eight months during which his parents visited him only once. Pilfering increased, and a couple of years later culminated in the theft of a bicycle which he used, then hid in a clump of bushes where it was found by the police. He was not prosecuted, but some months later stole from school and was suspended for a time. While away from school, he stole from his parents and from shops. His latest scoop before he was brought to us on the advice of his headmaster consisted of twenty-five pocket calendars, half-a-dozen telephone note-books and three bread knives. Immediately afterwards he stole fifty comic papers.

A few weeks after he started attending for treatment, his mother decided to go to the farm, ostensibly to look after her father who was in poor health. She had done so from time to time, and in the past used to take Barry with her. On this occasion, however, she decided to leave him behind because 'he upset' his grandfather. Her husband used his long hours at work as a pretext for refusing to take responsibility for Barry during her absence, and, against our advice, she arranged for the boy to stay with a friend, a kindly woman, who was asked not to let Barry out of her sight. The seriousness of his condition, however, was not explained to her; his pilfering was represented to her as an isolated incident. He was at that time suspended from school, and she had to take him with her when she went shopping. On one occasion she left him outside a shop and, on coming out, found that he had gone. He reappeared some couple of hours later with a bottle of lemonade which he said someone had given him. The same evening she found some tins of food in his room. When a similar thing recurred on another occasion, she became so alarmed that she wrote to his mother, asking her to take the boy home. The mother thus had to curtail her stay with the grandfather, and arrived home thoroughly exasperated and upset. There was a scene, and on the following day Barry stole a pound note from his mother with which he bought four clinical thermometers.

It became clear after two or three months that his parents would not co-operate in treatment: they were determined that the boy should go away. When he began to improve and his mother remarked on it to his father, her husband replied that Barry was behaving in some ways very much like her schizophrenic sister, that is, he talked to himself and imagined that people in the street were looking at him. By making her feel frightened and guilty, he stimulated her wish to get rid of the boy and escape from the responsibility for him.

We made great efforts to find a foster home for Barry, but it proved impossible. He was aware of what was happening, as his parents had often threatened him that he would be sent away. He stole another bicycle. His father's behaviour on this occasion gave us reasons to think that he intentionally brought this theft to the notice of the police, in order to force our hand. The police, he said, were going to prosecute unless the boy was sent away. We arranged for Barry to go to a hostel for children awaiting placing. He really had no right to be there, as his parents could well afford to pay for his keep, but we knew that no boarding school was likely to keep him for more than a few days.

Barry was well aware of his rejection, although he did not realize the full extent of his father's part in the affair. He had said on several occasions that he wanted to leave home. 'I want to get away from Mum. She's finding fault with me all the time.' Also: 'My mother said last night that she did not want me to go, but I said I wish I were going today. I want to get out of Mum's way. I'm not as cross with Dad as I am with Mum.' But, in reality, he dreaded the unknown and cried bitterly on the way to the hostel. In his first fortnight there he made two attempts to get back home and stole from shops, but settled down afterwards, joined the scouts and appeared to be reasonably happy. He continued attending for treatment with me, and was helped by the affectionate interest the staff of the hostel took in him, perhaps especially by the maternal personality of the matron.

His settled period, however, did not last long. He had to be moved, and went to a school for delicate children in the country. This change was followed by an outburst of pilfering and wandering. The headmaster's wife took a dislike to him, whereas the nurse living at the school mothered him. Barry's behaviour improved in response to affection, but when he was punished for some escapade in company with other boys, he reacted as he had always done—by pilfering and running away. During his wanderings, he stole from shops and was taken to court. He is now fifteen, and the latest news I had of him was that he had been committed to an approved school. This boy, I believe, could have been rescued from his fate by being placed

175

in a good foster home. He was too immature emotionally to profit by the inclusion in a larger group, and I fear that now he is well on the way to becoming a confirmed law-breaker.

Barry was one of the very few children who persistently refused to do my Family Attitudes Test. At first he professed an inability to make up stories, but later frankly admitted that he did not want to do it because he did not like the idea. Someone had told him that 'psychologists want to see what's inside your brain', and no proof of my concern for his welfare could dislodge suspicion from his mind. He was, like his mother and aunt, somewhat paranoid. On the other hand, he was pathetically eager for affection and recognition, and most reluctant to relinquish his claims on me when I had to close his case. In fact, he continued to arrive at the usual time after he was supposed to have stopped attendance. Any situation which revived his early experiences of rejection and deprivation was apt to bring about depression, wandering and stealing. His parents' infrequent visits to the hostel to see him were always followed by such outbursts.

I chose to describe these cases, out of a number of others, because these children were so different from one another in so many ways, yet the results of psychotherapy with them were almost equally disappointing. The two younger children, Robert and Hazel, were of good average intelligence, extraverted and cyclothymic in their emotional reactions, whereas of the two elder boys one, Gerald, was of superior intelligence, and the other, Barry, slightly below average, both introverted and schizoid in disposition, with some hysterical and obsessional traits.

All four, however, had some important traits in common: they were all persistent pilferers and destroyers, destructiveness predominating in the two younger children, pilfering in the two elder. With the exception of Robert, they all attended for treatment weekly for twelve months or more, yet none achieved a complete change over from the negative to the positive and creative forms of self-realization. They made attempts in that direction from time to time, but these attempts were sporadic and never became established as habits or attitudes of mind. Nor were they able, except intermittently, to respond to my offers of friendship, help and affection, as if the capacity for such a relationship had never developed, or had been deeply repressed at an early age.

The significance of this becomes clear if one calls to mind their family environment. Externally, their background was in many ways dissimilar: Robert belonged to a wealthy tradesman milieu; the other three had parents who, I think, could best be described as belonging to the skilled 'working class'. None of these children had been materially deprived, and all were well looked after physically. Robert and Gerald were jealous of their younger siblings; Barry and Hazel, on the other hand, were both 'only' children. What all the four families had in common was the mother's attitude towards the child, which I believe to be decisive in determining delinquent behaviour. In each one of the cases the mother's attitude could best be described as one of 'non-acceptance' of the child, with the resulting lack of a close emotional relationship between the mother and child—a bond which provides the basic pattern for the child's later relationships with others. These mothers were not merely ambivalent towards their children, as many mothers are, but rejected them fundamentally. They seemed to feel that their children were wicked and unredeemable, expressing their sentiments in words, as some of them did, or in action, by depriving them in various ways or sending them away, or handing the care of them to other people.

The causes and motives of these attitudes in mothers are most certainly complex and almost certainly rooted in their own childhood experiences. Strong feelings of guilt might have made them intolerant of the children's lapses; sexual frigidity, self-centredness and temperamental coldness might have contributed to the lack of warmth in their approach. To this the children reacted by a compulsive testing of maternal forbearance, and by destructiveness which followed from a state of mind amounting to despair.

Through lack of an earlier relationship and an established

defensive habit of emotional non-commitment, these children found it extremely difficult to accept a relationship with me, and I believe that in every case their treatment ought to have continued for a considerably longer period. Continuity of a relationship with the therapist and a gradual broadening of friendly contacts creating a stable circle of benevolent influences, might have strengthened their capacity to withstand temptation. It might have raised their sense of personal value to the extent of making them capable of caring what others thought of them.

As it happened, of the four children described, Robert, the six-year-old, was removed too soon for the treatment to have had any appreciable effect, whereas Barry, aged 12, was given no chance to settle down because of the several changes of 'home', and the breaking off of the good relationships he had begun to form with his mother substitutes. The parents of the eight-year-old Hazel were suspicious of psychological treatment and could never bring themselves to co-operate in it. The child was aware of their attitude and it constituted a serious obstacle to her forming a good relationship with me. In one only of the four cases, that of the ten-year-old Gerald, were both the length of treatment and the punctuality of attendance adequate for establishing a relationship which to some extent compensated the boy for the lack of a good relationship with his mother. Yet even in this case the parents broke off the treatment before the boy was ready for it. I have kept in touch with the parents and the boy, seeing them at intervals of about six months. Gerald was not very happy at the grammar school, and his lack of success in academic subjects constituted a danger and contained a possibility of a further breakdown. This had, in fact, occurred after he had been in his new school for about two years, as I have described earlier in this chapter.

There is little doubt that a change in Gerald's personality has been initiated through psychological treatment and his relationship with me. He developed consistency of interests whereas previously he seemed to take up hobbies only to drop them as soon as he was given tools and materials for their pursuit. Although he continued taking money from his parents without asking permission, he always admitted to having done so, while previously he stubbornly denied all knowledge of the matter. His manner and facial expression became more animated and open; he was able to feel and show affection both to his new baby sister and to a crippled boy neighbour, for whom he adapted an old bicycle.

The recurrence of stealing under stress, however, seems to indicate that a streak of immaturity remains—an inability to tolerate postponement of satisfactions. Nor is he free from sudden outbursts of violent temper, usually against the sister next to him, of whom he remains very jealous. His mother reported, however, that he is no longer violent towards herself, and able to control his anger if his father is present.

It is perhaps idle to speculate how much more Gerald might have profited by an extension of the period of treatment. I am convinced, however, not only by my experience with him, but through the treatment and study of a number of other delinquent children, that most of them need a much longer treatment than the majority of neurotic children, and that contact should be maintained after they have stopped attending regularly. One must make sure that they reach the stage of maturity at which they are able to postpone immediate satisfactions out of self-respect and a need for respect from others. Only recently I was forcefully reminded how risky it is to leave a former delinquent without support in times of emotional stress, before he reached the maturity sufficient to withstand it.

Paul, a boy of twelve, had a bad relapse into pilfering and truancy, after having made good progress over a period of two years. He attended for psychological treatment with me for about twelve months; then, as he was backward in school subjects and a poor reader, his parents confronted me with the demand of having him coached or stopping his attendance altogether. I arranged for him to have help with his reading, and saw him occasionally for another twelve months. Pilfering recurred immediately after this transfer and was doubtless related to it. However, the experienced psychologist who coached him was soon able to form a good relationship with the boy, and he continued to improve until, at the age of eleven, he had to go to a new school.

He liked it at first, but it soon became evident that he was not favoured by his class teacher, who 'shamed' him for his backwardness. Unfortunately, at the same time the psychologist, who had been coaching him, was obliged to leave. At home, there was worry and uncertainty on account of the grandfather's illness. This grandfather had been living with the family for years and contributing to the rent. Paul heard his father say that if grandfather died they would have to move house, as they would be unable to afford the rent. His young sister, too, fell ill, and the mother, who had been going out to work, had to stay in to look after her. Then the father had to stay away from work for a month with influenza followed by complications. The mother, with her time fully occupied, could give no attention to Paul, and the combined strains proved too much for him. He truanted regularly, took long rides on trains, and stayed out at night. I saw him again, and not having a treatment vacancy, arranged for him to have coaching with another psychologist, but he came only once, while truancy and pilfering continued as before. His parents meanwhile are pressing for his removal, and there appears to be now no other solution to this state of affairs.

Paul's case is very similar to that of Barry because the parents of both boys displayed an unwillingness and an inability to modify their attitude towards their sons. Paul, I am afraid, will go the same way as Barry unless a boarding school is found where he can be given individual attention and stay for several years. What he needs most of all at present is the security of a stable human relationship, the absence of which lay at the root of his trouble. His mother was one of those dissociated elusive women who baffle the effort to establish contact with them, and whose detachment is bound to create profound insecurity in their children. She went out to work when Paul was a toddler and while his father was away with the Forces during the war. Paul was looked after by his paternal grandmother, who was very fond of him. She died when he was seven, and this coincided with the birth of Paul's sister. He was sent away for a couple of months and returned to what was virtually a new family, with his father at home and a baby sister supplanting him and absorbing the mother's attention. He began pilfering then, and was thrashed by the father, a dull and heavy type of man, who could not understand why Paul should behave in this way, because he had 'quite a good home'.

For boys like Paul and Barry, whose parents are quite unable to modify their feelings and give them the security of a stable affectionate relationship, and whose disagreements or preoccupations create a family atmosphere of perpetual tension, there should have been a hostel, appropriately staffed and within reach of psychotherapeutic help and observation. Such an arrangement would have given them the best possible chance of recovery. As it is, by handing these boys over to the care of one group of people after another, we complete the process of estrangement begun in infancy and perpetuate the state of 'not belonging' which is the hall mark of a delinquent's character.

In describing the behaviour of delinquent children under treatment, I emphasized the difficulty of establishing contact with them and the length of time it took to build up a relationship. I do not think this was due to any constitutional trait, for not all of these delinquents were withdrawn, schizoid types. I believe it was due to the fact that they had to learn how to play their part in such a relationship from the very beginning, that is, to learn something which more fortunate children learn at their mother's breast. Their self-assertive activities, therefore, retained a negative character for longer periods than those of neurotic children. In drawing their 'curve of aggression', I would represent it as rising steeply and continuing on a plateau for months on end, whereas the neurotics' 'curve' would be high, sharply rising and just as sharply falling.

III. NEGATIVE SELF-ASSERTION IN NORMAL CHILDREN

Negative forms of aggression occur, of course, in the behaviour of normal children, but it has neither the intensity nor
the consistency shown by the neurotics and the delinquents. I
had an opportunity of observing several normal children under
the same conditions as the delinquent and the neurotic, that
is, in the same room, with the same freedom of choice of play
or occupation. They were sent for psychological examination
on account of isolated symptoms, but could not, by any stretch
of imagination, be described as neurotic, or seriously disturbed.

(a) Gordon

GORDON, aged ten, with an I.Q. of 115, was referred by
his headmistress because she thought he ought to be doing
better in school subjects. She described him as timid and lacking in confidence. He was, in fact, an introverted, sensitive,
thoughtful boy, who was not, however, abnormally withdrawn
and who made an excellent contact with me almost from the
first interview. On the Stanford-Binet scale his intelligence was
only 115, but his vocabulary was so large and his command of
it so good, that he might well have given his headmistress the
impression of being more gifted academically than he in fact was.

From the second interview with him I noticed that he had a
very determined streak in his character and that he neither
hesitated nor even asked permission when he wanted to break
something during play. He usually rationalized his destructive
action by giving a plausible reason for it: a middle rail was
wrenched out of a length of toy railway lines 'because it served
no purpose'; lead fencing was broken in two 'to make them all
the same height'. He took an old car to pieces 'to mend it', but
never returned to it again. Throughout the twelve sessions I
gave him, this mild destructiveness, with a professed constructive aim in view, continued. On one occasion I had to

prevent him from cutting off the base of a rather precious Russian doll, so that he could fit it inside another!

Yet for the most part of each interview his behaviour was friendly and co-operative and his play imaginative and constructive. The destructive aspect of it might have been a kind of protest against the exacting nature of his family environment.

He was an only child of middle-class Scottish parents, who were very fond of him, but thought it their duty to be strict. His father was ambitious for him; his mother critical. Gordon's early childhood was uneventful, but from the age of three onwards he had had a succession of shocks and changes of environment. A flat-iron fell on his head and his face was covered with blood; a bomb exploded in the next-door back garden; a hurried evacuation to Scotland with his mother followed these two incidents. The relatives with whom they stayed had two unruly children somewhat older than Gordon; there had been tension and friction between the two families. At the age of four Gordon had his tonsils removed in hospital; the mother was not allowed to visit. They returned to London during the quiet period of the war, but during the flying bomb attacks, his mother again took Gordon to Scotland. He was said to have greatly missed his father. Between the ages of five and six he had several illnesses, including pneumonia. As can only be expected he had had several changes of school. When he first started school, he developed a habit of rolling his eyes and contorting his face, but these habits cleared up spontaneously. He sucked his thumb until he was three and was enuretic until the age of four.

Gordon's case provides, in my opinion, a good illustration of the ways in which a harmonious family atmosphere and a genuine respect and affection for the child can minimize the effects of early traumatic experiences and of external insecurity. None of the minor symptoms of emotional disturbance which Gordon showed before the age of six had persisted into later childhood. The character traits he displayed at school, at home and in the clinic were by no means exaggerated in a child of introverted disposition, who had no child companions at home and whose parents set him high standards of behaviour and achievement. His shyness did not prevent him from making good contact with me and with other children whom, on several occasions, I took together with him. He was persistent in everything he undertook, with a tendency to perfectionism. His quiet manner did not exclude outbursts of gaiety and mischievousness, especially when another child was on the scene. He got on well with his companions, sometimes taking the initiative, sometimes following another child's lead.

His mother reported that at home his play was usually constructive and that he liked to carry on with his projects for several days. He was allowed to leave what he had built on the floor for two or three days if he wanted to. He was reluctant to take the first step in making friends, but responded quickly if the other child approached him, and he kept friends he had made. He preferred bringing them home to playing with them outside. He was eager to go camping with the school, and was very happy in the camp, although it was the first time he had been separated from his mother. In fact, he showed an amount of independence unusual in an only child, whose parents were wrapped up in him. Within the limitations of his age and his introverted disposition, Gordon was an attractive, well-developed, all-round personality.

His inclination to break, take to pieces or cut toys during his interviews with me was, however, a manifestation of immaturity, and was most likely due to the too early imposition of adult standards upon him. His parents would not have approved of it; and to do it in my presence was for him the means of asserting himself in the face of quasi-parental authority. His destructiveness, however, was always followed by a constructive effort: the breaking or cutting was always done for a purpose, and not, as with neurotic or delinquent children, for the sake of mere destruction, or with the aim of annoying me. Towards me he remained always friendly, and he was most reluctant to stop attending for weekly interviews.

(b) Patrick

PATRICK was another boy whose early childhood contained enough material to produce a serious emotional disturbance, and who, nevertheless, recovered fairly quickly from its effects.

When I saw him first, he was eight-and-a-half years old and his I.Q. was given as 121. He was tall for his age, good-looking, with delicate features and an engaging smile. He talked in a soft voice and moved gracefully; there was a suggestion of 'girlishness' about him. His mother brought him because he refused to go to school after a short illness at home. He refused to leave his mother, and, when frustrated, attacked her violently, kicked and screamed. He also had fears, especially of being left alone in the house. When his mother had to go out shopping, he would undress and get into bed.

His treatment with me fell into two periods separated by a ten weeks' interval. In the first period he had eight weekly interviews, during which he remained uniformly co-operative and constructive. Although obviously on his guard, he was prepared to talk about himself and to explain some of his behaviour which his mother regarded as 'peculiar'. It was true, he said, that he used to enjoy going to the children's cinema with a friend, but had recently decided that he did not want to go any more. One reason was that he did not like getting up early on Saturdays; the other, that in the last film he saw 'there were lots of snakes, and I didn't like that'. This objection may have been related to his occasional masturbation for which, however, he had not been scolded or punished. His reasons for objecting to being left alone in the house were also adequate: the family lived in a bungalow which had been burgled twice. Patrick admitted that he was 'a bit afraid' of another visit from the burglars and that he felt safer in bed 'because you can slip under the bedclothes'.

His play behaviour during these eight interviews was wholly constructive. He was competent with tools and spent some time on making a boat and on mending an old toy car. The only glimpse of a more boisterous aspect of his personality which I was allowed at that time, came through in his fantasy play with a family of dolls. The boy doll behaved in a 'naughty' and provocative way towards his parents, and usually got away with it. Occasionally Patrick himself took an exaggeratedly vigorous ride on a rocking horse, during which he managed to produce a great deal of noise.

When he came back to me after a ten weeks' break necessitated by my absence, his behaviour was boisterous from the very first interview. He rode the rocking horse very noisily for at least ten minutes, then asked for a game of cricket with me during which he became wildly excited. He flung the ball at my head instead of aiming at the wicket, laughed and danced about the room, and threw himself down on to the floor as if helpless with amusement. This type of behaviour continued for several weeks. On one occasion Patrick ran round the room hitting my desk and other furniture with a mallet; on another, he threatened to burn me with a piece of smouldering paper and struck me on the hands in a 'pretend' fencing match. He uttered other threats without any real provocation on my part: when I tried to prevent him from spraying me with water, he shouted that he was going 'to smash' my jaw and break my fingers.

All this alternated with constructive activities, imaginative play with boats and trains and friendly games with me. As time went on, negatively aggressive behaviour subsided and during his last two interviews Patrick's play and behaviour were entirely constructive.

The quick recovery of this boy from his symptoms—they had not recurred when I saw him a year later—his capacity to overcome initial shyness and make a good contact, his ability to control his aggressive outbursts and to switch over to constructive activities, all pointed to more than average capacity for integration. Why was he then impelled to behave in the way he did for a certain period? The answer, I believe, is contained in his family conditions.

Patrick was an only child of elderly parents. At the time of his treatment, his father was sixty-five, his mother fifty. The father was in poor health, suffering from asthma, and rather intolerant of noise. Although very fond of Patrick he, in the mother's words, 'couldn't romp with him'. The mother herself was unwell, uncertain as to whether she would have to undergo an operation, and Patrick's rough playfulness was not welcomed by her. She had, however, a good sense of humour, was intelligent, and understood the disadvantages he suffered through having elderly parents and no brothers or sisters.

Patrick was born eleven years after marriage and was a very much wanted baby. His mother, however, had to go to work when he was eighteen months old because her husband was too ill to work at the time. Patrick was left at home in charge of a mother's friend. He had many childish illnesses between the ages of three and eight, none of them serious. At three years, however, he had to stay in hospital for a couple of weeks, receiving treatment for ear abscesses, which must have been very painful. The parents visited him regularly, and he cried bitterly every time they left him. After returning home, he suffered from night terrors for some time. When he was four, his mother had to go to hospital for a serious operation, and he was sent to a day nursery which he liked. He started school at five, and at first went readily, but at the age of six he began to follow his mother about the house, as if afraid to let her out of his sight. He was eight when this behaviour culminated in a refusal to go to school, after he had been at home for a few days with a heavy cold. His mother said that he looked 'white and miserable', and that he pleaded with her, saying that she was 'cruel' to send him. She had to stay away from work for a fortnight, take Patrick to bed with her to pacify him, and escort him to school every morning and afternoon.

She has been working full time throughout Patrick's childhood.

Clinical experience accustoms one to expect a deep impairment of personality, perhaps neurosis or delinquency in a child with a background and early history of this type. Patrick, however, developed only a few transient symptoms. Diffident, yet trustful and friendly; sensitive and imaginative, yet eminently sensible; humorous and gay, yet thoughtful, he promised to

develop into a most delightful personality. For years he with-
stood the insecurity of a home with two ailing parents, a home
from which the mother absented herself for the best part of the
day. His protest against this state of affairs took the form of
trying to keep his mother at home, which he expressed verbally
by quoting a talk on the wireless, in which 'they said that
mothers with children should stay at home'. His fears were an
unconscious expression of insecurity intensified by probable
awareness that his mother's life was in danger. His behaviour
in the play-room was a release of pent-up self-assertion which
he had been expected to control from the age of two when he
first joined a group in a day nursery. Neither parent had been
able to tolerate 'roughness' or noise, and the freedom to in-
dulge in either without damaging me, a parent figure, must
have been very reassuring to Patrick.

Although the family background was responsible for Patrick's temporary breakdown, the good relationship between
the parents and their wise and steady affection made it possible
for him to recover quickly.

(c) *George*

In another case, that of GEORGE, the situation was com-
plicated by the presence of two siblings, one of whom was
George's twin, a boy, and the other, a very attractive little girl,
six years his junior. George was nine years old, with an I.Q.
of 115, a plain, virile little boy, with a mischievous grin.
The symptom for which he was brought for treatment was
described as 'bucking in bed'. Lying face downwards and
apparently sound asleep, he would make short, rapid movements with the middle of his body, so that his bed rattled and
disturbed the parents sleeping in the adjoining room. He was
said not to remember it on waking in the morning. He was
somewhat backward at school and did not have many friends.

He was passed on to me by another therapist and did not
particularly like the change. He was, however, friendly and
constructive, trying to mend broken toys and playing with

cars and trains in a normal way. The need to assert himself in opposition to me was expressed mostly in competition with me, and the choice of play was, undoubtedly, significant. He would construct two towers of many tiers out of bricks of various sizes, leaving some smaller bricks to be used as 'shells'. One tower 'belonged' to me, the other to him. The game consisted in bombarding each other's tower with bricks to see who would be the first to raze the opponent's tower to the ground. Deliberately and without trying to conceal it, but with a guilty giggle, George would build his tower with the biggest bricks, but with wide open tiers, so that my 'shells' would go right through them without striking the edifice. He always succeeded in grabbing the heaviest bricks to use as projectiles and in securing a lion's share of the available supplies. It was not surprising, therefore, that he nearly always won this game, that is, he was the first to destroy 'my' tower. He was not, however, without generosity, and, after having satisfied his thirst for victory, he would invite me to have a few extra 'shots' at his tower.

He worked himself into a state of great excitement during these games, would gasp and start whenever his tower tottered, would insist on smashing up whatever was left of both towers at the end of a round of bombardment, and did so with much force and gusto. He clearly derived great satisfaction from displaying his skill and vigour, but his choice of destructive play suggested the presence of negative emotions needing release. His family background provided an explanation.

His parents' married life was harmonious and happy. His mother was a pleasant sensible woman; his father, a charming extraverted man, who ran a fairly large business and kept an open house. When George was an infant, his elder brother, then a toddler, met with a fatal accident. The mother was guilt-stricken and depressed while she was nursing the twins; she found them 'rather a handful', and George was the more difficult of the two. Even now she was inclined to prefer the other twin.

The little girl was the favourite with her father. He played 'tickling games' with her after she had gone to bed, and her screams and laughter could be heard all over the house. She came into the parents' bed on Sunday mornings, and the boys, too, tried to follow suit. George was allowed to cuddle himself against his mother after the father had vacated the place, and she had remarked that he 'would get at her breasts if she had let him', but she 'gave him a good hug and kept his hands down'.

George and his twin got on quite well together, but George often got impatient with his small sister and tried to 'knock her about' for which he had been scolded by the father.

George's responses to the Family Attitudes Test were unusual in that the child in his stories was always 'a naughty little girl'. Yet, despite her naughtiness, she was very much wanted, not only by a man who tried to steal her, but also by the boy, who 'wanted to take her away, just to keep her for his own'. If the parents 'asked for her back, he would say "No".'

George was very interested in the question of the origin of babies, and at the time his treatment began, he knew that a baby 'started from a seed inside the mother'. He did not know, however, that the father also had to contribute 'a seed', and it became clear from his questions that the father's part in procreation has been occupying his thoughts for some time. His symptom, an unconscious imitation of coitus, suggested that his knowledge lay deeper than his ignorance. He seemed to be hoping that he could stake a claim on 'a naughty little girl', to own and treat as he chose, by taking his father's place in his mother's bed. That this belated Oedipus situation had not led to much more serious difficulties was no doubt due to the parents' good relationship between themselves and with the boy.

This was reflected in his attitude towards me which remained basically friendly throughout the short period of his attendance. He may have had moments of resentment against both his parents for preferring his small sister and 'spoiling' her, and he expressed it by smashing 'my' tower, for I represented to him adult privilege and authority. Yet this 'smashing up' alternated with long periods of constructiveness and co-operation, without an element of rivalry. He showed no 'peak of aggression', such as neurotic children have shown, nor 'plateaux of aggression', like the delinquent children.

These three boys were chosen for comparison with the neurotic and the delinquent children whom I described earlier because I was able to observe them under exactly the same conditions, i.e. the conditions of free play with nobody but myself to watch them. I described them as 'normal' not because they conformed to some well-defined standard of normality generally accepted, but because the symptoms they showed had not produced a serious distortion of personality, or grossly asocial behaviour. In intelligence, all three were of high average, or slightly above; in temperament they differed considerably, one being a strongly masculine, somewhat 'tough' personality, whereas the other two were of the introverted, sensitive disposition, which, however, proved no obstacle to sociability, or to practical pursuits. Their developmental histories were also different; in one case (George), no major upsets, illnesses or deprivation had occurred; in another (Patrick) there was a painful illness and in-patient hospital treatment at the age of three, followed by a separation from the mother at the age of four, because of her illness, and an early start at a day-school when his mother went to work; in the third case, (Gordon) there was an accident at the age of three, followed within a week by an explosion of a bomb in the next-door garden and his evacuation with the mother to the country. Such happenings are often found in the histories of neurotic and delinquent children, yet neither of these boys developed into a neurotic or a delinquent. The characteristics which their early histories and environment had in common were just those which were lacking in the histories and environment of the seriously disturbed children, described earlier, i.e. a harmonious family life and the sensible affection of their parents.

Part IV

Interpretation and Theory

*

I. THE ROLE OF MOTHER-CHILD RELATIONSHIP
IN DIRECTING AGGRESSION

In the following chapters I shall attempt to summarize the observations and conclusions which, I think, can be drawn from the studies described in the Second and Third Parts of this book, and to formulate more fully my theory of aggression.

Before I began to work as a psychotherapist with emotionally disturbed children, I was inclined to accept the generally held view that there was an instinct of aggression and that its inherent components were destructiveness and hostility. At the start, my experience with my young patients appeared to provide a wealth of material to confirm this view. It was only as I gained more experience and found that my patients' aggressiveness gradually changed in character and became constructive while their conflicts were being resolved, that I began to have doubts with regard to the primary nature of the destructive impulse itself.

In consequence of these doubts, I was prompted to make an attempt to discover what relationship, if any, existed between destructive aggressiveness and the child's early history. With this aim in view, I made some comparative clinical studies of my own patients, and also carried out an experiment in projection, using a set of pictures specially designed by myself.

I found that, as my studies progressed, I was obliged to split the concept of aggression into 'positive' and 'negative', to designate respectively the constructive and destructive drives shown by the children I was studying.

The principal facts brought out by these studies which I felt needed explanation and interpretation, were briefly these:

In the clinical study: (i) The much greater extent and intensity of destructiveness shown by the neurotic and the delinquent children compared with the normal; (ii) The greater predominance of ambivalence in the relation of the neurotic children towards the therapist, compared with the delinquent and the normal; (iii) The change from negative to positive aggression which occurred during treatment in most neurotic and some delinquent children.

In the projective study: The significant differences between the neurotic, the delinquent and the normal groups in their descriptions of family relationships. These were predominantly negative in the first two, and predominantly positive in the last group.

(a) Maternal Anxiety and Ambivalence as causes of Neurosis and Delinquency in Children

A certain amount of destructiveness in children is taken for granted and is usually explained as an outcome of frustration. The children I studied, however, were in no way frustrated by me: they were treated with friendliness and courtesy, and were free to choose what they wished to do. They did nevertheless destroy and spoil toys and other objects deliberately and on a fairly extensive scale when they found that prohibition and punishment were not forthcoming. It was justifiable therefore to assume that their destructiveness was transferred from some other situation which inhibited its expression. It was perhaps inevitable that one should have turned to the study of the child's family.

The relationship between the parents was the first relevant fact to ascertain. In three of the four cases of neurotic children (Martin, Bernard and Margaret) the parents did not get on at all well together. In Martin's case this amounted to an intense and open hostility; in the other two cases there were frequent, sometimes violent quarrels between the parents. In the fourth case (Geoffrey), the parents disagreed about the child's upbringing.

The second relevant fact was the parents' attitude towards the patient and to their other children. In three of the four cases there were younger siblings, who were favoured by the parents, and of whom the patients were intensely jealous. In the fourth case, the child had had a twin brother who died at birth, and of whom his mother had spoken with much grief.

The personality of the mother and her handling of the child in infancy was the third relevant fact. Regular interviews with the mothers, most of whom were seen weekly over periods of eighteen to twenty-four months, produced a great deal of material to show that not one of them could be described as placid, contented, or even moderately happy. On the contrary, each was, in a greater or less degree, an unhappy, anxious and insecure person. Between them, they showed almost as great a variety of symptoms and neurotic character traits as the children whom they brought for treatment. These included compulsive fears, tendency to excessive worry, obsessional tidiness, irritability, a habit of persistent nagging, a hasty temper, and a readiness to smack.

One might try to imagine the emotional climate which such an over-anxious mother creates for her young child. Doubtless, her state of mind communicates itself to the infant in a vague but all-pervading way. We all have seen at some time or other a screaming child in the arms of a mother, who vainly tries to pacify him, and who calms down at once when handed over to a placid person. Parental quarrels, even if not understood, would fill the child with a sense of impending danger, would keep the feeling of insecurity perpetually reinforced and renewed. Then, as the child began to reach out towards the external world, the anxious mother would tend to check and to prohibit most activities. Activities, which in the beginning are merely associated with pleasant bodily sensations, such as grasping, tearing, slapping, throwing, emptying bowels and bladder, would, if the mother shows anxiety about them, tend to acquire aggressive meaning in the narrow sense, that is, of being dangerous, 'bad', harmful to others. Yet, because they are still pleasurable to the child, a conflict of wills between him and the mother would be almost bound to arise, and might become so absorbing to the child that the natural transition to constructive forms of self-realization and self-assertion would be obstructed.

This drift towards neurosis would be precipitated by the arrival of a sibling. An anxious mother is rarely able to prepare her child adequately for the birth of a new baby, to answer his questions with frankness and confidence, for in addition she is apt to feel guilty and ashamed of sexual life. Her reticences and evasions would inevitably lead to the heightening of anxiety in the child, who would be living in a state of alarmed expectation, keyed up for a dangerous encounter. Perpetually unsure of his mother, he can hardly regard the new baby as anything but a rival produced specially in order to displace him. Like 'John' in the story quoted further on p. 220, he would tend to assume that his mother 'was not satisfied' with him. The anxious mother, on the other hand, would be unable to re-assure him, or to deal in a constructive way with the first signs of rivalry. She is liable to condemn jealousy out of hand, especially if she herself had been a jealous child.

In this way, the birth of a sibling becomes a centre of an additional disturbance in the mother-child relationship, and a point of regression, instead of advance. The child, whose dependence on the mother remained excessive through anxiety, finds himself quite unable to accept an even minor degree of renunciation, and is thus confirmed in immature forms of self-assertion, that is, in his neurosis.

My own observations confirm the view that the abnormal aggressiveness of many neurotic children during treatment represents repeated attempts at relieving anxiety. That the capacity for constructive self-realization is not lost, however, but is merely in abeyance, even in the seriously disturbed children, becomes obvious as treatment goes on. As the therapist accepts sibling jealousy and links it with the child's feelings of insecurity, guilt feelings in the child are relieved and anxiety lessened. While destructiveness and hostility are interpreted as inadequate efforts at self-reassurance and self-assertion and met with tolerance, the child is given proof that he is accepted by the adult despite his 'badness', and his sense of personal value is gradually restored.

Yet, not until this process of explanation, reassurance and mutual acceptance has stood the test of time, can the way be open to constructive effort and thus to positive aggression. Recovery cannot be hurried. In my experience, however, the recovery of neurotic children generally took less time and was more certain than that of the delinquents. I believe that the personality of the mother was the decisive factor in this. The relationship between the neurotic children and their mothers was highly unsatisfactory, but it was not entirely barren. The mother, though ambivalent in her feelings towards the child, was genuinely concerned about him, sometimes even excessively so, in direct proportion to her anxiety. A degree of mutual understanding existed between the mother and child. There was therefore a basis on which a more mature relationship could begin to be built, and, as the treatment progressed, this greater maturity was reflected in the child's relationship with his mother. In the modification of this relationship the help of a psychiatrically trained social worker can be invaluable, and in a clinical team it is usually she who carries the brunt of work involved in eliciting the information about the child's family which the therapist then uses in treatment.

The interpersonal relationships in the families of the delinquent children studied were not very different externally from those found in the families of the neurotics. They were by no means happy families, even though the parents of the delinquents seemed to get on rather better together. This was clearly so in Robert's case, and to some extent in Gerald's, although his father complained of his wife's nagging and seemed to be dominated by, and afraid of her. Hazel's mother confessed to hating her husband when he made sexual demands on her, whereas Barry's parents quarrelled continually and were planning a separation.

The essential difference between these families and those of the neurotic children lay in the mother's feeling for the child.

Warmth seemed to be absent, and the mother gave the impression of having completely failed in creating a bond between
herself and the child. It was no doubt significant that some of
the characteristics these mothers shared were sexual frigidity,
shallowness of feeling, a remoteness of manner, a difficulty in
making contact with others, and the excessively high standards
of tidiness and cleanliness in the home. Barry, for instance, was
not allowed to go out into the garden for *three days* after it had
rained, in case he brought in some mud on his shoes. He was
also forbidden to do painting, for which he had a gift, for fear
he 'made a mess' on the table. Toilet training was extremely
rigid in three of the four cases; feeding almost forcible. Thus,
Hazel was made to eat up all she was given, as a toddler, and
took to pushing her food inside a dirty-linen basket. Barry was
brought up on a rigidly applied Truby King method.

The lack of feeling and the virtual rejection of the children by
the mothers were shown in their leaving the care of the child
to other people for several years, as Gerald's mother did, or in
planning, and sometimes succeeding in sending him away from
home, as was the case with Barry and Robert. Such actions and
intentions represent, in fact, a confession of failure, an abro-
gation of maternal duties and responsibilities. In discussing
their actions these mothers gave some evidence of guilt feelings
by making such remarks as 'I suppose I am to blame for what
has happened', but they also sought relief from these feelings
by projecting the guilt on to the child. They wondered whether
the child was not, after all, 'born wicked' or bad, and whether
anything at all could be done to make him better.

Such condemnation, combined with the rigidity in feeding
and toilet training, would complete the estrangement between
the child and the mother who lacked warmth for him from the
beginning.My strong impression from studying these particular
cases was that toilet training had become a focus in which all
the force of the negative emotions of both mother and child
had become centred. This may be true of a large proportion of
delinquent children. It is well known that even if the relationship between child and mother is an affectionate one, toilet

training can easily become a source of conflict and of a distortion of character. The change in the mother's attitude from early acceptance of the infant's 'gifts' to later disapproval and rejection of them can be both painful and confusing to a young child. When the mother is remote, over-fastidious and cold, when she demands such 'gifts' with an insistence amounting to cruelty, and rejects them with disgust, the child would tend to react with compulsive stubbornness. He would soon realize, as well, that such situations are the only ones in which he can rouse his mother to strong emotional reactions. He would therefore tend to exploit them for the purpose of making contact with her, for she had given him no help in discovering a more positive way of reaching her.

If separation occurs at this stage, or soon afterwards, the child would be confirmed in his awareness of rejection, his feelings of guilt and his conviction that only by shocking or upsetting the mother can he establish some kind of contact with her.

I am, therefore, inclined to regard the persistent aggressiveness of the delinquent children during treatment as compulsive attempts to make contact with someone who represents a parent to them, and so to break out of the isolation into which they had been driven by maternal rejection and condemnation, and by their own feelings of guilt arising from this. Their destructiveness, especially of their own work, may be symbolic of the destruction of their 'gifts' by the mother. It is, no doubt, also a sign of despair: they feel so 'bad' that nothing which comes from, or is made by them, can be worth preserving. Such feelings probably constitute one of the chief obstacles to the emergence of positive aggression; they may even be intensified for a time by the therapist's tolerance. The treatment of delinquent children is handicapped from the beginning by the absence of a relationship, however imperfect, between the child and his mother, a relationship which could provide a basis for building up a new and more harmonious relationship. It has to be created from the foundations up, and the child awakened to its possibilities. This is, of a necessity, a very slow process, and it may explain the relative lack of success in the treatment of delinquent children which discourages many therapists. Parents and teachers frequently hope for an immediate improvement in behaviour when a delinquent child is accepted for treatment, and, when relapses occur, tend, in their disappointment, to take premature and sometimes fateful decisions, such as sending the child away, or using corporal punishment, which merely confirms the child in his asocial tendencies.

The three normal children whom I studied under clinical conditions came from united families. Two of them (Gordon and Patrick) were 'only' children, whereas one (George) had a twin brother and a sister six years his junior. Patrick's family suffered from the disadvantage of both parents being elderly and from his father's delicate health which necessitated his mother going out to work during the boy's early childhood. The parents of both Gordon and George were happily married.

Not one of these three boys showed during treatment the degree of negative aggression characteristic of the neurotic and the delinquent children described earlier. It was clear that their need to relieve anxiety by testing my tolerance and to reassure themselves as to their position in my esteem, was much less pressing than that of the others. Doubtless, their symptoms, no less than those of the others, arose from the mistakes made by their mothers early in their upbringing, for their mothers gave evidence of some rigidity in habit training, and of some degree of anxiety. They were not, however, strongly ambivalent in their feelings towards their children, nor rejected them or regarded them as 'bad'. On the contrary, in each case the child was very much wanted, and a genuine affection existed between him and his parents.

I have mentioned in another context the significant fact that in the histories of these three children there occurred events and experiences which could have been traumatic. In George's family it was the preference his parents showed for his young sister; in Patrick's—his mother's absence from home in the day-time while he was being cared for by a relative from the age of eighteen months; in Gordon's, a painful accident he suffered and a change of home before he was four years old. Both Gordon and Patrick had been in-patients at a hospital before the age of four. Yet these experiences failed to produce lasting and damaging effects, for, when at home, the children lived in an atmosphere of protective kindness and consideration. In this kind of mental environment children can experiment without anxiety and guilt, and so discover for themselves the positive ways to self-realization.

In these 'normal' cases the symptoms were so relatively easy to remove because they were not rooted in a development which had become distorted at an early age, but were an outcome of more or less accidental happenings. During treatment, anxiety aroused by these events was being 'ventilated': the children were seeking reassurance that the affection of the adult would not be withdrawn as a result of their 'naughtiness'. It may be that every child, because he is aware of his vulnerability, needs such reassurance from time to time, and is impelled to seek it.

On the other hand, it was impossible not to be impressed by the preference these normal children showed for positive forms of self-assertion, by the spontaneity with which they turned even destructive acts to constructive purposes, and by the evident satisfaction which they derived from their achievements. It was difficult not to feel that, in the security of an affectionate and harmonious family, most of the self-assertive energy of the child would be spontaneously directed into creative channels, and his negative aggression limited to insignificant episodes.

(b) *The Effects of Mother-Child Relationship on the Success of Treatment*

The link between the destructiveness shown by the neurotic and delinquent children during treatment interviews and their family relationships was made even clearer by the development of their relationship with me, as their therapist.

In so far as I embodied for them some of the parental attributes, it was perhaps inevitable that some of the feelings, desires and demands which they experienced towards their parents, should have been transferred on to me. Frequently, these feelings, wishes and demands were the very ones the child dared not express to his mother, for fear of rejection, refusal, punishment or condemnation. They resented and feared me in so far as they expected me to react in the same way. On the neurotic children, the discovery that I did not punish or condemn, had the effect of removing their inhibitions, gradually, or in some cases suddenly, and releasing the repressed emotions. The timid, inarticulate, cowed little boy Martin, who dared not raise his voice at home or at school, screamed abuse at me, called my room 'this vile place', glared at me with intense hostility and did his best to hurt me when he acted 'the teacher' with a 'cane'. Margaret, the little girl who had a phobia of strangers, smeared my desk with paints and threatened to 'drown' me with paint water.

As treatment went on, however, their hostility gradually gave place to ambivalence, and finally to sustained friendliness. They began to want me to participate in their activities or at least to watch and sanction them. They were eager to come and reluctant to go; they tried to prolong their interviews and were sad at the termination of treatment.

I do not regard treatment as completed until, in addition to the resolution of inner conflicts, and the achievement of better integration, to which the disappearance of symptoms is only incidental, there is also the broadening of the circle of personal relationships. In these cases, the effects of a better relationship with me spread to other persons in the child's environment. After an initial stormy period, the children in question were on better terms with their mothers than when the treatment began, for they became more free, mature and complete personalities. They were also on better terms with their teachers and schoolmates.

In this, as in the gradual change from the destructive to constructive activities during treatment, there was evidence of latent powers which could be employed in positive relation-ships—creatively, instead of destructively.

The delinquent children in this group differed from the neurotics in that they kept me at a distance even after they had been given many proofs of my tolerance and sympathy with their difficulties. This could hardly be explained by tempera-mental differences, for only one of the four children, Gerald, could be described as schizoid, or withdrawn. Barry showed some hysterical traits, while Robert was manically excitable. Hazel, on the other hand, appeared to be an all-round little person, with a mischievous sense of humour and a charm of her own. The rapport between us, however, remained slight, and the children showed little change in their attitude towards me throughout the period of treatment. This may not be significant in the case of Robert, as he attended only twelve times. The other three, however, attended for eighteen months —a period sufficiently long for a relationship to develop. Yet, unlike the neurotics, they showed little hostility towards me at the beginning and not much friendliness at the end of the treatment period. Their attacks on me, usually with water, sand, or ball, appeared to be inspired more by curiosity than by anger. They showed no desire to share their play with me, or have me participate in their activities, although they liked displaying their skills or their mischievousness before me. The two younger ones particularly enjoyed teasing and trying to provoke me.

Whereas the neurotic children were able, after a time, to treat me as a play companion, the delinquents tended to assume that I was there to do things *for* them. Thus Robert would demand that I should cut out paper aeroplanes for him, or draw the portraits of his family, so that he could scribble over them. Hazel would get into the water tray and order me to lift her out of it. Barry would set me tasks, such as making tiny dolls out of pipe cleaners, which he then took away. None of the four ever made an attempt to render me any kind of service, such as putting toys and materials away. None ever volunteered an admission that they liked coming. Gerald and

Barry said they 'didn't mind it', whereas Hazel often declared that she did not like it at all and would not be coming again.

A superficial way of describing these children would be to call them selfish and lacking in capacity for affection, perhaps even for any deep emotion or feeling. Their own remarks about themselves tended to support this impression. Gerald, for instance, would never admit that he enjoyed, or strongly disliked anything. His favourite comment on a holiday was: 'It was all right', and on some less pleasant event: 'I didn't mind it.' When questioned about his preferences, he would reply: 'It's all the same to me', or 'I don't mind what I have.' Barry too, asserted that he 'would rather like' to go away from home. Yet, in times of crisis, such as an imminent danger of being sent away, or of appearing before a court, both these boys showed clearly that they were capable of strong feeling, even if it were only self-pity or fear. When I saw Barry after he had been placed in a hostel, he cried bitterly as he talked about the light domestic tasks his mother used to set him at home, and compared them with what he felt to be the dreadful drudgery of peeling several pounds of potatoes for supper at the hostel. Gerald, after he had been found out stealing savings stamps from his teacher's desk, presented a front of apparent indifference to my comments on the subject. Yet, when he rose to leave my room, there was a pool on the chair and on the floor underneath it, indicating his emotional state and a loss of control from which he had not suffered for years.

I do not think, therefore, that it is possible to be sure that such children are incapable of strong feeling; all we can say is that they are much less accessible than other disturbed children. This holds of the majority of the delinquents I have treated, and may be true of delinquent children in general. Remembering the evidence obtained from the interviews with their mothers, one would hardly think it surprising. The child, whose mother had been unable to meet him half-way in his outgoing, object-directed impulses, would have no opportunity of learning how to respond when a good relationship is offered.

Any sign, however, on the part of a delinquent child of

seeking praise for his appearance, or his work, may be an indication of concern for another person's opinion of him, and so a starting point for the development of true self-esteem. Thus, I felt that I was getting somewhere with Gerald when I heard that he had had a scene with his mother because she would not allow him to wear his first pair of long trousers when coming to see me. A trivial point, one might say—but, possibly, also a first step to a discovery, an all-important one for a delinquent, that certain things which please him and make him feel 'good' or attractive, might also be a source of satisfaction to others, and so add to his own satisfaction.

It is most significant in this connection that delinquent children, although they often go about in gangs, very rarely have friends who really care for them, or of whom they are fond. All four in the group I described were lone wolves, and either complained that other children would not play with them, or asserted that they did not like other children. Hazel was a Brownie, and Gerald belonged to a boys' club, but this did not help them in making friends. Towards the end of their treatment, only Gerald showed signs of increased capability for forming relationships. A year or two after his case was closed, his mother reported that he was very fond of his new baby sister, and very friendly with a crippled boy in the neighbourhood for whom he adapted an old bicycle. It is, therefore, possible that if the treatment of these children had not been discontinued at the parents' wish, their capacity for making friends might have developed more fully.

The contact which the normal children made with me was different in quality from that of both the neurotics and the delinquents. In the beginning, they had to overcome a certain amount of shyness and self-consciousness, for, not unnaturally, they were somewhat puzzled and a little anxious about the whole business. This, however, did not inhibit their essential friendliness for long. Although two of the boys, Patrick and Gordon, were of a distinctly introverted disposition, they talked readily, and wanted me to participate in their play as soon as they saw that I was prepared to do so.

Our relationship developed quickly: like the seriously disturbed children, they tested my tolerance by being noisy, or messy, or provocative, but their negative aggression had neither the hostility of the neurotic, nor the calculated slyness of the delinquent. Usually, it was followed by the offer to put things away or to clear up the mess. Unlike the neurotics, these children needed no proofs of my goodwill, or forgiveness, in the form of small gifts, nor did they show awareness of guilt in an excessive readiness to render services. They made no attempts to destroy or depreciate other children's work, on the contrary, when they made simple toys, such as wooden boats or aeroplanes, they usually left them behind 'for others to play with'. They never gave displays of violent emotion, like the neurotics, or of uncontrolled mischievousness, like some of the delinquents. They were friendly in a warm, undemonstrative, steady manner.

From the reports of their parents and teachers, I knew that all the three boys were able to make and keep friends. Gordon was said to love having children to play in his parents' garden, or house, and, although he tended to choose children somewhat younger than himself, he had greatly enjoyed a camping holiday with schoolmates of his own age, despite the fact that it was the first time he was away from home without his mother. Patrick was delighted when, on one or two occasions, I saw him together with another boy. He played well with him, and was eager to accompany him home part of the way. George, although he was said to be 'rather solitary' in school, was on very good terms with his twin brother. These reports, as well as the ease with which these boys were able to enter into a good relationship with me, were a proof of their capacity to form satisfactory relationships—a capacity, no doubt, developed through a secure, warm and satisfying bond they had with their mothers. They possessed, as it were, a fund of affection, sympathy and considerateness on which they could draw and which they had accumulated through the generous giving by their mothers. This may be a prosaic way of describing the situation, but I believe it to be fairly accurate.

To summarize: the relationship, which these three groups of children were able to form with me, was deeply influenced by the early relationship which each child had had with his mother and it reflected it in its most essential features. Thus, the neurotics were strongly ambivalent, the delinquents detached and mistrustful, and the normal, friendly and confident.

(c) Decrease in Negative Aggression as a result of Improved Relationship

I referred earlier (p. 181) to differences in the curves of negatively aggressive behaviour shown by these three groups of children during treatment. For the neurotics it could be represented as steeply rising and just as steeply descending; for the delinquents, as a high plateau with a series of small curves; for the normal, a similar series of small curves on a base line representing positive behaviour. The meaning of these curves may, perhaps, be expressed in terms of the emotional conflicts underlying behaviour. The steeply rising curve of the neurotics may reflect anxiety, which mounted rapidly while negative emotions were expressed and made conscious by interpretation, and which decreased, sometimes as rapidly, when reassurance was given. The high level of negative aggression, continuing over a long period with only minor fluctuations, shown by the delinquents, may reflect feelings of guilt, which are less accessible to consciousness, and might be for a time intensified by the absence of restraint or retribution. The slight fluctuations of negative aggression shown by the normal may represent immature responses to frustration, common enough in adults, as well as in children.

The curves of positive aggression for these three groups could also be drawn. For the neurotics, it would show a slow and steady rise after the peak of negative aggression has been reached, and it would gradually attain a high plateau well above the descending curve of the latter. For the delinquents, it would show slight rises and falls well below the level of the plateau of negative aggression. For the normal group, the position of the two latter curves would be reversed, that is, slight fluctuations of positive aggression would appear well above the low level curves of negative aggression.

This is not intended to imply that such curves would be the same for each individual case, but merely that tendencies or trends of this kind might be observed in the neurotic, delinquent and normal children. Certainly a few neurotic children show curves of aggression more common in delinquents. Significantly, however, they usually are children whose neurosis has paranoid features, and who had established, almost from infancy, a pattern of reacting to danger by attacking. They are apt to regard every adult as an enemy. It is interesting, too, that, like many delinquents, they often had, in infancy, a very rigid training in cleanliness.

Some delinquents, on the other hand, may refrain from open aggression and remain merely unresponsive, resisting all attempts to obtain their co-operation in treatment. This resistance, however, is in itself a form of negative aggression, for it is a refusal to yield their trust, a hostile rejection of the help offered, a silent declaration of war. The patient cannot conceive a relationship in other terms except those of a battle of wills, and pits his will against the therapist's with every intention of winning. The curve of negative aggression for these children would be a plateau similar to that of the more openly hostile delinquents, and just as much, if not more, extended in time.

The point which must be stressed, however, is that—if the treatment is continued long enough—the curve of negative aggression begins to descend, that even a plateau drops to a lower level, whereas the curve of positive aggression rises gradually. This, of course, like any other change in personality, can be attributed, at least in part, to maturation. But if we infer that maturation would have brought about these changes without the help of the therapist, we would have to explain why it failed to have this effect in so many cases of adult neurotics and criminals, who most probably were neurotic or delinquent as children. In other words, is not all neuroses and delinquency a sign of emotional immaturity, and is not psychotherapy a process which assists and accelerates emotional maturation?

(d) Qualities of 'Creativity', 'Realism', and Balance in Free Composition of Normal Children revealed by Projective Technique

The projective technique which I used, in addition to clinical studies, to explore the children's awareness of relationships within the family, brought out differences between the normal, the neurotic and the delinquent in several important respects. These differences were apparent not only in the attribution of positive or negative emotions to adults and children in the stories, which represented projections of the patients' own emotions, but also in the qualities of the stories which stood in no direct relation to such emotions. I am referring to the qualities of balance, realism and creativity, in all of which the stories of the normal children were superior to those of the delinquents and the neurotics.

The following three very brief stories can serve as illustrations of the different ways in which three children interpreted the scene represented on Picture 4, of a big man facing a rather small woman who is holding up a child.

> *Normal.* 'The father is having fun with the little boy, he's trying to teach him how to box. The mother is holding the little boy up high, so that he can get level with his father.' (Boy, aged 11, 5; I.Q. 110.)
>
> *Neurotic.* 'The lady is holding up the baby and the man is going to fight them. ("Why?") Because he wants to. Yes, he's the baby's father. The lady's holding him up because she wants the man to fight them. The man's fighting them because he doesn't like them.' (Boy, aged 8, 10; I.Q. 102.)
>
> *Delinquent.* 'A man is hitting the baby severely because he's cruel and so is his wife. They don't like the baby very much, and they punish him most severely than any other mother would.' (Boy, aged 12, 2; I.Q. 85.)

These stories speak for themselves. A significant point in the second story is the uncertainty about the attitude of the woman, a mother figure, shown by the neurotic boy. She is said to want the man 'to fight them', as if she were far from averse to the idea of the child being hurt, yet obviously she and the child are in the same camp, as the man 'doesn't like *them*'.

In the story by the delinquent boy, both the man and the woman are 'cruel' to the baby: the parents and the child are in opposite camps. The woman is clearly seen as the betrayer of the child.

I do not think that the interpretation of these stories can be limited to projection by the children of their own hostile emotions on to the parent figures in the pictures. I believe some of the feelings of the real parent, as the child becomes aware of them, are also projected. Thus, maternal anxiety and ambivalence introjected by the neurotic child, are subsequently projected on to the mother figure in the picture, whereas the more complete estrangement between the delinquent child and his parents might be projected by him on to the parent figures as a wish to send him away, or as unnatural cruelty. Nothing of this appears in the story by the normal child. The children of the normal group most consistently saw this scene as one of play, or boxing practice.

But as was shown in the second part of this book, the differences in interpretation of these pictures were not limited to parent figures. They included also the relationship between siblings as the following three stories illustrate. The stories are about Picture 2, in which a woman is represented nursing a baby while a man and a small boy are looking on.

> *Normal.* 'She's like the lady next door. She's just had a new-born baby. The father's looking at it. The boy is watching them. He's thinking he'll play with the baby when it grows up, and take it out in the pram when it's little. It's a brother. The boy wants a little brother. He's a nice boy. The father and mother like the baby best when it's little. It's a good baby.' (Boy, aged 8, 2; I.Q. 101.)

> *Neurotic.* 'When John came back from school and saw the baby, he shouted, "Hie! I thought you weren't going to have another one!" His mother said, "But it isn't a boy, it's a girl."

John said, "Aren't you satisfied with me?" His mother said, "Of course I am." The father told John, "Will you be quiet?" And John said to him, "The same to you." Then they started a game, chasing round the furniture and John burst a couple of springs in the settee. Then his father caught him, and he had to go to bed. No, it wasn't a joke; his father was angry because John has been naughty—cheeky. It seems as if the father liked the baby better. The mother—she, too, might like the baby better just now—because of these broken springs." (Boy, aged 9; I.Q. 129.)

Delinquent. 'Father and mother sitting down. The mother's holding the baby and the little boy's dossing. The father is also dossing at the baby. ("What is the boy thinking?") He's thinking that he hates the baby. He is naughty. He slings the baby about on the sofa and kicks her. Yes, it is a little sister. His father and mother hit him for it.' (Boy, aged 8, 3; I.Q. 98.)

The first of these stories is characteristic of the normal child's tendency to overcome sibling rivalry by taking over some of the parental functions and deriving pleasure from being protective. The second story is interesting for the light it throws on the intense feelings of insecurity of the neurotic child. The arrival of the new baby is interpreted by him as a direct consequence of his mother's dissatisfaction with him. The father, too, prefers the baby. The boy in the story reacts to this by negative aggression—an attack on the parents, symbolized in the story by 'bursting' the springs of the couch on which the parents had been sitting. The third story is direct and primitive in its expression of resentment against the sibling who monopolises the parents. The boy in the story makes no attempt to win the parents back, as if he had given up this hope long ago. Stories like this suggest that although, as a group, delinquent children appeared less intensely jealous and more tolerant of sibling rivalry, this apparent tolerance may have been due to a deeper repression of hostility.

The creative urge may well be an impulse in its own right, but it appears to be linked with the urge to self-realization. When self-realization assumes negatively aggressive forms, creativity becomes inhibited. Of the three groups, the normal composed their stories with the greatest ease, however much they varied in imaginative capacity and verbal ability. The neurotics were the most unpredictable, some eager to pour out their fantasies, others too self-critical to achieve even a small measure of spontaneity. The delinquents were the least articulate and needed most prompting. That this lack of spontaneity was not entirely due to their, perhaps natural, mistrust, was shown in their inability to play imaginatively or constructively. The material produced by the boy Donald may serve as an illustration.

Donald was seven years old when I first saw him and had an I.Q. of 90 on Stanford-Binet scale. Though not yet a pilferer, he showed many signs of becoming a delinquent. He was backward in school subjects, truanted, 'blackmailed' his schoolmates into giving him their toys and sweets, attacked children in the street violently and without provocation, giving as a reason that he 'just didn't like them', destroyed his clothes by cutting them up deliberately, and was, in addition, a bedwetter and a masturbator. His mother was determined to send him away, but was persuaded to try a period of treatment first.

In a room which contained sand-and-water trays and an assortment of toys, Donald could not bring himself to do anything. He would go through the boxes of toys just standing them up and looking at them. All my suggestions were met with a whispered: 'I can't do it'. Only after I had managed to steer him towards the sand and praised the first sandcastle he built, did he reveal the constructive urge which had been so completely overlaid by the patterns of negativism and destructiveness. For many interviews afterwards he went on making bigger and better castles, until one day I put a sheet of paper and some crayons before him. His confidence was built up sufficiently by then for him to attempt the usual drawing of a house, then of a ship. They were poor drawings, but I praised them, and he was immensely pleased. A new field was thus open for creative activities. Soon he was ready to try putting together a simple jig-saw puzzle, then cutting out and pasting, and finally he arrived with a cotton reel and a ball of wool, doing French knitting! His mother reported that he 'just couldn't stop doing it'. He discovered the pleasure of *making* things—something he had hardly attempted before, oppressed as he was by the weight of adult criticism and disapproval.

His stories reflected the same inhibition of the creative impulse, and an inability to let himself go. I had to use persuasion to get him to say something about each picture. This is what he said about Picture 1.

> 'The man's coming to take the boy away. (A long pause. "Why?") Because he's a naughty boy. (Another long pause. "Where is he going to take him?") To a home. ("What kind of home?") A home for naughty boys. ("What about his Mum and Dad?") They are sad. ("Will they let the boy go?") Yes, they will let him go. ("You mean they are sad because he is going?") Yes. ("Tell me more about the boy.") He is seven years old. He's English. ("You said he is a naughty boy. What sort of thing does he do when he is naughty?") He throws spoons and knives at the wall. ("Why does he do that?") Because his father hits him. ("What happens first?") His father hits him first because he is naughty.'

Each statement had to be dragged out, phrase by phrase, and the projected image was that of a child trapped into accepting his own naughtiness, and despairing that his parents could help him, for they were 'letting him go'.

This boy had, in fact, an appalling early history. When his mother was pregnant with him, his father had to go to prison for petty forgery. Donald could not be breastfed and almost from birth was left in the care of other women while his mother went out to work. He was a sickly baby and had all the childish illnesses in succession. Before he was four years old, he had pneumonia and was an in-patient at a hospital for several weeks. He had three elder siblings, one of whom, a brother, had to be sent away because of behaviour difficulties. His younger brother was much favoured by the mother and was taller and stronger than Donald. His mother, unwisely, frequently and openly compared him unfavourably with his siblings, and she did not conceal her intention of sending him away because he was a 'bad boy'. Everything in this boy's environment seemed to conspire to make life difficult for him. Yet, he responded well to treatment, and when I saw him six years later, there were no complaints whatever about his behaviour. He was holding his own in school subjects, though still somewhat backward in English, and he was the captain of the school football team. His ambition was to become a professional footballer.

This boy had had psychological treatment for about twelve months. It came at a decisive moment when he was being threatened with separation from his family and a life in an institution at the age of seven. During his treatment he had experienced, perhaps for the first time in his life, the satisfaction of a positive achievement, both in a human relationship and in constructive activities. This experience proved to be so worth while, that it induced him to abandon gradually the precarious pleasures of destructiveness and negativism, for the sake of these other satisfactions. The effects of treatment were more rapid in his case, probably because it began when the boy was still very young, and because his mother, although lacking in understanding, was not a remote, frigid type of person, nor was she grossly unstable or devoid of sympathy.

Although the stories of the neurotic and the delinquent children were projections of real feelings, the form into which they were clothed was often unrealistic, both in their frequent use of fairy-tale themes and in their character of improbability, if a contemporary setting was chosen. Murderers killing the child or the whole family, truculent, child-eating giants, fierce lions attacking children, appeared more frequently in the fantasies of the neurotics and the delinquents than in those by the normal, who chose their themes mostly from the events of everyday life. Selling, starving or desertion of the child by the parents, was treated by the intelligent neurotics and delinquents as something which could easily happen in real life. This points to a faulty development of the reality function in the emotionally disturbed children, compared with the normal. On the other hand it cannot be said, on the basis of these responses, that the emotionally disturbed showed a tendency to cling to the 'pleasure principle', for their unrealistic fantasies were predominantly of the gruesome, sado-masochistic type.

The quality of balance is doubtless related to the reality function. In their stories, the normal children showed a pronounced tendency to balance unpleasant happenings with a happy ending. This has a parallel in my findings concerning the responses of adolescent girls to a similar test, which were described in the beginning of Part II of this book. The younger children showed the same trends. Thus, in the story by Jean, quoted on p. 111, the heroine of the story, Susan, loses her privileged position in the family owing to the birth of a brother, but later becomes 'the most popular girl at school'. In another story, by a boy aged seven years ten months, the little girl has to scrub floors for her mother but 'then she can go into the garden and play till dinner time'.

The disturbed children, on the other hand, showed a preference for a balance of a more primitive kind—tooth for a tooth, and eye for an eye. Thus, a neurotic girl, aged eleven years eleven months, with an I.Q. of 106, describes how a boy was sent to a boarding school by an uncle, in punishment for teasing his cousins. The father of the boy rescues him from the school, then entices the uncle's children to his home and sends *them* to a boarding school 'in revenge'. The deliberate use of the phrase 'in revenge' is very significant. Whereas in the stories by the normal children punishment for naughtiness is usually followed by reconciliation, the delinquents and the neurotics most often end their stories with a harsh 'settling of accounts'. Here is a typical story by a delinquent boy aged 10, 1 with an I.Q. of 100, about Picture 5.

> 'A little girl's playing with the fire. Her father comes along and gives her a good smacking and sends her to bed. Because he (meaning the child) was playing with the fire. His father does not want him to play with the fire because he might set the house alight. The mother won't give her any tea.'

The change of the personal pronoun from the feminine to the masculine in the third sentence of the story is an interesting indication of the operation of projection. The scene described, although familiar enough, suggests an alliance of the parents against the child, and the final phrase has a forlorn ring.

I think it is clear from the examples quoted that an early misdirection of the aggressive urge affects not only the child's relationships with persons, but influences his mental functioning in a variety of ways, dominating his value judgments and inhibiting or distorting his constructive and creative capacities. Such misdirection is usually the result of a bad relationship between mother and child.

On the other hand, the free constructive use of aggressive energy by the child, and subsequently by the adult, seems to result only if the relationship between mother and child is good. Both these outcomes thus depend almost entirely on the personality of the mother, and on her capacity to enter into relationships entirely creative, generous, free from anxiety and rich in warm feeling. It is a capacity which can be developed, but as a rule is largely determined by the mother's temperament and her early childhood experiences with her own parents. It also determines to a great extent her relations with her husband and the whole family atmosphere in which their children will grow up, thus intensifying whatever effects her own personality has on the child's development.

The implications of this view might appear rather discouraging, for how can wide-reaching results be achieved in this sphere except by eugenic measures which, in the present state of our knowledge and public opinion, are both uncertain and impracticable? There is little doubt that where seriously neurotic, or near psychotic mothers are concerned, nothing short of deep psychological treatment is likely to help them in their relations with their children. This may not be available or acceptable to them. Less seriously disturbed women, on the other hand, can be helped a great deal by explanation and reassurance. Their anxiety can be relieved, their guilt lessened and their inhibitions reduced in scope and intensity, thus opening a way for greater spontaneity and warmth to which the child rarely fails to respond. Here is a wide field for psychiatric

social work. It is of such great importance because the therapist's efforts to restore the child to health can be most seriously
handicapped by the inability or unwillingness of other adults—
parents and teachers—to play their part in this undertaking,
even if the child's own co-operation can be secured. The
therapist's art depends to a large extent on his ability to
establish a relationship with the child, in which neither seduc-
tion nor domination play a part, and which would provide a
basis for the establishment of similar, mature and satisfactory
relationships between the child and other people in his environment. In building up this relationship, the therapist has
to take the initiative in virtue of his greater age and experience,
and because the child usually comes to him burdened with the
feelings of mistrust and failure.

The delinquent child is at a particular disadvantage, for his
experience of human contacts has no deep foundation in the
early bond with his mother, and he is not merely unpractised
in the art of making friends, but simply has no inkling as to
what friendship is about. He does, however, see other children
happy in the company of their parents, or of their schoolmates,
and is aware that he is lacking something important, be it
affection, or the material proofs of it, such as the giving of
money, toys or food. His very delinquency, in one of its several
meanings, is an unconscious attempt to secure a substitute for
this intangible lack of something very important. It is also the
only effective way he knows of getting in touch with others, of
breaking out of the isolation into which he had been forced
originally by parental rejection, and subsequently by his own
delinquencies. It is an obscure and desperate appeal to society
for help.

The predicament of the neurotic child is not quite so serious,
for in his case failure in relationship is limited to excessive
ambivalence, and parental rejection is only partial, or inter-
mittent. The child's negative aggression is circumscribed within the bounds of his own family and school, and has not, as in
the delinquent, spread to a larger community. Nor has it
assumed patently anti-social forms, although in the amount of

friction, unhappiness and disruption it causes, it often has a nuisance value in no way inferior to that of delinquent behaviour, and its repercussions, in later years, on the life of the community might be just as widespread and harmful.

While the normal child is neither excessively involved nor prematurely detached and isolated from his family, the neurotic child's strivings can be described as centripetal: he is too dependent on his family, he cannot free himself from cravings belonging to infancy. The strivings of the delinquent child, on the other hand, can be described as centrifugal: his infantile cravings have become projected to the outside world and to society at large, from which he tries to wrest the satisfactions his family denied him; he is prematurely and superficially detached from the family.

For those reasons the aims of treatment of the delinquent and the neurotic may lie in opposite directions. For the delinquent, treatment would aim at building up a good child-parent, or parent-substitute, relationship, and by this means bring him into the larger community as a full, socially effective member. For the neurotic, it would be directed to loosening the infantile bond with the family which had come to constitute an obstacle to further development. My belief is that these aims could only be achieved through a positive relationship with the therapist which, however, may be initiated by a phase of intense hostility or ambivalence on the part of the patient. Neither the parents nor the therapist need feel discouraged if this phase lasts a long time. This is common with the delinquent, the paranoid and the obsessional child, and it sometimes occurs also with the hysterical. It usually means that the relationship between the child and his mother, or both parents, is greatly at fault, or that the child's hostility towards them has been repressed for a long time.

The fear and dislike which such hostility inspires, naturally enough, in both the parents and the community as a whole, are in themselves obstacles to the effective treatment of negative aggression in children and young people. Aggression is condemned wholesale and its positive aspects go unrecognized.

218

The position might alter if it were accepted that hostility and destructiveness are originally reactions of the child to the clumsy handling of the urge to self-realization which, at its biological source, is identical with the survival urge. They are, as it were, wrong moulds into which the liquid of neutral but dynamic energy had been poured. If allowed to remain in them long enough, it is liable to set so firmly, that all subsequent efforts to modify the pattern of individual behaviour may prove ineffective. The habitual criminal, the psychopathic personality, the incurable neurotic may be as much the products of such initial misdirection of vital energy, as of the intangible constitutional trends.

II. CONCLUSIONS

I described in the preceding pages the evidence and the process of reasoning which led me to conclude that the widely accepted view of aggression, as an urge which is primarily destructive, has no firm basis in reality. To summarize: this inquiry originated in theoretical interests allied to a practical problem. The questions I asked myself were: was aggression what it was commonly assumed to be? how arose the negative, that is, destructive and hostile forms of aggression? was it inevitable that aggression should assume such forms? how could destructiveness and hostility be transformed into constructiveness and friendly co-operation?

These are large questions, and I cannot claim to have found full answers to them. The theoretical question of the origin of aggression may not be one that can ever be answered with certainty, but I hope to have shown at least that the evidence adduced in favour of innateness of negative aggression—of destructiveness and hostility—is far from convincing, and that by describing the behaviour of infants and young children in adult terms we may be projecting on to them our own emotions and unconscious urges, and unjustifiably treating their mental states as equivalent to our own.

My experimental work with children seems to me relevant to theories of aggression in so far as it demonstrates objectively —in the children's free responses to pictures—the close link between negative forms of aggression in children and the parent-child relationship.

My projection Test of Family Attitudes has shown that significant differences exist between the neurotic and delinquent children—who are addicted to negative forms of aggression—and the normal—who are aggressive in a positive way—in their conceptions of family relationships, and, perhaps inevitably, in their basic attitudes towards people and the world in general. The neurotic and delinquent children conceive these relationships in terms of mutual hostility with all that it involves, i.e. the inner mechanisms of defence, the strong sado-masochistic trends, and the canalization of self-assertion into asocial channels. The normal conceive the same relationships in terms of mutual goodwill and co-operation, with all that it involves in social adaptation and positive achievement.

What is the meaning of these differences if we view them from the standpoint of a theory which assumes destructive aggressiveness to be innate? If we accept the hypothesis that all children are born with a fund of destructive aggressiveness and hostility in their mental constitution, how are we to explain the apparent absence of these trends in normal children? Are we to suppose that the parents of normal children were able to deal with such trends at an early stage in such a way that they became transformed into positive forms of aggression, and that the parents of neurotic and delinquent children were unable to deal with their hostility and destructiveness in the same way? This is, of course, a possible and even likely explanation. It is, however, hardly a complete one, for the differences in responses of the delinquent and the neurotic on the one hand, and of the normal on the other, appear in this test at the age of about six years. Hence if transformation, or sublimation, of destructiveness and hostility has taken place as a result of parental influence, it has presumably occurred before that age. The hypothesis of innate destructiveness, however, gives no account of the inner mechanisms by which destructiveness is sometimes 'converted' into constructiveness and sometimes is not. I believe my hypothesis has the advantage of being the more economical—not to say the more sensible—of the two, in postulating the existence of *one* kind of innate urge, i.e. a forward-pressing urge to self-realization, rather than *several*, one of which—the so-called 'aggressive' urge, is wholly negative. Not even the appearance of negativism and contra-suggestibility in young children between their second and fourth year provides, in my opinion, sufficient proof for the existence of innate hostility. Rather does it suggest attempts at self-realization appropriate to that age, at which the child first becomes aware of his individuality and which can be turned into the channels of negative aggression by rigid and unsympathetic handling.

I realize that to give more force to this argument projection studies should have been made of children between the ages of two and six, which unfortunately I have had no opportunity of carrying out. My view, however, is supported by the evidence of recent anthropological studies, especially by the work of Margaret Mead (40). She found that in one of the primitive communities she studied, social relationships were almost entirely free from negative aggressiveness, i.e. hostility, rivalry and uncharitableness of every kind. This she relates to the custom of infant nurture prevailing in that particular culture, which maintains an uninterrupted, close, physical and psychological contact between mother and child throughout infancy, and avoids situations liable to arouse anxiety and feelings of insecurity in the child, such as separation, frustration at the breast and shock of sudden weaning. Another primitive society, on the other hand, in which infants were by custom deliberately subjected to such disturbing experiences, was characterized by just these traits of negative aggressiveness—quarrelsomeness, combativeness, ruthless competition, liability to anger and violence—from which the first group were free. The fact that negative forms of aggression failed to appear in the first group, whereas in the second group very disturbing conditions were necessary to bring them out, goes far, in my opinion, to support the argument against the existence of innate destructiveness and hostility.

I believe that my clinical studies of emotionally disturbed children also support my theory, in so far as the destructiveness and hostility of those children were gradually and almost wholly transformed during the course of treatment into constructiveness and friendly co-operation, not only in the children's relationship with me but also with other people in the child's environment. How is this to be explained? Should we, on the analogy with chemistry, postulate a transformation of a simple (wholly negative) urge into its opposite—a wholly positive one? It seems more reasonable to suppose that re-direction rather than transformation has taken place and that it was only the form, not the substance of the urge which was negative—the primary, powerful innate urge to self-realization, mis-directed in early life, has been helped to flow again in its natural channels, leading to creativeness and positive relationships with other human beings.

This view is further supported by the evidence provided in the histories of these children, showing that in every case such mis-direction had taken place. Had it been otherwise, there might have been more substance in the assumption that these delinquents and neurotics were merely showing an exaggeration of an urge which was originally negative, i.e. hostile and destructive. And I think it is relevant to this argument that even the most hostile and destructive of these children made spasmodic attempts at being constructive and friendly, as if the original positive character of the urge to self-realization was asserting itself despite all inner and external obstacles.

I doubt that this argument will convince a firm believer in the duality of human nature, but I shall be satisfied if he at least is led to admit the practical usefulness of a conception which views aggressiveness as primarily a positive force. For it has been amply shown by experience that negative aggression cannot be permanently disposed of by violent measures, or by repression, either in individuals or in nations, and that only by accepting it as a potentially creative force and re-directing it accordingly can we hope to make use of the vast fund of energy it represents.

APPENDIX

TABLE I

Showing the data for 600 Normal subjects, 150 boys (or girls) in each of the groups (a), (b), (c) and (d).

Subjects	No. of Responses given of the types:				Total
	'0'	'1'	'2'	'3'	
(a) Boys (Normal), 8–10 years of age	1852	2739	574	385	5550
(Means) ..	12·30	18·21	3·84	2·56	
(b) Girls (Normal), 8–10 years of age	1829	2858	539	324	5550
(Means) ..	12·19	19·05	3·60	2·16	
(c) Boys (Normal), 10–12 years of age	1611	2811	730	398	5550
(Means) ..	10·70	18·70	4·86	2·65	
(d) Girls (Normal), 10–12 years of age	1670	2870	639	371	5550
(Means) ..	11·13	19·13	4·23	2·47	
(i) Totals for all cases (Boys and Girls a, b, c, d) ..	6962	11278	2482	1478	22200
	31·3%	50·8%	11·2%	6·7%	100%
(ii) Total for all cases: (a, c) Boys ..	3463	5550	1304	783	11100
(b, d) Girls ..	3499	5728	1178	695	11100
(iii) Total: Boys and Girls aged 8–10 (a, b)	3681	5597	1113	709	11100
Boys and Girls aged 10–12 (c, d)	3281	5681	1369	769	11100

TABLE I (supplementary)

Showing percentages of responses of types '0', '1', '2' and '3' for the Normal group of subjects as a whole (section '*a*'), and for the same group divided according to sex (section '*b*'), and age (section '*c*').

(*a*) Total of all 600 cases (see Table I (i)).

The '0' responses (very positive and thus somewhat unrealistic) are selected in   31·3% of the total

The '1' responses (positive and realistic) are selected in   50·8%   ,,

The '2' responses (negative, somewhat harsh but still realistic) are selected in   11·2%   ,,

The '3' responses (strongly negative and thus, generally speaking, unrealistic) are selected in   6·7%   ,,

(*b*) Difference in responses of the two sexes

The following table gives the same data but with the sexes separate (see Table I (ii).)

Subjects	% number of responses of types:				Total
	'0'	'1'	'2'	'3'	
All Boys (300) ..	31·2	50·0	11·7	7·1	100%
All Girls (300) ..	31·4	51·6	10·6	6·4	100%

(The figures in columns '2' and '3' are each significantly different (P=0·01) from the 'chance' values for the columns. Those in columns '0' and '1' are not significantly different from 'chance' values for these columns.)

(c) Difference in responses due to age

The following table gives the same data but with the age groups separate (see Table I (iii)).

Subjects	% of responses of the types:				Total
	'0'	'1'	'2'	'3'	
Boys and Girls (aged 8–10) ..	33·2	50·3	10·1	6·4	100%
Boys and Girls (aged 10–12) ..	29·5	51·3	12·4	6·9	100%

(The figures in columns '1' and '3' are not significantly different from 'chance' values; but those for columns '0' and '2' are highly significant at P <0·01.)

TABLE II

Showing the data for 150 boys and girls in each age-group, i.e. 600 subjects in all, classified as 'A' (bright), 'B' (average) and 'C' (dull).

No. of subjects	Intelligence level	No. of responses given of types:				Total
		'0'	'1'	'2'	'3'	
109	A	1181 (1264) 5·45*	2111 (2049) 1·88	481 (451) 2·00	260 (269) 0·30	4033
374	B	4414 (4340) 1·26	7065 (7030) 0·17	1476 (1547) 3·26	883 (921) 1·57	13838
117	C	1367 (1358) 0·06	2102 (2199) 4·28*	525 (484) 3·47	335 (288) 7·67*	4329
		6962	11278	2482	1478	22200

(The only data significantly different from 'chance' values are those marked with an asterisk (*).)

TABLE III

Showing the data for 600 boys and girls classified as (a) 'only' children, (b) youngest of the family, (c) middle of the family, (d) eldest of the family.

No. of subjects	Position in family	No. of responses given of types:				Total
		'0'	'1'	'2'	'3'	
125	'Only' children	1427 (1450) 0·36	2328 (2350) 0·21	559 (517) 3·41*	311 (308) 0·03	4625
184	Youngest children	2091 (2135) 0·91	3476 (3458) 0·09	771 (760) 0·16	470 (453) 0·64	6808
127	Middle children	1525 (1474) 1·76	2374 (2387) 0·07	496 (525) 1·60	304 (313) 0·26	4699
164	Eldest children	1919 (1903) 0·13	3100 (3083) 0·09	656 (678) 0·71	393 (404) 0·30	6068
		6962	11278	2482	1478	22200

(No value is significantly different from 'chance'. The most 'significantly' different is marked with an asterisk (*).)

TABLE IV

Showing the data for 600 Normal, 108 Neurotic and 172 Delinquent subjects, compared as to number of responses of the types '0', '1', '2' and '3', given by each group.

Subjects	No. of responses given of types:				Total
	'0'	'1'	'2'	'3'	
Normal (600) aged 8–12 years ..	6962	11278	2482	1478	22200
Neurotic (108) aged 8–12 years ..	1078	1755	628	535	3996
Delinquent (172) aged 8–12 years	2013	3010	855	486	6364

X^2 test applied to this table gives highly significant deviations from 'chance' values. If the data for all 880 subjects are used as a basis for arriving at 'chance' values, the results are as shown in Table V.

TABLE V

Subjects	No. of responses given of types:				Total
	'0'	'1'	'2'	'3'	
Normal (600) ..	6962 (6854) 1·70	11278 (10938) 10·57	2482 (2704) 18·23	1478 (1704) 29·97	22200
Neurotic (108) ..	1078 (1234) 19·72	1755 (1969) 23·26	628 (486) 41·49	535 (307) 169·33	3996 .
Delinquent (172) ..	2013 (1965) 1·17	3010 (3136) 5·06	855 (775) 8·26	486 (488) 0·01	6364

(The table gives 'chance' values in brackets with the X^2 value underneath. Clearly there is an overall enormous significant difference from 'chance', involving differences far greater than any encountered for age, sex, intelligence, or position in the family, in the Normal group.)

As Table V stands, the greatest deviations from 'chance' values are shown by the Neurotic group, the least by the Delinquent. This, however, depends upon how the data are analysed. A better basis for comparison would be provided, probably, by considering the 'normal' responses as 'norms' representing the 'expected' values, and to re-examine the data, in order to see how far the results for the Neurotic and the Delinquent subjects differ from 'norms' or 'expected' values.

The results of this re-examination are shown in Table VI.

TABLE VI

Subjects	No. of responses given of types:				Total
	'0'	'1'	'2'	'3'	
Normal (600) ..	6962	11278	2482	1478	22200
Neurotic (108) ..	1078 (1253) 24·44	1755 (2030) 37·25	628 (447) 73·29	535 (266) 272·03	3996
Delinquent (172) ..	2013 (1996) 0·14*	3010 (3233) 15·38	855 (711) 29·16	486 (424) 9·07	6364

(The only value *not* significantly different from Normal is marked with an asterisk (*). The table gives 'chance' values in brackets with the X^2 value underneath. All the figures are significantly different from 'expected' values except for the Delinquent for responses '0'.)

TABLE VII (from Tables IV or VI)

Showing percentage deviation from Normal of the Neurotic and Delinquent subjects in giving responses of the types '0', '1', '2' and '3'.

Subjects	Type of response:				Total
	'0'	'1'	'2'	'3'	
(i) Normal (No. of responses)	6962	11278	2482	1478	22200
(ii) Neurotic (No. of responses)	1078	1755	628	535	3996
(iii) On 'expected' basis . .	1253	2030	447	266	
Difference (ii)–(iii)	−175	−275	+181	+269	
% on 'expected' basis	−14·0%	−13·5%	+40·5%	+101·1%	
(iv) Delinquent (No. of responses)	2013	3010	855	486	6364
(v) On 'expected' basis . .	1996	3233	711	424	
Difference (iv)–(v)	−17	−223	+144	+62	
% on 'expected' basis	−0·9%	−6·9%	+20·3%	+14·6%	

(The percentage differences are much greater for the Neurotic subjects indicating that they differ more from the Normal on this test than do the Delinquent.)

REFERENCES

1. ADLER, ALFRED: *The Neurotic Constitution*, London, Allen & Unwin, 1921.
2. ALLEN, F. H.: 'Aggression in Relation to Emotional Development, Normal and Pathological', *Paper read to the Congress on Mental Health*, London, 1948.
3. BAGOT, J. H.: *Juvenile Delinquency*, London, Cape, 1941.
4. BOVET, PIERRE: *The Fighting Instinct*, London, Allen & Unwin, 1923.
5. BOWLBY, JOHN: *Maternal Care and Mental Health*, Geneva, World Health Organization, 1951.
6. BOWLBY, JOHN: 'Forty-four Juvenile Thieves', *International Journal Psycho-analysis*, 1944, vol. XXV.
7. BUEHLER, CHARLOTTE: *From Birth to Maturity*, London, Routledge, 1935.
8. BURT, CYRIL: *The Young Delinquent*, London University Press, 1925.
9. BURT, CYRIL: 'The Factorial Analysis of Emotional Traits', *Character and Personality*, vol. VII.
10. CARR-SAUNDERS, MANNHEIM and RHODES: *Young Offenders*, London, Macmillan, 1942.
11. DARWIN, CHARLES: *Mind*, vol. II, p. 287.
12. DEARBORN, G. V. N.: *Moto-Sensory Development*, p. 5, Baltimore, 1910.
13. DOLLARD, J., DOOB, L. W., MILLER, N. E., MOWRER, O. H., and SEARS, R. R.: *Frustration and Aggression*, London, Kegan Paul, 1944.
14. FISHER, R. A.: *Statistical Methods for Research Workers*, Edinburgh and London, 1936.
15. FLUGEL, J. C.: 'Freudian Mechanisms in Moral Development', *Brit. Jrnl. Psychol.*, vol. VIII, pp. 480–8, 1913.
16. FOULKES, S. H.: 'Psycho-analysis and Crime', and KARPMAN, B.: 'Case Studies in the Psychopathology of Crime', *Psychol. Abstracts*, 1944.
17. FRIEDLANDER, KATE: *The Psycho-Analytical Approach to Juvenile Delinquency*, London, Kegan Paul, 1947.
18. FREUD, SIGMUND: *Beyond the Pleasure Principle*, London, Hogarth Press, 1922.
19. FREUD, SIGMUND: *Three Contributions to the Theory of Sex*, Nerv. and Ment. Diseases Mon. Series, No. 7, N.Y., 1948.

REFERENCES

20. FREUD, SIGMUND: *Totem and Taboo*, London, Routledge, 1935.
21. FREUD, SIGMUND: *Collected Papers*, London, Hogarth Press, 1937.
22. FRY, S. M.: *The Ancestral Child*, The Fifth Clarke Hall Lecture, London, 1940.
23. GOODENOUGH, FLORENCE: *Anger in Young Children*, Oxford University Press, 1931.
24. GORING, C.: *The English Convict*, Cambridge University Press, 1913.
25. HARROWER-ERICKSON, M. R., and STEINER, M. E.: *Large Scale Rorschach Techniques*, U.S.A., 1945.
26. HEALY, W., and BRONNER, A. F.: *Mental Conflict and Misconduct*, London, Baillière, Tindall & Cox, 1917.
27. HEALY, W., and BRONNER, A. F.: *New Light on Delinquency*, Oxford University Press, 1936.
28. HENDERSON, D., and GILLESPIE, R. D.: *Textbook of Psychiatry*, Oxford University Press, 1927.
29. HENRY, WM. E.: 'The Thematic Apperception Technique in the Study of Culture-Personality Relations', *Genet. Psychology Monog.*, February, 1947, 35, 7–135.
30. HORNEY, KAREN: *New Ways in Psychoanalysis*, London, Kegan Paul, 1939.
31. HUXLEY, JULIAN: 'The Uniqueness of Man', *Essay in Eugenics and Society*, London, 1941.
32. ISAACS, SUSAN: *Social Development in Young Children*, London, Routledge, 1933.
33. JACKSON, LYDIA: 'Investigation into Factors Influencing the Direction of the Aggressive Impulse into (*a*) Delinquency, (*b*) Neurosis, (*c*) Positive Achievement', *D.Phil. Thesis*, Oxford University Library, 1949.
34. JACKSON, LYDIA: 'Analysis of Aggression among Problem Children: its Incidence and Immediate Nature', *B.Sc. Thesis*, Library of the Institute of Experimental Psychology, Oxford, 1942.
35. KRETSCHMER, E.: *Physique and Character*, London, Routledge, 1936.
36. LANG, ANDREW: *The Origins of Religion and other Essays*, London, Watts & Co., 1908.
37. LANGE, J.: *Crime as Destiny*, London, Allen & Unwin, 1931.
38. LOMBROSO, C.: *Criminal Man*, translated by Ferrero, G. L., London, Putnam, 1911.

233

39. McDougall, William: *Introduction to Social Psychology*, London, Methuen, 1931.
40. Mead, Margaret: *Sex and Temperament in Three Primitive Societies*, London, Routledge, 1935.
41. Murray, H. A.: *Thematic Apperception Test Manual*, U.S.A., Cambridge, Mass., 1943.
42. Ordhal, George: 'Rivalry, Its Genetic Development and Pedagogy', *Pedag. Semin.*, 1908, vol. XV, b. 4.
43. Pailthorpe, G. W.: 'Studies in the Psychology of Delinquency', *Med. Research Council Spec. Report Series*, No. 170, 1932.
44. Piaget, Jean: *The Moral Judgment in the Child*, London, Routledge, 1932.
45. Powdermaker, F., Turner Levis, H., and Touraine, C.: 'Psychopathology and Treatment of Delinquent Girls', 1945, *Amer. Jrnl. Orthopsychiatry*, vol. VII, pp. 61–2.
46. Rivière, Joan: 'Hate, Greed and Aggression', in *Love, Hate and Reparation* by Melanie Klein and Joan Rivière, Epitome No. 2, London, Hogarth Press, 1937.
47. Sears, R. R., and Sears, P. S.: 'Minor Studies in Aggression; V. Strength of Frustration-Reaction as a Function of Strength of Drive', *Jrnl. Psychol.*, 1940, 9, pp. 297–300.
48. Sears, Robert R., Hovland, C. I., and Miller, Neal E.: 'Minor Studies of Aggression', *Jrnl. Psychol.*, 1940, 9, pp. 215–95.
49. Sherman, M. and I. C.: 'Sensori-motor Responses in Infants', *Jrnl. Comp. Psychol.*, vol. V, 1925.
50. Spearman, Carl: *The Nature of Intelligence and the Principles of Cognition*, London, Macmillan, 1923.
51. Stern, M.: 'Some Differences between Neurotic Delinquents and other Neurotic Children', *Psychol. Abstracts*, 1944.
52. Stott, D. H.: *Delinquency and Human Nature*, Carnegie Trust, Dunfermline, Fife, Scotland, 1950.
53. Sully, K. M.: *Studies in Childhood*, p. 408, London, Longmans, 1895.
54. Suttie, Ian: *The Origins of Love and Hate*, London, Routledge, 1935.
55. Valentine, C. W.: *The Psychology of Early Childhood*, p. 286, London, Methuen, 1942.
56. Willemse, W. A.: *Constitutional Types in Delinquency*, London, Kegan Paul, 1932.
57. Zukerman, S.: *Social Life of Monkeys and Apes*, London, Routledge, 1932.

INDEX

For Product Safety Concerns and Information please contact our EU
representative GPSR@taylorandfrancis.com
Taylor & Francis Verlag GmbH, Kaufingerstraße 24, 80331 München, Germany